COOKERY
YEARBOOK
1986

INTRODUCTION

If you are interested in cooking, then you will want to know what's new in food today. The Cookery Yearbook has information on new ingredients and techniques, advice from professionals and lots of recipes to try.

Presenting food so it pleases the eye is a trick every good chef knows. In Menu Planning, you get advice on balancing foods to make appetizing meals, and hints on table layout and decoration to create a mood and impress your guests. Wines and Spirits explains how to match up food and wine to round off a meal.

There has been a lot of controversy about food and health. Diet and Nutrition clears up the misconceptions, answers your questions and offers practical advice on getting the most from your food while improving your health.

Many celebrations are centred around food. The Great British Cookery Year explains, month-by-month, what foods are in season and incorporates these into holiday dishes and menus.

Microwave cooking is one of the fastest growing trends in food today. You can get advice on choosing a microwave and hints, tips and recipes to make cooking by microwave a success.

There is a host of other information, such as advice from a professional on designing your perfect kitchen, a favourite menu from a well-known cookery writer and a review of the latest in kitchen equipment. There's even Kids in the Kitchen, with lots of recipes for children to make. With the Cookery Yearbook, you can choose the right ingredients, make the most of your equipment and learn the latest techniques – and be sure of perfect meals for every occasion.

THE EDITOR

ISBN 0-86307-452-9

© MCMLXXXV Marshall Cavendish Limited

Published by Marshall Cavendish House
58 Old Compton Street, London, W1V 5PA

Typeset by Bookworm Typesetting, Salford, England
Printed and bound in Milan, Italy by New Interlitho Spa

COOKERY YEARBOOK
1986

MARSHALL CAVENDISH
LONDON · SYDNEY · NEW YORK

CONTENTS

DIET AND NUTRITION

Caroline Schuck is a writer and editor specializing in food and health. She has worked on the Good Housekeeping cookery books, Madhur Jaffrey's most recent Indian cookery book, A La Carte magazine and a recent health book, Bodycare. She has also contributed to the Oxford Companion to Food.

KITCHEN EQUIPMENT REVIEW

Beverly Le Blanc is a freelance cookery editor and writer. She has worked on the Good Housekeeping Cookery Book, the Harrods Cookery Book, a food processor book and a number of books for Tesco.

MICROWAVE COOKING

Pat Alburey has been a home economist for 23 years, during which time she has created, tested and written thousands of recipes. She was assistant cookery editor on Woman's Realm and worked on the Time-Life Good Cook series for seven years. She has owned a microwave cooker for four years.

KIDS IN THE KITCHEN

Coralie Dorman has been a cookery writer and editor for over eight years. She has worked on the Harrods Cookery Book, a number of cookery books for Boots and a series of books for Tesco. She is currently a cookery writer for Woman magazine.

THE PERFECT KITCHEN

Jane Suthering has been a home economist for over 10 years. She has written a number of books, including Delicious Desserts and Step by Step to Cake Decorating. She is a regular contributor to the Radio 4 Woman's Hour, Cook's Weekly magazine, and produces recipes for Colman's of Norwich. Most of her work as a home economist consists of consulting, preparing food for photography sessions and testing and developing recipes.

IN THE SUPERMARKET

Supermarkets today offer more than ever before. With the wide range of products available, and special services to help you make wise choices, shopping can now be a one-stop affair.

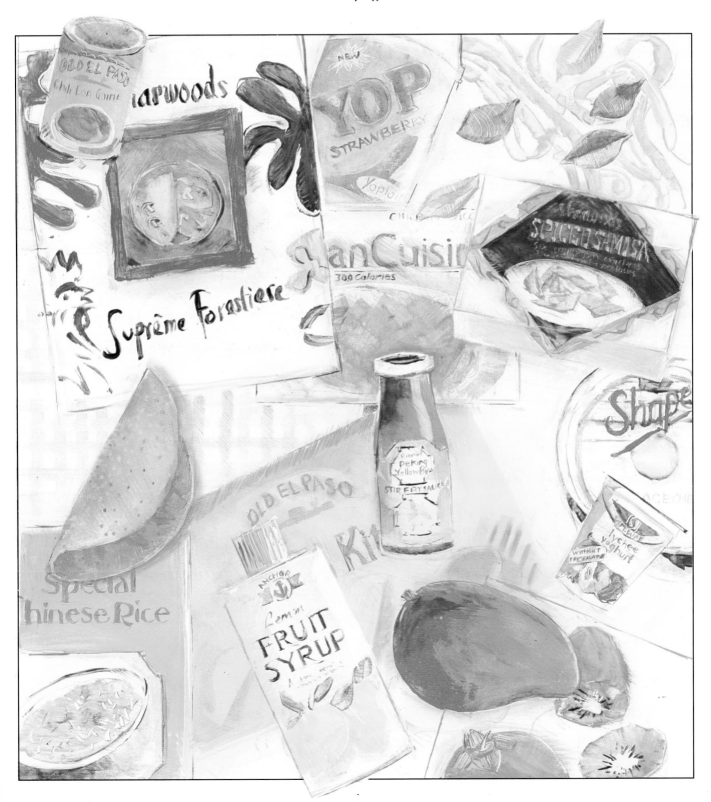

Shopping used to be an all-day affair. You would have to go to many different local shops to get all the ingredients you needed for a meal, or to get your family's weekly food supply. But supermarkets have changed drastically over the past few years. With new marketing innovations and an ever-increasing stock, shopping can now be a one-stop affair.

If you have a household to run or a job that takes up most of your time, you will have little energy left to fight the crowds in shops at the end of the day. Most supermarkets now have much later hours, with at least one late night a week. And with the possibility of Sunday trading being allowed, supermarkets may soon be open seven days a week. And some of the newer branches are being planned to include banks, creches and even post offices.

Although most supermarkets have self-contained bakeries, delicatessens and well-stocked off-licenses, supermarkets also have an incredibly wide range of products. They are filled with foreign delicacies from around the world, such as noodles from China, vine leaves from Cyprus and exotic fruits and vegetables. One store even stocks edible nasturtiums! You can find baby care supplies, shampoos and bubble bath, car oil, cookware and clothes, all in your local supermarket.

One of the best aspects of supermarkets' changing faces has been that they have picked up on Britain's new awareness of nutrition and health. They all have their own range of foods, many of which focus on health and slimming products. In the past you may have had to go to health food shops to get special food if you were carefully watching what you or your family ate, or if you had special dietary requirements. Today, most supermarkets have 'own brand' skimmed milk, low fat yoghurt and cottage cheese in a variety of flavours. They have no-sugar canned fruits and no-salt canned vegetables, as well as food that is appropriate for diabetics and vegetarians.

But aside from all the foods that are available in the supermarket today, they now provide additional services to help you select food products for a healthier way of eating.

Tesco, for example, has devised a Healthy Eating Programme. All of their own brand foods are labelled clearly with nutritional information. Along with this information are the Healthy

Eating logos, which appear on Tesco products that have a particular benefit which can contribute to a healthy diet. These logos contain such words as Low Fat, Vitamin Fortified, Low Calorie and High Fibre, which are easy to see at a glance. A booklet called the Tesco Guide to Healthy Eating is available, which explains the basis of the programme and and the reasoning behind it. It illustrates all of the logos, explains what they mean and how to use them in conjunction with the nutritional labels. In addition to this booklet, the consumer advisory service at Tesco has published fact sheets on a number of different types of food such as fruits, vegetables, fish and bread. They explain the different foods and tell you how they should be prepared as well as giving recipes. All of these booklets are available from your local Tesco.

While Safeway doesn't yet have nutritional labelling on most of their own brand products, they do have some invaluable information available about them. Most people have little idea about the hidden ingredients in foods. Although eggs are an obvious addition to a frozen cheese flan, do you know what canned or packaged foods also contain eggs, if you are not allowed to have them on your diet? Safeway will provide a list of products that are egg-free, so you can safely choose the foods you want. They also have information on milk-free and gluten-free products, and even a list of foodstuffs that are suitable for lacto-ovo vegetarians. They will also provide you with a list of the preservatives, by E numbers, in Safeway products. Although this labelling will be required on all food products in 1986, Safeway has compiled it voluntarily for its customers.

Marks and Spencer is known for their food halls and the quality of their products. The food packaging, though, contains little nutritional information. What they do have available is a sheet of information on St Michael food products which gives the calorie, carbohydrate and dietary fibre count in their foods. If you shop at M&S regularly for food but have wondered how many calories are in their Chicken Kiev, for example, ask for a copy of these listings.

Boots is a relatively new entry into the supermarket game. They have introduced a new department in over 100 of their branches called Foodcentres, which have a selection of healthy and

nutritious foods. These include fresh bread, dairy produce, high fibre foods, low sodium foods and vegetarian foods as well as a selection of foreign foods and ingredients. They have a series of fact sheets available, explaining about fibre, salt, fats and sugar, with tips on reducing or increasing the amount of this nutrient in your diet. In addition, Boots has a service that will analyze your diet. You simply fill out a form describing your typical daily diet and a few other pertinent questions. The form is then either sent by post to be analyzed by computer or can be taken into one of the Advice Centres where they will help you plan a better way of eating.

Although ultimately the choice of what you eat is your own, supermarkets have made it easier than ever before to make wise choices. They help you to plan diets, give you more information about food in packets and tins, and offer you a much wider selection of foods to choose from. What you will find on your supermarket shelf today is unlike that which you have seen before.

THE E ADDITIVES

Food additives need to be listed on a food label along with the ingredients. In 1986, the food labelling regulations require listing these additives (except flavourings) by 'E numbers'.

These additives are included for a variety of reasons. Some are colourings to make food more attractive, and others act as preservatives to keep the food from going off, and are essential for safety reasons.

A number of physical reactions and responses are traced to these additives, especially in people who are sensitive and allergy-prone. The Ministry of Agriculture publishes a list of E numbers and what they stand for, but it does not explain what these chemicals do to the body or in which foods they are found. To properly understand the E numbers, and find a comprehensive list of what foods they are in and what their possible side effects can be, Maurice Hannsen's *E for Additives* will prove useful.

FOOD LABELS

One of the most important factors in choosing prepacked or convenience foods is understanding what they are made of. The way to understand these foods is to understand the labelling system. Although it may appear complicated at first, there are a few basic guidelines to follow that will make shopping easier and ensure that you choose the foods you want.

All labels must list the following information — the food name, the ingredients, the net quantity, datemark, name and address of manufacturer, packer or seller in the EEC, and any special conditions for storage or use.

All prepacked foods must show the name of the food. Some names are prescribed by law, such as sugar, chocolate or honey. Others are customary names, that is the name by which we usually know the food, like pizza or fish fingers. Foods which do not have either of these listed must have a descriptive name and should tell the shopper the true nature of the food. Usually the condition of the food, such as smoked, dried or powdered is also required.

There has been recent controversy over misleading names. A food product is not allowed to call itself 'chocolate' or 'chocolate flavoured' unless chocolate has actually been used to provide the taste and flavour. If artificial methods have been used to provide the flavour, the product must say 'chocolate flavour'.

Labels must also include a complete list of ingredients in descending order of weight. Food additives must also be included on the ingredients list.

It is now compulsory for most foods to be datemarked. This indicates the minimum durability of the food. The datemark will usually say Best Before, followed by the day, month and year. Perishables may be marked with the words Sell By. The label should also tell you that the food is best if eaten by a specific number of days after purchase, and include any storage conditions that apply to keep the food fresh. Datemarks are based on the assumption that the products will be properly stored.

With all the information required by law, it is possible to see from the label how long most foods will keep and under what conditions. But there is often additional information listed on labels, some voluntary and some required by law.

Many foods now claim to be made especially for slimmers. Such claims must be backed up with information. They must state how much energy they provide per 100 grams and per helping, and also state that they can help slimming and weight control *only* as part of a controlled diet.

Due to an increased awareness of health, many foods now include nutritional information. The usual listings are energy, protein, carbohydrates and fat content, in that order. Vitamin and mineral content is appearing more and more, usually with the percentage of the Recommended Daily Allowance (RDA) of each the food provides. By mid-1986 most food labels will include the total fat content and the saturated fatty acid content which is required by law.

In addition to all this information, the generic terms 'low' or 'reduced' may appear. These should not be part of the nutritional information. 'Low' means that the product has less than half the amount of the nutrient found in parallel normal foods, such as low fat cottage cheese. 'Reduced' means that the product has less than three-quarters of the amount of nutrients in parallel foods.

Food labels are intended to help the consumer. They should be easy to read and to understand. The information should be legible and easily visible.

Today, with the choice of prepacked and convenience foods available from all over the world, informative labels are more important than ever. Food labelling laws are being updated on a regular basis, and they are there to protect you. If you want to be a smart shopper and be sure of what you are buying, learn to look at the label.

Name of food

Ingredients

Net quantity

Instructions for use

INGREDIENTS
Beans, Water
Tomatoes, Sugar
Salt
Modified Starch
Spirit Vinegar
Spices

Free from
artificial colour
and preservative

⊖ 580 g
1.28 lb

GUARANTEE
Price refunded,
without affecting
your statutory
rights, if any
Heinz variety
fails to please

TO SERVE
Empty
contents into
a saucepan
and stir gently
while heating.
Do not
add water or
overheat as this
impairs flavour

Made in England
H. J. HEINZ CO. LTD.
Hayes, Middx. UB4 8AL

Name and address of manufacturer, packer or seller in the EEC

● Datemarks are required on most food labels. The main exceptions are long-life foods, such as baked beans.

TROPICAL FRUITS

The consumption of many exotic fruits such as mangoes, pomegranates and kiwifruit, has doubled over the past five years. Many people are still unsure of how to recognize, choose and prepare these unusual fruits.

Following are some details and descriptions about a selection of exotic fruits you might find in your supermarket. Once you experiment with a few, you will realize how much these fruits have to offer.

1 Avocados originated in Central and South America. They are highly nutritious, and are widely available all year round. They can be purchased ready to eat, but if bought when still firm, ripen at home in a warm place.
2 Cape Gooseberrys originated in South America, and have a distinctive sharp-sweet taste. The small golden berries are surrounded by a paper thin husk. If left in their husk, the berries will remain sweet and sound for many weeks. The fruit is ripe when the husks have turned a straw colour.
3 Carambolas are sometimes known as the star fruit, because when the fruit is cut widthways the slices resemble yellow five-sided stars. It is not necessary to peel carambolas, just wash and slice widthways to achieve the star shape.
4 Dates are among the world's oldest cultivated fruits. They are available fresh all year round, and should be plump and moist. Fresh dates can be eaten as they are or peeled by pinching the skin gently at one end until the date pops out.
5 Figs are one of the most ancient plants in civilization. Fresh figs have a high water content and only 12 per cent sugar. When dried, the sugar content raises to 50 percent. Fresh figs have a tender thin skin and should be handled with the utmost care.
6 Guavas are highly scented, with an aromatic sweet-acid taste. They can be eaten raw by simply cutting in half and scooping the flesh from the skin.
7 Kiwifruit originally came from China and were once known as the Chinese Gooseberry. The flesh is an emerald green colour with a refreshing tangy taste. It is usually best to peel off the skin before cutting into slices.

8 Limes are a member of the citrus family and are extensively cultivated in the West Indies. Limes can be used in much the same way as lemons. The juice has a delicious flavour, but is stronger than lemons so always use less quantity in a recipe that calls for lemon juice.
9 Mangoes have a history that goes back almost 6,000 years and have close connections with the Hindu religion. They are rich in vitamin A and are best eaten when ripe and soft to the touch.
10 Mangosteens are not related to the mango, despite its name. The thick skin can be easily cut away to expose the five pearly white segments, each with a seed, which are arranged in the same way as an orange. It has a delicate scent and flavour and is usually eaten raw
11 Passion fruit also has a wonderful scent and flavour. They are simple to eat. Just cut them in half and scoop out the juicy seeds with a spoon. They can be eaten on their own or added to fruit salads and ice cream.
12 Paw paw, or papaya, is a native of tropical America. The taste is said to be a cross between peaches, melons and strawberries. They are soft to the touch and need to be handled carefully to avoid bruising.
13 Persimmons originated in Japan, and must only be eaten when fully ripe. They have a sweet date-like texture and contain a high percentage of protein and glucose. To eat persimmons, just slice off the top and scoop out the pulp.

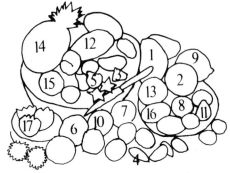

14 Pineapples are a native of Brazil, but are widely grown in all tropical regions. Pineapples contain vitamin C and an enzyme which aids digestion. A good test for ripeness is when one of the bottom leaves of the plume pulls out easily and the pineapple scent is apparent, even before slicing.
15 Pomegranates are originally from Persia, and have been connected to many religions for centuries. Simply cut the fruit in half and spoon out the soft pink jelly and seeds. Pomegranates make a refreshing drink, but when making the juice do not crush the seeds – they can make the juice bitter.
16 Prickly pears are sometimes known as Indian figs. They are a member of the cactus family, and since the skin is covered with tiny prickles, they should be handled with caution.
17 Rambutan is sometimes known as the hairy lychee, and it is of the same family. A small cut should be made in the skin which can then be easily peeled away to reveal the white flesh inside.

MEXICAN FOOD

Although Mexican food has been popular in America for quite some time, it is a relatively new taste for Britain. Some people may already be familiar with it, having tried Mexican food on holiday or sampled it in one of the Mexican restaurants that have recently opened.

There are many misconceptions about Mexican food, the major one being that all Mexican food is hot. It isn't, and doesn't have to be. Just like curries, you can go to town on the fiery flavours or stick to one of the milder dishes.

A new range of products has been introduced in Britain, called Old El Paso, which include tortilla chips, taco shells, refried beans and packaged seasonings. They are available in most large supermarkets and smaller grocers. As you get more familiar with Mexican food and its various tastes, you will be able to experiment and discover a new and exciting way of cooking.

Included here are two well known Mexican dishes, guacamole and tacos. Guacamole is an avocado dip that is usually served with tortilla chips, raw vegetables or as a topping for tacos or enchiladas. A taco, which means 'snack' in Mexico, is a folded corn tortilla that is cooked until crisp and filled with meat, salad or cheese. The variety of fillings is endless. Minced beef, shredded chicken,

refried beans, lettuce, tomatoes, onions and cheese can all be used to fill tacos. A vegetarian taco, filled with beans, lettuce and other vegetables, is included.

Guacamole
SERVES 4-6
2 large avocados, peeled and pitted
1 jar/8 oz Old El Paso Mild Taco Sauce
1 onion, chopped
1 tablespoon lemon or lime juice
1 teaspoon salt
1 teaspoon garlic powder
tortilla chips for serving

1 Mix all the ingredients together in a large bowl until well blended.
2 Cover with cling film and chill until ready to serve. Serve with tortilla chips.

Florida Chicken Taco
SERVES 4
4 Old El Paso Taco Shells
shredded lettuce
4 tablespoons sweetcorn kernels
16 thin slices cucumber
6 oz/175 g cooked chicken, cut into strips
peeled segments from 2 oranges
Old El Paso Mild Taco Sauce
halved stuffed olives, to garnish
fresh mint sprigs, to garnish

1 Heat the oven to 180C/350F/Gas 4.
2 Place the taco shells on the oven shelf, rounded side uppermost. Warm through for 3-4 minutes.
3 Turn the taco shells cup sides uppermost. Put a layer of shredded lettuce into the base of each, then top

with the sweetcorn, cucumber, chicken strips and orange segments. Spoon over a little taco sauce, if liked. Garnish and serve at once.

Basic Mexican Taco
SERVES 4
4 Old El Paso Taco Shells
4 tablespoons Old El Paso Taco Filling, warmed
shredded lettuce
2 large tomatoes, seeded and chopped
1 large red or green pepper, seeded and finely chopped
1 onion, finely chopped
4 oz/100 g Cheddar cheese, grated
Old El Paso Hot or Mild Taco Sauce
sliced jalapeño pepper and black olives, to garnish

1 Heat the oven to 180C/350F/Gas 4.
2 Place the taco shells on the oven shelf, rounded sides uppermost. Warm through for 3-4 minutes.
3 Turn the taco shells cup sides uppermost. Put a spoonful of warm taco filling into each one. Add a thin layer of shredded lettuce, followed by a sprinkling of chopped tomato, red and green pepper, onion and grated cheese. Spoon over a little taco sauce and garnish with sliced jalapeño pepper and black olives. Serve immediately.

Vegetarian Taco
SERVES 4
4 Old El Paso Taco Shells
4 tablespoons Old El Paso Refried Beans warmed
shredded lettuce
1 yellow or red pepper, seeded and finely chopped
2 oz/50 g button mushrooms, thinly sliced
1 large courgette, thinly sliced
mung bean sprouts
2 tomatoes, seeded and chopped
Old El Paso Mild Taco Sauce
chopped fresh parsley

1 Heat the oven to 180C/350F/Gas 4.
2 Place the taco shells on the oven shelf, rounded sides uppermost. Warm through for 3-4 minutes.
3 Turn the taco shells cup sides uppermost. Put a layer of warm refried beans into each one, and top with a layer of shredded lettuce. Add a sprinkling of chopped pepper, sliced button mushrooms, sliced courgettes, mung bean sprouts and chopped tomatoes. Spoon over a little taco sauce and sprinkle with chopped parsley and serve immediately.

INDIAN FOOD

Indian food needs little explanation. Having been popular for years, and with Indian restaurants in almost all cities, most people have tried it at one time or another.

Although Indian cooking may look complicated and difficult, it really isn't. The techniques are actually quite simple and the ingredients are familiar and readily available. The charm of Indian food lies in the spicing, which must enhance but not overpower.

Many areas of India follow a vegetarian diet due to religious laws. The recipes given here create an exciting and flavourful vegetarian meal using Sharwood's Indian food products. Their range of over 40 products includes curry powders, chutneys and condiments. Each can be used to create authentic Indian food in your own home.

Rice with Chick Peas
SERVES 6 AS AN ACCOMPANIMENT
6 oz/150 g Sharwood's Basmati Rice
1 teaspoon salt
2 tablespoons oil
1 heaped teaspoon Sharwood's Mild or Medium Curry Powder
4 onions, sliced
1 teaspoon Sharwood's Garam Masala
6 oz/150 g canned chick peas
3 oz/75 g butter

1 Cook the rice in boiling salted water for 5 minutes, then drain.
2 Heat the oven to 180C/350F/Gas 4.
3 In a flameproof casserole, heat the oil, then add the spices and cook for 10-20 seconds.
4 Stir in the onions, rice and chick peas and fry for 2-3 minutes.
5 Place a small knob of butter on top of the rice, cover and bake for 45 minutes.

Masoor Dall
SERVES 6
½ lb/225 g lentils, washed
1 teaspoon salt
6 oz/150 g butter
1 large onion, sliced
1 heaped teaspoon Sharwood's Hot or Extra Hot Curry Powder
fresh coriander leaves for garnish

1 Place the lentils in a large saucepan with the salt and 2 pints/1 litre water.

Cover and simmer for 1½-2 hours, until all the water is absorbed.
2 Fry the onion in 2 oz/50 g of the butter and the curry powder. Stir in the lentils and simmer for 10 minutes.
3 Meanwhile, melt the remaining butter.
4 Divide the lentils between six dishes and pour the butter over. Garnish with fresh coriander and serve at once.

Marrow Kofta Curry
SERVES 6 AS AN ACCOMPANIMENT
1½ lb/¾ kg marrow flesh, grated
4 tablespoons gram flour or plain flour
2 heaped teaspoons Sharwood's Garam Masala
1 teaspoon salt
oil for shallow frying
1 can Sharwood's Vegetable Curry
pinch Sharwood's Garam Masala

1 Mix the marrow, flour, garam masala and salt together, then form into 6 patties. Place on a plate, cover with sheets of absorbent paper and chill for 2 hours.
2 Heat the oil in a large frying pan and fry the patties until golden on both sides. Drain on absorbent paper towels.
3 Heat the vegetable curry in the rinsed-out pan or a flameproof casserole and place the patties on top. Cook over low heat for 15 minutes. Serve hot with extra garam masala sprinkled over the top of the curry.

Banana Masala
SERVES 6
2 bananas, peeled and sliced
6 tablespoons natural yoghurt
1 teaspoon Sharwood's garam masala

1 Coat the bananas in the natural yoghurt and sprinkle with the garam masala.
2 Cover with cling film and chill until ready to serve.

CHINESE FOOD

Most people enjoy eating Chinese food but few try to recreate the food at home. Part of the secret of Chinese food lies in the unusual way of contrasting textures and tastes, such as sour and sweet, soft and crisp and pungent and bland.

Another major secret is in understanding the Chinese method of seasoning. Sugar is used more generously than salt, while garlic, spring onions and ginger are often introduced to add zest to dishes.

The methods of cooking are familiar — boiling, braising, poaching, steaming and stir-frying. Stir-frying, which is usually done in a wok, is simply a rapid sauté of finely cut ingredients which are then coated with a rich glaze.

The menu offered here includes familiar dishes such as sweet and sour pork. It has been chosen for its contrasting flavours, textures and colours, which is the hallmark of a good Chinese meal.

Sharwood's, better known for its Indian food products, also has a range of authentic Chinese ingredients. They will enable you to produce, quickly and easily, many dishes that are found in Chinese kitchens.

Chicken in Yellow Bean Sauce

1 lb/450 g chicken, boned, skinned and diced
4 tablespoons vegetable oil
3 tablespoons cornflour
2 oz/50 g cashew nuts or peanuts
1 jar Sharwood's Yellow Bean Stir-Fry Sauce

1 Rub the chicken with a little oil, then dust with the cornflour.
2 Heat the remaining oil in a wok or large frying pan and fry the nuts until lightly coloured.

3 Increase the heat, add the chicken and stir-fry for about 2 minutes. Add the Yellow Bean Sauce and heat through. Serve at once.

Sweet and Sour Pork

½ lb/225 g lean pork, cubed
4 tablespoons cornflour
1 teaspoon salt
pinch of baking powder
1 egg, beaten
1 jar Sharwood's Hong Kong Sweet and Sour Stir-Fry Sauce
oil for deep-fat frying

1 Toss the pork with the cornflour, salt and baking powder until evenly coated.
2 Dip the pork in the egg and toss in cornflour again.
3 Heat the oil in a deep-fat fryer and cook the pork in batches for 2-3 minutes, until crisp and golden.
4 Meanwhile, heat the sauce in a small saucepan. Re-crisp the pork balls and glaze with the hot sauce. Serve at once.

Almond Floats

2 tablespoons powdered gelatine
½ pint/250 ml milk
2 tablespoons sugar
1 teaspoon almond essence
1 jar Sharwood's Tropical Fruits, chilled
2 kiwifruit, peeled and sliced

1 Place ¼ pint/150 ml warm water in a small heatproof bowl and sprinkle the gelatine over the surface.
2 In a small saucepan, heat ¼ pint/150 ml water with the milk, sugar and almond essence. Remove from the heat and cool, then add the gelatine mixture and stir for 1 minute.
3 Pour the mixture into a rectangular glass dish and set aside until set.
4 To serve, cut the almond flavoured gelatine into diamond shapes and serve with the fruits.

Celery-Pearl Paradise

6 tablespoons beef stock
2 teaspoons salt
1 tablespoon cornflour
1½ lb/700 g celery or Chinese cabbage, chopped
4 tablespoons vegetable oil

1 Blend together the beef stock, salt and cornflour.
2 Heat the vegetable oil in a wok or large frying pan and stir-fry the vegetables over high heat for 2 minutes.
3 Add the sauce, stir and cook over medium heat for 4-5 minutes. Serve.

LEAN CUISINE

The British public's interest in healthy eating has heightened dramatically within the past few years. A new product that will meet the needs of a growing band of people who enjoy their food, but at the same time are conscious of what they eat, has been introduced.

Dieting and weight watching can be one of the most tedious chores for a cook. Preparing low calorie dishes for one, or separate dishes for dieters, can be difficult and time consuming. Packaged and convenience foods are not usually suitable for dieters, since they contain added sugar, salt and preservatives. They may be convenient, but they are not always healthy.

Findus, makers of frozen and packaged convenience foods, have introduced a product that will make weight watching easier and enjoyable.

Lean Cuisine is a range of 12 individual frozen meals, based on meat, fish, vegetables and pasta. Lean Cuisine combines good cuisine with selected top quality fresh ingredients and the latest in nutritional expertise. The collection of prepared dishes is not only appetizing and satisfying, but also low in fat and sugar, and each Lean Cuisine meal contains less than 300 calories.

All 12 Lean Cuisine dishes are quick and easy to prepare straight from the freezer, either by baking or using the boil-in-the-bag method. Alternatively, the majority of these products are suitable for microwave cooking, and the instructions for both methods are included on the package.

Priced from around £1.15 to £1.60 per single serving, Lean Cuisine dishes give value for money both in terms of quality and quantity. The range is available in most major supermarkets, including Sainsburys, Waitrose, Tesco, Asda and Safeway, as well as most other supermarkets, grocers and co-ops.

For those trying to lose weight, Findus had devised the 14 day Lean Plan, a booklet available free of charge to purchasers of Lean Cuisine. The Lean Plan incorporates all 12 dishes in a two week calorie controlled diet. It also provides information on the wider aspects of dieting and keeping fit.

The Lean Plan was devised by nutritionists and dieticians, and provides a well balanced diet using the British recommended daily intakes of essential vitamins and minerals. It provides a calorie controlled eating plan to help with weight loss, and at the same time ensures that the levels of fat, sugar, salt and dietary fibre are in line with those suggested by British health experts.

In addition to the Lean Plan, there is also a special Lean Plan for diabetics. There are over a million diabetics in Britain, and many are trying to lose weight as an essential part of the control of their diabetic condition. Diabetics must also be constantly aware of precisely what they eat. If you or a member of your family is a diabetic, the Lean Plan for Diabetics can be of great help.

The plan is a free, 12 page guide to sensible eating for diabetics, and was produced by Findus with the help of the British Diabetic Association. The plan for diabetics provides a variety of suggestions for meals centred on Lean Cuisine dishes.

For a free copy of the Lean Plan for diabetics, send an SAE to:
The British Diabetic Association
10 Queen Anne Street
London, W1M 0BD.

SHAPE

Along with a reduction of salt and sugar in the diet, reducing the amount of fat consumed plays a major part in improving health. A diet high in saturated fats is associated with many heart and circulation disorders.

Fats account for almost 40 per cent of the daily calorie intake in Britain. The National Advisory Committee on Nutritional Education (NACNE) suggests that this figure should be reduced to 30 per cent. Some authorities recommend that it be reduced even further.

Reducing the amount of fat in the diet is also an aid to weight reduction. Foods with a low fat content equals fewer calories — fat has roughly twice the calories, ounce for ounce, of carbohydrate or protein. So whether you are trying to lose weight, or improve your health and that of your family, it is wise to reduce your fat intake.

St. Ivel is the first company in Britain to introduce an entire range of low fat dairy products, each containing at least half the fat of their traditional counterparts. Their use enables the entire family to eat well while reducing their fat intake, without sacrificing taste, nutritional value or versatility. These products supply the same amount of protein and calcium as full cream products but with half the fat. Many are suitable for freezing, and can be used extensively in cooking.

The Shape range includes a number of products. Shape Low Fat Milk has less than half the fat of full cream milk. Shape Cheese is made with pure dairy ingredients. It has the taste of traditional Cheddar but half the fat. Shape Cottage Cheese is indistinguishable from standard cottage cheese. It is available in natural flavour, or Onion and Chives, Pineapple and Onion. Shape Low Fat Soft Cheese has the versatility of cream cheese and is similar in taste and texture. It contains only 9% fat compared to 46% in cream cheese. The varieties include Onion and Chives and Garlic and Herb. Shape Yoghurt comes in a variety of flavours. These include strawberry, raspberry and peach along with more unusual flavours such as Melba, Rhubarb and Tropical Fruit. Shape Double and Shape Single are low fat alternatives to double and single cream. They are blends of skimmed milk, butter fat and vegetable fat, with half the fat of standard cream.

Tangy Rice and Almond Mould
SERVES 6

1 orange, peeled and segmented
1 pint/600 ml Shape low fat milk
4 tablespoons clear honey
2 oz/50 g pudding rice
few drops almond essence
1 tablespoon Bemax
1 tablespoon gelatine
¼ pint/150 ml Shape Double
1 egg white
1 lime and mandarin oranges, to garnish

1 Put the orange rind into the low fat milk and bring to the boil. Infuse for 10 minutes, then strain.
2 Return milk to the pan, add the honey, rice, almond essence and Bemax. Bring to the boil and simmer until the rice has softened. Cool in a bowl.
3 Dissolve the gelatine according to the package instructions, then stir into the rice.
4 Whip the Double until it holds its shape. Fold into the rice and add the orange segments.
5 Whip the egg white until thick, fold into the rice and spoon into a 1 litre/2 pint mould or dish.
6 Chill for several hours before turning out. Decorate with mandarin oranges and lime.

ARTIFICIAL SWEETENERS

One of the problems with artificial sweeteners is that they are so much sweeter than sugar when compared by weight that cooking and using them spoon-for-spoon has always proved difficult. A new product has been introduced recently which helps to eliminate these problems.

Canderel Spoonful, an artificial sweetener made with NutraSweet, is a granulated one-for-one sweetener that can be used in much the same manner as sugar.

One teaspoon of Canderel Spoonful is equivalent in sweetness to one teaspoon of sugar, making it easier to obtain the desired amount. It can be sprinkled directly on to cereals or fruit or into beverages. It can also be used in baking and cooking. Included here are some recipes for three different sweets, all using Canderel Spoonful. There is also a recipe book available by Hilary Walden called *The Sweet Taste of Life*.

Melting Snow
MAKES 35
2 teaspoons gelatine
8 tablespoons Canderel Spoonful
½ egg white

1 Place 7½ fl oz/215 ml water in a saucepan and sprinkle over the gelatine. Stir gently, the leave to stand for 10 minutes.
2 Heat the mixture over a very low heat, stirring constantly, until the gelatine has dissolved, then bring to the boil and simmer for 5 minutes.
3 Remove from the heat and cool slightly, then sprinkle in the Canderel Spoonful, stirring the mixture continuously. Leave to cool until just on the point of setting.
4 Whisk the egg white until standing in stiff peaks. Pour in the gelatine mixture in a slow steady stream, whisking constantly. Continue to whisk until the mixture is very thick and frothy and nearly on the point of setting.
5 Place teaspoonfuls, or pipe the mixture, on a large non-stick baking tray or on to greased baking parchment and leave to set.
6 Store in a covered container in the refrigerator for up to 3 days.
● 2 calories each

Rose Delight
MAKES 40 SQUARES
4 teaspoons gelatine
15 tablespoons Canderel Spoonful
approximately 1½ teaspoons rose water
few drops of pink food colouring (optional)

1 Place 15 fl oz/425 ml water in a saucepan and sprinkle the gelatine over the surface. Stir well, then leave to soak for 10 minutes.
2 Bring the liquid slowly to the boil, then simmer for 5 minutes. Remove from the heat and leave to cool slightly.
3 Sprinkle in the Canderel Spoonful, a tablespoon at a time, stirring continuously. Stir in the rose water.
4 Either colour all the mixture pink with food colouring or pour half into a square or rectangular tin, and colour the remaining half before pouring into another tin.
5 Leave to set in the refrigerator for several hours until set. Cut into squares just before serving. Keep in a covered airtight container in the refrigerator for 1-2 days.
● 3 calories each.

Coffee and Nut Bonbons
MAKES 16
1½ oz/40 g skimmed milk powder
2 teaspoons instant coffee powder
3-4 teaspoons Canderel Spoonful, to taste
1 or 2 drops almond essence
2 tablespoons finely chopped toasted hazelnuts or almonds

1 Stir the milk powder, coffee powder and Canderel Spoonful together.
2 Sprinkle over 2 tablespoons water and almond essence, then bind all the ingredients together to form a stiff paste.
3 Leave for 2-3 minutes, then form into 16 small balls. Roll the balls in the nuts until they are lightly coated and gently press so the nuts are secure.
4 Wrap the balls in individual pieces of cling film, and place in the refrigerator for 1 hour. Serve immediately or store in an airtight container in the refrigerator for up to 3 days.
● 14 calories each.

CHEF'S CHOICE

Gail Duff, cookery writer, shares one of her favourite menus. Based on traditional British food, the menu offers a choice of starters and desserts, with a simple but spectacular main course.

I first started cooking for the love of it. When I left home for college (to study a completely different subject) at the age of eighteen, I had hardly ever even boiled an egg. My school had dictated whether you studied cookery or needlework, and their choice for me was needlework.

I stayed for a brief two weeks with a friend's aunt in Highgate. She was a health food nut. I say 'nut' because this was a long time ago. Health and diet were rarely put together in people's minds, and if you ever thought of basing a main meal on a nut roast or even bought biscuits with 'Healthlife' written on them, you were thought to be cranky indeed.

I have always had fruit juice in the mornings, and throughout my sixth form years my breakfasts had consisted of crispbreads, honey and oranges, so I suppose my mind was ripe for learning more. I enjoyed the salads and fresh flavours of the meals that I was given by friends. I didn't associate them with 'health' food, but these brief two weeks had a great influence on what was to come in later years.

My next stay was with a Jewish actress and drama teacher. This lasted for two years. The first meal that I was given in this house was something consisting of aubergines, rice and lamb. Now a meal such as that sounds perfectly normal today, but I had never seen or tasted such a thing. Lamb chops were something to be baked in the oven and served with roast potatoes and home grown English vegetables. I tried not to look surprised. I acted as though I ate meals of this kind every day — and found myself thoroughly enjoying it!

Before long I was asking questions, poking about in spice cupboards and enjoying the run of the kitchen. Every-one else was out in the early evenings so I could try out lots of new recipes. I explored the North London markets and delicatessens. Even the supermarkets looked exotic compared to those I had left behind at home. A favourite aunt bought me Katharine Whitehorn's excellent book *Cooking in a Bedsitter*. I used it straight for a while and then started to play around with ingredients and techniques. A whole new world had opened up for me. Life would never be the same again.

I got married straight out of college and found another joy — entertaining. Not the formal type of dinner party entertaining, but always having a house full of friends who would stop by for a chat and end up staying for a meal. After a year, I gave up work and took over my husband's shop and photographic studio while he went to college. During the quiet times, I had my nose buried deep in a Cordon Bleu cookery partwork. The house was always full of students and I could experiment to my heart's content. Soon my experiments fell into a pattern which became my first book, *Fresh all the Year*, published by Macmillan.

I received a further cookery 'education' by the fact that my husband photographed a series of articles by top chefs for *Caterer and Hotelkeeper* magazine. Acting as his assistant, I spent many happy hours in the kitchens of famous hotels and restaurants just watching chefs such as Anton Mossiman at the Dorchester or John Tovey up at beautiful Miller Howe on the shores of Lake Windermere.

My interest in wholefood did not at first leap ahead as quickly. I still used brown rice instead of white, never bought white bread, and many of my recipes were based on fresh vegetables. All this was purely a matter of taste. The fresher and more natural the ingredients, the better they were. I frequently visited the local health food shop for bread and locally made yoghurt, and gradually began looking along the shelves for other ingredients. Then I became curious as to why they were considered to benefit health, and so began a series of wholefood books.

My lack of formal training has been both an advantage and a disadvantage. It definitely enabled me to be more creative. I could devise my own methods and combinations of ingredients without the restrictions of a textbook. But when magazines started to commission work on basic cookery techniques, I then had to spend many long hours poring over books and typing out notes until I knew how to properly line a flan tin or for how many minutes to boil a carrot.

My other passion besides cookery is the history and folklore of the British countryside. My reading and research in this field made my meals that of a medieval baron on one day and a 19th century cottage on another. Despite my cosmopolitan student days, I now use mainly British ingredients and am never more happy than when delving into regional cookery books.

My favourite style of cooking is a combination of British country food and wholefood, and my menu reflects this. I cook very much with the seasons, and so have included one warming soup and one light tomato first course. There is also one hot and one cold sweet, the first warming and traditional, the second cold and made from the best of wholefood ingredients. I chose pigeons for the main dish because they are the cheapest and most readily available game, and can be purchased all year round. My husband shoots and I enjoy beating with the dogs and so we always have pigeons in the freezer. They are also available from many supermarkets and country butchers. I pick my own blackberries, too, but again you can buy them, and frozen ones are available all through the year.

The influences that have come to bear in my cookery have come from far and wide. I am constantly researching and experimenting with food, and cooking never ceases to be a pleasure.

MENU

Stilton and Onion Soup
or
Stuffed Tomatoes in a Parsley Field

Pigeon Breasts with Blackberry Sauce

Juniper Cabbage

Apple Rum Cake
or
Apricot and Almond Tart

Stuffed Tomatoes in a Parsley Field

Stuffed Tomatoes in a Parsley Field
SERVES 4
8 small or medium-sized tomatoes
Stuffing
2 x 3 3/4 oz/110 g tins sild, drained
2 oz/50 g curd cheese
pepper
grated zest and juice of ½ lemon
2 oz/50 g parsley, finely chopped

1 Cut off and reserve a slice from the top of each tomato. Using a teaspoon, remove all the seeds and flesh from the insides of the tomatoes and discard.
2 To make the stuffing, use a fork and mash the sild. Work in the cheese and season with the pepper and lemon zest and juice, beating well.
3 Fill the tomatoes with the stuffing, then position the reserved slices as lids so the stuffing is visible on one side. Gently press some of the parsley on to the side of the stuffing that is visible.
4 Serve each person 2 tomatoes on individual plates and sprinkle round the remaining parsley.
Note If curd cheese is unavailable, use any low fat soft cheese. The parsley is not just for garnish and should be eaten with the tomatoes and stuffing. The combination of flavours is superb.

Stilton and Onion Soup
SERVES 4
1 oz/25 g butter
2 onions, finely chopped
1 tablespoon wholewheat flour
1¼ pints/725 ml vegetable or chicken stock
bouquet garni
¼ pint/150 ml dry white wine
4 oz/100 g Stilton cheese, finely grated
4 tablespoons finely chopped watercress for garnish.

1 Melt the butter in a large saucepan over low heat. Add the onions and sauté until soft but not brown.
2 Stir in the flour, then add the stock and bring to the boil, stirring. Add the bouquet garni and simmer, uncovered, for 15 minutes.
3 Place the Stilton into a deep bowl. Remove the soup from the heat and remove the bouquet garni. Add the wine to the soup and stir.
4 Gradually stir about one-quarter of the soup into the Stilton, then return all the mixture to the saucepan.
5 Gently reheat the soup without boiling. Serve in individual bowls, garnished with watercress.
Note This may also be made with all stock instead of half stock and half wine.

Stilton and Onion Soup

Pigeon Breasts with Blackberry Sauce

Pigeon Breasts with Blackberry Sauce
SERVES 4

1 oz/25 g butter
4 pigeon breasts, each cut into 2 pieces and skinned
1 onion, finely chopped
7 fl oz/200 ml dry red wine
2 tablespoons red wine vinegar
½ lb/225 g blackberries
bouquet garni made with sage and thyme sprigs

Pigeon Stock
4 pigeon carcasses
1 onion, cut in half but not peeled
1 carrot, split lengthways
1 stalk celery, broken
1 teaspoon black peppercorns
bouquet garni

1 To make the stock, put all the ingredients in a large saucepan with 2½ pints/1.4 litres water. Bring to the boil, skim the surface and simmer gently for about 1½ hours. Skim the surface with a large metal spoon as often as necessary.
2 Melt the butter in a large frying pan over high heat. Add the pigeon breasts and cook for about 5 minutes, until well browned on both sides. Remove the breasts from the frying pan and set aside and keep warm.
3 Spoon off a little of the fat from the frying pan and put a thin layer in the base of a large heavy-based saucepan over medium heat.
4 Add the onion and stir until it is soft and brown. Add the wine, wine vinegar and 7 fl oz/200 ml of the stock and bring to the boil. Add 6 oz/175 g of the blackberries to the liquid with the bouquet garni.
5 Boil, uncovered, until the mixture is reduced by half.
6 Strain the sauce into a large sieve over a large bowl, using a large wooden spoon to press down hard on the blackberries and onions, to extract as much purée as possible.
7 Return the sauce to the rinsed-out pan and simmer for 2 minutes.
8 Slice the pigeon breasts into thin slices; they should be tender and pink in the middle. Arrange the slices on a large serving dish with the blackberry sauce in the middle with the remaining blackberries sprinkled over the top. Serve at once.
Note To remove the breasts from the pigeons, use a sharp knife and cut down the breastbone. Gently ease the knife between the breast meat and bone so each half of the breast comes away in one piece. The skin should pull off easily if you hold the meat firmly in one hand and gently pull away the skin with your other hand.

To complete this meal, serve these delicious pigeon breasts with jacket potatoes and buttered braised cabbage flavoured with lightly crushed juniper berries.

Juniper Cabbage
SERVES 4

1 oz/25 g butter
1 medium head cabbage, shredded
6 juniper berries, crushed
1 clove garlic, crushed
salt and pepper (optional)

1 Melt the butter in a large heavy-based saucepan over high heat.
2 Mix together the cabbage, juniper berries and garlic, then add ¼ pint/150 ml water and stir until all the flavourings are evenly distributed.
3 Cover and cook over low heat for about 10 minutes, until the cabbage is tender. Season with salt and pepper, if desired, place in a warmed serving dish and serve at once with the pigeon.

Apple Rum Cake
SERVES 4-6

4 oz/100 g wholewheat flour
1 teaspoon baking powder
1 teaspoon ground cinnamon
4 oz/100 g butter, softened
4 oz/100 g Barbados sugar
1 egg, beaten
3 fl oz/75 ml white rum
3 oz/75 g raisins
2 large Bramley apples
extra butter for greasing the cake pan
single cream or custard for serving

1 Heat the oven to 180C/350F/Gas 4. Thickly butter a 9 inch/23 cm cake pan.
2 Toss the flour with the baking powder and cinnamon, then beat it into the butter, alternately with the egg. Beat in the rum, a little at a time, then fold in the raisins, using a large metal spoon.
3 Peel and core the apples, then cut them lengthways into thin slices. Decoratively arrange the apples in the base of the prepared cake pan, then spoon the batter over the top and smooth the surface.
4 Bake for 30 minutes, until the cake is firm and begins to shrink away from the sides of the pan.
5 Turn out the cake on to a large, flat plate so the apple slices are on top. Serve hot with cream or custard to pour over the top.

Almond and Apricot Tart
SERVES 4

4 oz/100 g dried whole apricots
¼ pint/150 ml natural orange juice
3 oz/75 g ground almonds
2 oz/50 g pear and apple spread (see Note, below)
½ pint/275 ml double cream
2 squares of sugar-free carob bar

Pastry
6 oz/175 g wholewheat flour
pinch of salt
3 oz/75 g chilled margarine, cut into small pieces

1 To make the pastry, put the flour and salt into a large bowl and rub in the margarine until the mixture resembles fine breadcrumbs. Sprinkle over 2-3 tablespoons cold water and mix to make a soft dough. Turn out on to a lightly floured surface and knead. Wrap in cling film and chill for at least 30 minutes.

2 Meanwhile, put the apricots into a saucepan with the orange juice. Bring to the boil, then remove from the heat and set aside for 4 hours.

3 Heat the oven to 200C/400F/Gas 6.

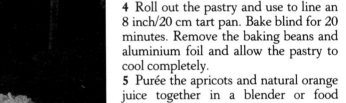
Almond and Apricot Tart

Apple Rum Cake

4 Roll out the pastry and use to line an 8 inch/20 cm tart pan. Bake blind for 20 minutes. Remove the baking beans and aluminium foil and allow the pastry to cool completely.

5 Purée the apricots and natural orange juice together in a blender or food processor.

6 Place the almonds in a bowl and stir in the pear and apple spread and the apricot purée. Continue stirring until all the ingredients are well mixed.

7 Remove the pastry shell from the pan and carefully put it on to a flat serving plate. Spread the almond and apricot mixture evenly over the base.

8 Stiffly whip the cream, then decoratively pipe it over the top of the tart. For an extra fillip, grate the carob squares over the top of the cream. If sugar-free carob bars are difficult to find, you can use ordinary plain carob bars or a bar of plain chocolate.

Note All of the ingredients used in this recipe can be bought in a health food shop, with the possible exception of double cream. Pear and apple spread is a thick, sticky syrup made from concentrated pear and apple juice. Carob is a health food alternative for ordinary plain chocolate, which is made from the long, flat pods of a Mediterranean evergreen tree.

WINES & SPIRITS

You don't need to be a gourmet or connoisseur to appreciate wines and spirits. A little knowledge about how they are made, and an understanding of the different types and how best to serve them, will increase your pleasure considerably.

MAKING WINE

In recent years, many advances have taken place in wine making, both in the vineyard and in the actual production of the wine. These developments have led to an increase in yields, have made the quantity and quality more reliable, and increased the availability of reasonably priced, better standard wines. They have also brought a greater uniformity to wines. Not only in those wines that are mass-produced, but also in the fine wine field.

Red wines are produced by including the grape skins during fermentation to extract the pigment. At the same time, a substance called tannin is drawn out of the skins. It is this substance that gives red wines a harsh, acid flavour, and enables them to live much longer than most white wines. During ageing, the tannin softens, mellows and becomes much less noticeable.

The ripe grapes are picked in the autumn and then quickly taken to the press house or winery, where they are crushed and the stalks are removed. The juice, called 'must', and the crushed grapes with their skins and pips, are pumped into temperature-controlled fermentation vats. During fermentation the sugar in the must is converted into alcohol. For red wines, the fermentation continues until all the sugar has been used up. The time this takes depends on the temperature and the style of wine being made. The longer the time of fermentation, the 'bigger' the wine.

When fermentation has finished, the new wine is pumped into large vats or casks where the particles left in the wine will settle to the bottom. The wine is syphoned off the sediment at regular intervals until it is clear, and will then be left to age.

The ageing time varies from wine to wine. If a light, modern wine is being made, it will age for just a few months. But if a traditional claret or Burgundy is being made, the wine will age for up to two years. Before the wine is bottled it will be filtered and refined to remove the last traces of particles that could make the wine cloudy.

White wine is made in basically the same way as red, except that the skins are usually removed before fermentation, and fermentation takes place at a lower temperature for a shorter time. It may be stopped before all the sugar has been used up, to leave a wine that is sweet. White wines are also kept for less time than red before they are bottled.

VINTAGES

The date that appears on the main label, neck label or cork of a wine is called the

vintage. This shows the year in which the grapes used for making the wine were gathered, and also the year that the wine was made.

In countries where the climate is more or less consistent, vintages are not as important as in those countries that have greater climate fluctuations, such as France and Germany. The weather affects the quality and quantity of the grapes, influences the character of the wine, determines how long it should be kept before it is at its best for drinking, and how long it will last. Vintages are also less relevant for the cheaper, mass-produced wines, since many of the differences caused by the weather are ironed out during the production and blending process.

KEEPING WINE

The vast majority of wines are ready for drinking as soon as they have been bought. They are not very likely to improve with age, and will in fact deteriorate after about a year. These wines are the ones that cost less than about £3, are non-vintage, and light in colour and style.

Slightly more expensive wines, such as those in the £3.50-£4 price bracket, are ready for drinking when about 2-3 years old. They may have already reached this age when you see them on the shelves, so look for the vintage. Some wines, such as good white Burgundies, Rhône wines, good Chianti, good German wines and many Cabernet Sauvignons, are at their best when about 3-5 years old. Others, such as good Bordeaux and Burgundies, need to be kept for 5-10 years before they are ready for drinking, and can last for much longer.

Price is a reliable, if not always foolproof, guide to the keeping potential of a wine — the lower the price the younger the wine should be drunk. White wines are almost always drunk younger than red ones of the same style and quality, lighter-styled wines are drunk sooner than full-bodied ones, and lesser quality wines should be drunk sooner than those of superior quality.

GRAPE VARIETIES

An increasing number of wines are being labelled with their main grape variety, so it pays to know the characteristics of a particular grape, although these will vary according to where the wine is made. Following are the main grape varieties that appear on labels.

GRAPES FOR WHITE WINES
Riesling
When used in German or Alsace wines, this grape produces wines that are fragrant and fruity, sometimes dry, sometimes sweet, always good and sometimes magnificent. They can last for many years. Similar-styled wines are also made in Austria, South Africa and California. True Rieslings are never cheap, so if you see a wine labelled with the word Riesling at a very modest price, it will have been made by a different grape altogether. This will probably be the Laski, Lutomer, Welsch or Olasz grape, depending on the country of origin. The wine will be lighter, less distinguished and suitable for casual drinking.
Chardonnay
This is the grape that is used for white Burgundies, and it always produces wines that are similarly full-bodied, often with an almost buttery richness. Chardonnays from California have a tendency to be very powerful wines, high in alcohol, and expensive, while those from Bulgaria are very good value.
Chenin Blanc
This grape makes flowery wines, usually with some sweetness, that have a hint of honey to them.

GRAPES FOR RED WINES
Cabernet Sauvignon
Traditionally, the Cabernet Sauvignon grape produces wines that contain a lot of tannin. They are hard when young, but mellow with age to a complex flavour that has a hint of cigar-box or cedar wood and blackcurrants. However, with modern wine making techniques, Cabernet Sauvignon wines are being made that are far more easy to drink when young. Reasonably priced, especially good examples come from Bulgaria and Chile.
Merlot
This grape makes soft, fruity wines, and is used for fine Bordeaux.

BUYING WINE

CHOOSING WINE

When buying a wine you must be able, by law, to find out certain basic information about it from the label. All wines must be labelled with the nominal volume, the country or countries of origin, the name and address of the bottler or importer, and an appropriate description of the wine.

In addition, there may be other authentication information, such as an 'e' mark which shows the wine has been bottled according to EEC regulations. If it is simply called 'table wine' it will be a blend of wine from different EEC countries. Wines from non-EEC countries will be even more simply labelled as 'wine', unless the country has a recognized quality grading system.

The EEC groups its wine into two categories — basic table wines, which are inexpensive, everyday wines, and quality wines, which carry a lot more information on their labels and are the product of a particular region.

Quality wines may be further controlled by the grading system that is in operation within that country. Comparisons between the various grades of quality in different countries cannot be made since the grading systems of each country differs in the way they assess the wines and in their thoroughness.

All of the above information provides, as it were, the birth certificate and pedigree of the wine, but does not actually tell you what it tastes like. The first clue to the style of the wine can be the shape of the bottle. Some shapes are so automatically associated with a particular type of wine that it is assumed that any wine within a certain shape of bottle will be in that style. Dark green bottles with squared-off shoulders are used for clarets and so tend to be used for wines with similar characteristics, while sloping shouldered dark green bottles indicate a Burgundy style of wine. Germanic-style wines come in tall, slim bottles — traditionally, brown is used for Rhine wines and green for Mosels.

Some labels do carry a description such as 'crisp and dry', but remember, these are very subjective. Recently, several large chains of wine merchants have introduced systems of grading and grouping types of wine according to their sweetness, with each group having a number (see below).

STORING WINE

Almost all wines are adversely affected by the shaking up they get when taken from the place of purchase to the place where they are to be drunk, and will taste better if they are allowed to rest for a day or so. Therefore, if at all possible, plan to buy wines a short while in advance, especially for dinner parties.

A good way to have a stock of wines always at hand to suit any occasion or guest is to buy in bulk and keep the bottles at home. In bulk very often means by the case, which is always 12 bottles, and it is invariably cheaper to buy like this than individual bottles. The 12 bottles do not usually have to be all of the same type of wine, but can be a mixture of any style that you like. However, places such as wine warehouses which specialize in this type of selling very often have a 'wholesale' licence which means they can only sell in units of 12. If 12 bottles is too large a purchase for you to make at one go, a friend, neighbour or colleague may be very happy to come in with you.

When keeping wine at home, whether for a few days or a few months, keep it on its side in a consistently cool place (fluctuations in temperature are very harmful to wine) away from direct light and draughts and free from vibrations. Remember that hot air rises so the top of a cupboard is not a suitable place while the bottom can be draughty. Wine racks can be bought very reasonably from a number of shops.

NEW WINE GUIDE

The Wine Development Board, a non-commercial independent body, has developed a dry-to-sweet guide for white wines which has the endorsement of the wine trade. The major white wines of the world, as well as rosés, sherry and vermouth, have been numbered from 1-9 in terms of dry to sweet. Number 1 signifies very dry white wines and Number 9 indicates maximum sweetness. The guide is used by many wine merchants and supermarkets, though in some outlets you may find wines numbered slightly differently to the numbers suggested, because their wine is drier or sweeter.

The numbers and symbols will usually appear on a description card underneath the wine. It is hoped in the future that the symbol will appear on the actual bottles, to help you choose the wine you prefer and to allow you to taste unfamiliar wines without the liklihood of disappointment.

1	2	3	4	5	6	7	8	9
Muscadet	Soave	Brut Sparkling wine	Vinho Verde	Vouvray Demi-Sec	Demi-sec Champagne	Asti Spumante	Austrian Beerenauslesen	Malmsey Madeira
Champagne	White Burgundy	Gewürztraminer d'Alsace	Moselle Kabinett	Liebfraumilch	Spanish Medium	Rhine Auslesen	Spanish Sweet White	Muscat de Beaumes de Venise
Chablis	Fino Sherry	Dry Amontillado Sherry	Rhine Kabinett	Medium British Sherry	All Golden Sherry types	1ères Côtes de Bordeaux	Sauternes	Marsala
Dry White Bordeaux	Sercial Madeira	Medium Dry Montilla	Yugoslav Laski and Hungarian Olasz Riesling Medium Dry	Verdelho Madeira		Tokay Aszu	Barsac	
Manzanilla Sherry		Dry White Vermouth	Portuguese Rosé			Pale Cream Sherry	Cream and Rich Cream Sherry types	
Tavel Rosé		Anjou Rosé				Montilla Cream		
						Bual Madeira		
						Rosso, Rose and Bianco Vermouths		

READING A WINE LABEL

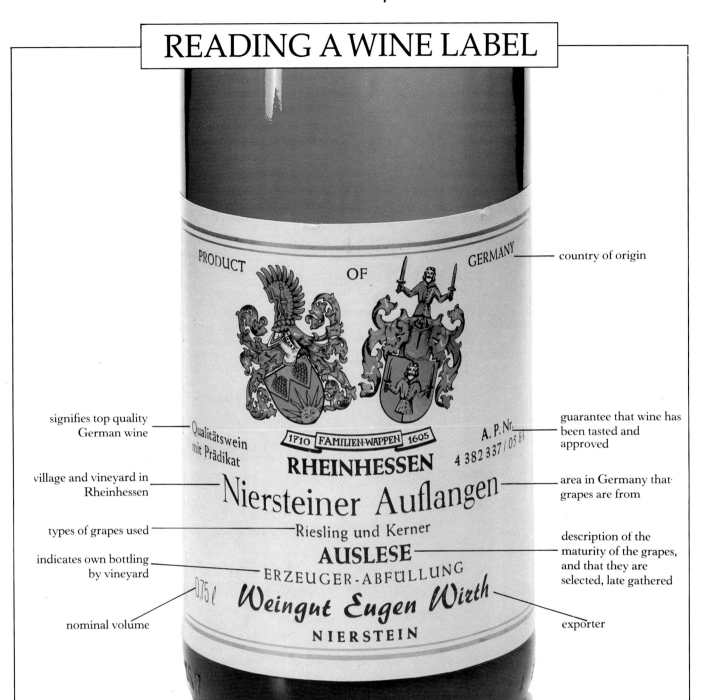

country of origin

PRODUCT OF GERMANY

signifies top quality German wine — Qualitätswein mit Prädikat

guarantee that wine has been tasted and approved — A. P. Nr. 4 382 337 / 05 84

1710 FAMILIEN-WAPPEN 1605

RHEINHESSEN

village and vineyard in Rheinhessen — Niersteiner Auflangen — area in Germany that grapes are from

types of grapes used — Riesling und Kerner

AUSLESE — description of the maturity of the grapes, and that they are selected, late gathered

indicates own bottling by vineyard — ERZEUGER-ABFÜLLUNG

0,75 ℓ — nominal volume

Weingut Eugen Wirth — exporter

NIERSTEIN

WINE LABEL GLOSSARY

Appellation Contrôlée (AC) This is a legal assurance that a superior French wine fulfils a region's specific growing, harvesting and quality requirements.

Délimités de Qualité Supérieur (DQS) This is the qualification for less superior French wines.

Denominazione di Origine Controllata Garantita (DOCG) This is the Italian classification for best quality wines.

Denominazione di Origine Controllata (DOC) This Italian classification is similar to the French DQS.

Chianti Classico The inclusion of 'classico' assures an authentic Chianti from a specific area of Tuscany. Each bottle is sealed with the local vinters association's crest.

Qualitätswein mit Prädikat (QmP) This is the top grade of German wine and has no added sweetener.

Qualitätswein bestimmter Anbaugebiete (QbA) This is the second grade of quality German wines.

Vins de Pays, Tafelwein, Vino da Tavola The French, German and Italian designation of basic table wines. They are usually inexpensive and drinkable.

Table wine If the label also includes an 'e' mark, the wine will be a blend from several different countries.

SERVING WINE
Temperature Wines are always more enjoyable if they are served at the temperature that shows off their characteristics to the best advantage. Coolness enhances the fresh crisp acidity of white wines, whether they are sweet or dry, while a certain degree of warmth is needed to bring out the aroma and flavour of red ones.

Within each category, different wines will benefit from being served at slightly different temperatures. Generally, the cheaper or sweeter the white wine, the cooler the temperature should be, with a

minimum of about 7°C/45°F, while full-bodied good white wines should be served at about 11-13°C/52-55°F. Fruity, light red wines such as Beaujolais, red Loires and Valpolicella can be served cool, everyday red wines are usually served at about 15-16°C/60°F, and more full-bodied red wines are most enjoyable if they are served at about 17-18°C/63-65°F.

Whether warming or cooling wine, any change in temperature should be gentle. Leave a red wine at room temperature for a number of hours before it is required — do not put it in

front of a fire, over a radiator or too close to the cooker. About 1-1½ hours in the refrigerator is long enough to cool good-medium quality wines, and about 2 hours for the cheaper wines. Obviously, the initial temperature of the wine and the temperature within the refrigerator will influence the time it will take to reach the right temperature. As an alternative to placing the wine in the refrigerator, the bottle can be placed in a bucket filled with water and ice cubes — this is more effective than just ice cubes. When serving the wine make sure the glasses are at a suitable temper-

GLASSES

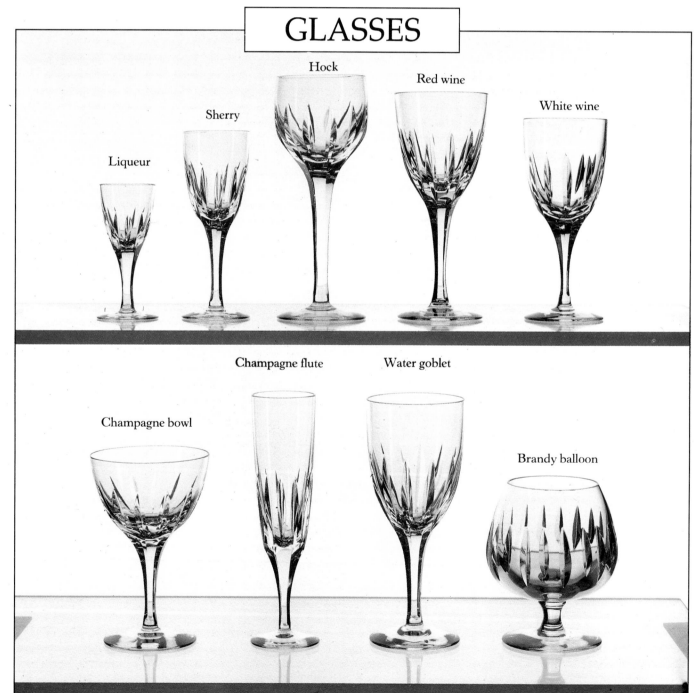

ature. A warm glass will soon undo the chilling of a white wine while a cold glass will chill a red. Also, use clear glasses that are stemmed — holding the glass by the bowl overwarms wine.

Decanting There are some sound reasons for decanting wines in certain instances. First, to remove any sediment that may be at the bottom of the bottle — as in, for example, an old claret or vintage port — which would make the wine cloudy when it was served. Second, decanting will aerate the wine and speed up the maturing process, making it softer and easier to drink. Robust wines such as Bulls Blood or a full-bodied Rioja and young, harsh wines are the main beneficiaries here. If you find when you taste a wine that it is too hard, simply pour it into another bottle, jug or carafe and you will find that it becomes much more drinkable.

Moderately priced, medium-bodied red wines should be decanted about 1-2 hours in advance. With better quality medium-bodied red wines, decant about 2 hours in advance for younger wines and allow slightly less time for older wines. Full-bodied red wines of good quality should be decanted about 4 hours in advance, and leave 2 hours for inexpensive full-bodied red wines.

If the cork of a bottle remains firmly in place, hold the neck of the bottle under fairly hot running water for a minute or two until the glass expands. A special gadget called a 'decorker' is available for removing corks that fall into bottles. Alternatively, hold the cork back inside the bottle with a knitting needle or long, pointed knife and pour the contents into a clean bottle, jug or carafe. If pieces of cork fall into the wine, pour it through a coffee filter, cheesecloth or muslin.

Keep a cork stopper of the type used for sherry bottles for re-closing opened bottles of still wines — there are special stoppers on sale for sparkling wines. Keep any partly used bottles of wine in the door of the refrigerator. If they are more than half full, pour the wine into a smaller bottle that it will just fill. Wines closed with a screw-cap will keep for 2-3 weeks, full-bodied and sweet wines for about 3 days, and lighter wines for about 2 days.

If serving a number of wines the general advice is to serve light-bodied before fuller-bodied, white before red, dry before sweet, chilled wines before those served at room temperature, and younger before older.

WINE WITH FOOD

MATCHING WINE AND FOOD

Any wine can be drunk with any food, but it is always worth at least considering the old conventions and general guidelines. They are the result of years of other people's eating and drinking experience, and so are reliable and will save you from any real disasters.

One of the main reasons to match up food and wine is chemical. White wine has an appetizing, refreshing quality that is provided by acids. These acids will enhance the flavour of fish, and the saltiness of the fish will emphasize the fruity flavours of the wine.

The tannin in red wine, though, will react badly with the salt in the fish and make it bitter. Often, it will react with the fishy oils and leave a metallic taste in the mouth. By the same token, red wine and sweets is also not a good match. Sugar, as with salt, reacts badly with tannin and makes it taste bitter.

When planning a menu with food and wine, you will need to consider the aesthetics of the meal. Balancing pale colours of food with a pale colour of wine, and strong colours of beef and game with a rich red wine make sense. A meal should be pleasing to both the eye and the palate, and foodstuffs will usually have their own appropriate colour.

There are a few basic rules to follow when matching food and wine. Balance the wine and the food so that neither overpowers the other. A light meal is best matched by a light wine, while richer, more highly flavoured food calls for a robust wine.

GOOD COMBINATIONS

Shellfish
A very dry white wine such as Muscadet
Light fish dishes
A dry white wine such as a white Burgundy or Sancerre
Richer fish dishes
Fuller flavoured white wines such as Graves, Orvieto or white Rioja
White meat
A dry, fairly full bodied white wine such as white Burgundy, white Rhône, Chardonnays, Rieslings or stronger rosés
Ham
As above
Duck and goose
A light red wine

Red meat cooked plainly
A medium bodied red such as Chianti Classico or Barbaresco
Rich beef and game dishes
A full bodied red wine such as red Rhônes, Barolos, stronger Riojas or South African Pinotage
Cheese
With soft cheeses, a light red wine is suitable, with hard cheese a medium-bodied red, and with goat's cheese a crisp dry white such as Sancerre
Desserts
With desserts that are not too creamy, non-citrus desserts and ones without chocolate, serve a sweet white wine such as Sauternes, Baumes de Venise, Monbazillac or a sweet sparkling wine.

COMBINATIONS TO AVOID

Some foods are more like enemies to wine than natural partners, and they can spoil the taste of wines that are served with them. Acidity in a food makes wines taste very sharp, so avoid using too much dressing on a salad, too much lemon juice with fish, and citrus fruits such as oranges and lemons. Raw tomatoes can also cause problems.

Watercress and eggs are two other difficult foods, so if you are planning to serve a wine with them, choose one that is simple and on the robust side, such as a Côtes du Rhône. With highly spiced foods and not-too-hot curries, serve a full-flavoured white wine, and a good match for Chinese food is a light, slightly sweet rosé.

Really strong cheese will kill all but the most robust of red or fortified wines, and chocolate spells death to all wines. Avoid serving full, tannic red wines with fish, although light red wines can partner rich fish like salmon. Also, avoid red wines with Chinese food and in general, desserts, although they can be matched with strawberries, peaches and pears.

WINE CHOICE OF THE YEAR

My wine choice for the year is the 1982 Gewurztraminer, from the vineyard Herrenweg Turckheim and made by Zind Humbrecht. The gewurztraminer grape always makes soft, appealing wines with a distinctive fruity-spicy flavour, but this one is particularly elegant since its flavour is more restrained than some. It is given a real touch of class by a fresh, underlying acidity.

Served lightly chilled, this wine is an ideal drink to sip without food, but it can also be served quite happily with light chicken, fish and shellfish dishes. It is especially good with cold dishes, provided they do not contain mayonnaise, and is an ideal late spring/summer wine.

Wines from the 1982 vintage in Alsace are maturing quickly, and this one is ready for drinking now. But with its acidity, it will last well into 1987. It is definitely worth buying some now and storing it for a future occasion.

The main source of supply for my wine choice of the year is *Le Nez Rouge, 12 Brewery Road, London N7, (01) 609-4711.*

SPARKLING WINES AND CHAMPAGNE

Sparkling wines are available in a wide range of prices and styles, from very dry to sweet, white, pink or red. In all of them, the sparkle is caused by carbon dioxide bubbles that are trapped within a wine. Several methods are used to introduce the bubbles into the base wine, and each method produces wines of different qualities at a different price. The method used is always appropriate for the quality of the base wine. For example, the most expensive method cannot make a good sparkling wine out of an inferior base wine.

The best method is the one that is known as the 'methode champenoise' since this is the one that is used to produce champagne. All champagnes are produced by this method, but not all of the wines that are made by it are allowed to call themselves champagne. This privilege is reserved for wines that are made in a small area north-east of Paris where the production is tightly controlled. The sparkle is the result of a secondary fermentation that is induced to take place in the bottle. Since the process is lengthy and laborious, sparkling wines made by the 'methode champenoise' will never be cheap.

Champagnes command an even higher price because of the superiority of the vineyards, the quality of the grapes and the length of time the wines are stored before they are sold. Good 'methode champenoise' wines are also made in Saumur and the Languedoc in France; in Spain the method is used in the making of 'cava' wines.

A quicker and cheaper way of getting bubbles into a wine is to induce the secondary fermentation to take place in large sealed vats and then to pump the sparkling wine into bottles. This is known as 'cuve close' or the 'method Charmat', after the Frenchman who invented it. It is used in the making of Veuve de Vernay, German 'Sekt' wines and Italian Asti Spumante — any bottle with the word spumante indicates it is a sparkling wine. Cheaper still is injecting carbon dioxide into the wine, but the bubbles quickly disappear once the wine has been opened.

The level of sweetness of the sparkling wine will be indicated on the label — 'brut' or 'nature' is very dry, 'extra dry', 'extra sec' and 'tres sec' show that the wine will be dry, 'sec' medium dry, 'medium dry' and 'demi-sec' indicate that it will be medium sweet while 'rich' or 'doux' describes a very sweet wine.

OPENING A SPARKLING WINE

To avoid an exploding cork and wastage of wine when it foams out of the bottle, make sure the bottle is well chilled and has not been shaken. Also, have cold glasses at hand — if they are warm the wine will froth up when it is poured. Carefully and gently remove the foil and untwist the wires of the metal cage that holds the cork in place. Keep your free hand over the cork while doing this to make sure it does not fly out. Then hold the cork firmly in your right hand, or left if left-handed, and twist the bottle around it with the other hand. Hold the cork firmly until it starts to give, then gently ease it out of the bottle.

FORTIFIED WINES

Fortified wines are wines that have been fortified or 'strengthened' by the addition of alcohol. This increases their alcohol content from the normal 9-14% of table or light wines to, on average, 16-24%, and gives them a longer life. As well as having a high alcohol content they also have a more concentrated flavour. They are served in smaller amounts than table wines, usually as an aperitif before a meal or a digestif afterwards. The most popular fortified wines are sherry, port, Madeira, Marsala and vermouth.

Sherry

Drinks labelled as sherry can only come from the Jerez area of Spain although sherry-style wines are made in many other parts of the world, notably Cyprus and South Africa. With these, the name of the producing country must always appear directly before the word sherry, such as South African sherry.

All sherries are naturally dry but most are sweetened and coloured before they are sold. Fino is the palest, lightest and driest style and has a distinct tang to its flavour. Finos should be drunk while they are still young, and once a bottle has been opened the sherry should be consumed within 2-3 weeks. Amontillados are medium dry, olorosos are richer and more full-bodied, and cream sherries are the sweetest.

Port

Port is the fortified wine of Portugal. The fermentation of the base wine is stopped by the addition of grape spirit before all the sugar has been used up. This gives the fortified wine its characteristic sweetness. As port ages, the sweetness becomes less obvious as the wine dries out. The main styles of port that are available are rubies. They are the youngest, and the least expensive.

Traditional tawny ports are aged in wooden casks for 20 or even 40 years. They become smoother, drier and more nutty with age. The cheap tawnies that are on sale are a blend of ruby and white ports, and lack the character and distinction of a true tawny.

Vintage port is only made in years that are considered to be especially good. The wine will be bottled after 2-3 years in a cask, and may be kept for 15-20 years before it is ready for drinking. These are the ports that should be decanted before they are drunk because they have a deposit that settles to the bottom of the bottle. Late bottled and vintage character are two styles of port that have recently become very popular.

Madeira

Madeira is made by an unusual method that involves heating the wine in special chambers for a minimum of 90 days. This produces wines that are particularly long-lived with a characteristic flavour that has an underlying caramel note to it and an acidity or dryness, even in the sweeter styles. Although often thought of as a sweet drink, only two of the four styles of Madeira are sweet — bual and malmsey. Of the other two styles, sercial is dry and verdelho is medium-dry. Both are drunk chilled.

Marsala

Marsala comes from Italy but it was created by an Englishman, John Woodhouse. It is dark brown or deep golden in colour with a full, rich, slightly nutty flavour that has a slight tang and burnt aftertaste. Marsala is best known as an ingredient in zabaglione.

Vermouth

Vermouths are made from wines that are lightly fortified and flavoured with blends of herbs and spices and sweetened to varying degrees. An Italian vermouth does not necessarily come from Italy, but will be sweet and red whereas a French vermouth will be dry and white. Biancos can vary from medium dry to medium sweet while rosés may be sweet or dry.

SPIRITS

Spirits are produced all over the world from a wide range of materials — grains, tubers such as potatoes, sugar cane and even cactus. Spirits are produced by distillation, a process that involves heating the fermented base material until the alcohol in it turns to vapour, which is then collected and condensed to turn it back into a liquid again. Since alcohol boils at a lower temperature than water, a liquid that is progressively more and more potent can be produced by repeated distillations. The spirits that are most popular are whisky, gin, rum, vodka and brandy.

Whisky

Whisky is produced from various grains which may or may not be malted. It can

be made in any part of the world where grain is available and there is a suitable water supply. In fact, the Scots claim that this last element is the critical one in determining the style and the quality of the whisky.

Scotch whisky — all whisky produced in Scotland can be called Scotch — can be distilled from barley or maize and it may or may not be malted. There are two different types of Scotch — grain and malt. Grain whisky accounts for a major part of the production. It is distilled from barley and maize and has a pale colour and mild flavour. Almost without exception, the grain whiskies are used for mixing with the cheaper blends.

Malt whiskies are made from malted barley. It may be sold as the product of just one distillery, the name of which will appear on the label, or it may be a

blend of malts from different distilleries. Malts are made in four main areas of Scotland, and each area not only gives its name to the whiskies produced in it, but also gives them their own individual character. Highland malts — which include the distilleries of Speyside, home of the famous Glenfiddich and Glenlivet — are generally considered to be the finest. Lowland malts are gentle and delicately flavoured and mainly used for blending. Cambeltown malts were popular at one time, but now there is only one distillery that produces an unblended product. Islay (pronounced Eye ler) malts have a strong peaty smell and flavour.

Irish whiskey is made from a blend of malted and unmalted barley with perhaps a little wheat and rye added. The flavour is more mellow than Scotch, but it has a certain class and distinction of its own. Bourbon is a style of whiskey that is produced in the United States according to very strict regulations. Bourbon tastes quite different to Scotch, often having a penetrating, slightly fruity flavour with a touch of sweetness. It can be sold 'straight' as the product of just one distillery or it may be blended. When rye whiskey is produced in the United States it must contain at least 51% rye, but Canadian rye is not subjected to any controls over composition or production.

Rum

Rum is distilled from sugar cane. Although it is made wherever this crop is grown, most of the commercial rums come from the West Indies and mainlands surrounding the Caribbean. Originally, rums produced in different areas had their own particular characteristics. For example, Jamaican rum was dark in colour with a pungent flavour, Barbados and Trinidad rums were dark in colour but considerably less pungent, while those from Cuba were very light. Today, although some rums made by traditional methods in the various areas are available, the majority of rums on sale are blended to a fairly consistent style — the most popular is white rum.

Gin

Gin is a grain-based spirit that gets its name from the main flavouring agent that is used — juniper. Other herbs and spices are also blended in to give brands their own particular characteristics. The words 'London Dry' on the label does not indicate where the gin was produced, but refers instead to its style — very pure and unsweetened, and much

lighter than the early gins. Dutch, Holland or Geneva gin, with their fuller, heavier, sweeter style are more in keeping with the traditional products, particularly those labelled as 'oude'. These gins are usually drunk on their own, being too strong and flavoured for use in cocktails and mixed drinks. Plymouth gin, the style associated with the Royal Navy, is now only made by one company, but it is the one that should be used when making 'Pink Gin' (gin with a dash of angostura bitters).

Vodka

Vodka is a very pure spirit that is usually distilled from grain, but can also be distilled from potatoes or any other fermentable product. The traditional home of vodka is believed to be Poland or Russia and the products from both these countries, and Finland, have quite a pronounced flavour and high alcoholic content. They are drunk chilled and knocked back in one go. The widely distributed brands that are increasing in popularity are a fairly recent development, and somewhat different in style having very little flavour or body.

Brandy

Brandy is distilled from wine. It can be made anywhere that produces a reasonable amount of wine, although much of the brandy that is made is very rough and only intended for local consumption. The best known brandies are cognac and armagnac. Both are produced in their own particular area of France according to strictly controlled methods. Cognac is often more highly regarded than armagnac, but each has its own distinctive style and it is a mistake to make comparisons. Cognac is generally lighter and more delicately flavoured, while armagnac is heavier and more pungent.

Do not take too much notice of grand-sounding names such as emperor, Napoleon etc., since they are usually no more than marketing ploys. Even the star ratings are not a guarantee of quality since they only indicate the minimum age of the product. Under French law a 3-star cognac need only be 18 months old but in Britain it must be at least 3 years and, in reality, is often much older. V.O. (very old) come next followed by V.S.O.P (very superior old pale) which is cognac that must be at least 4½ years old. An Extra, Napoleon (when used as a description and not as part of a name as in Napoleon Bonaparte) and Vieille Reserve must be at least 5 years old. The armagnac system

is 3 years for a 3-star, 5-10 years for a V.O., 10-15 years for a V.S.O.P. and at least 25 years for an 'hors d' age'.

With very few exceptions, spirits are ready for drinking as soon as they are bottled and do not improve once bottled. However, if bottles are kept unopened, store them upright in a cool place away from direct light. In the past few years the white spirits — gin, vodka and white rum — have gained in popularity. Their lighter, drier styles make them easier to drink, they leave less of a hangover and they blend well with many other flavours to make the cocktails and mixed drinks that are currently so popular.

LIQUEURS

Along with spirits, these are the other major component of cocktails. Liqueurs are sweetened, often coloured, alcoholic drinks that are made either by infusing the flavouring ingredients in a spirit such as brandy or by distillation. They vary quite considerably in alcohol content, and the traditional ones such as Cointreau and Benedictine are stronger than ones that have recently been introduced. Chartreuse was originally used as a medicine and as a comfort for mountain travellers. It is now a drink for connoisseurs, and is still made by monks at the monastery of the Grande Chartreuse in Dauphiné, France.

Hot Indulgence   Mulled Red Wine

DRINKS TO MAKE

Hot Indulgence
SERVES 1
3 fl oz/75 ml ginger wine
1½ fl oz/40 ml brandy
1 tablespoon double cream
3 inch/7.5 cm cinnamon stick
½ teaspoon finely grated orange rind

1 Gently warm the ginger wine and brandy to just below boiling point.
2 Pour into a warmed glass or mug, then gently pour the cream over the back of a spoon on to the surface of the drink. Add the cinnamon stick and sprinkle orange rind on the surface.

Mulled Red Wine
SERVES 8-10
1 orange
1 lemon, thickly sliced
8 cloves
2 bay leaves
2 inch/5 cm cinnamon stick
26.40 fl oz/75 cl bottle red wine
4 fl oz/100 ml ruby port
approximately 1 oz/25 g soft light brown sugar

1 Preheat the oven to 190°/375°/Gas 5.

2 Bake the orange for 30 minutes
3 Put the orange, lemon slices, cloves, bay leaves, cinnamon stick and the wine into a saucepan and heat gently to just below the simmering point. Cover and leave over a low heat for 20 minutes, taking care not to let it reach simmering point.

4 Gently heat the port and sugar in a small saucepan, stirring, until the sugar has dissolved. Strain the wine into a warmed heatproof bowl, then pour in the port. Test for sweetness and stir in extra sugar if desired. Serve in warmed glasses.

Orange Sunset
SERVES 1
2 ice cubes, crushed
1½ fl oz/40 ml gin
1½ fl oz/40 ml white vermouth
1½ fl oz/40 ml unsweetened orange juice
1 orange slice for decoration

1 Put the ice cubes into a cocktail shaker or screw-top jar. Add the gin, vermouth and orange juice and shake.
2 Strain into a glass and place the slice of orange on the rim. Serve at once.

Caribbean Kir
SERVES 1
2-3 ice cubes, cracked
2 fl oz/50 ml white rum
1½ tablespoons crème de cassis
soda water
half a slice of lemon, to decorate

1 Put the ice cubes in a tall, slim glass.
2 Add the rum and crème de cassis. Stir, then top up the glas with a dash of soda water.
3 Decorate the rim of the glass with half a slice of lemon and serve.

Orange Sunset   Caribbean Kir

MENU PLANNING

Food should create an atmosphere, and please the eye as well as the palate.
With careful planning, you can create meals that are attractive,
appetizing and nutritious.

Starter
Smoked
Salmon
Paté.

Flowers.

Napkins.

Dessert
Apple
Strudel.

Wine
Moselle.

Main Dish
Stir fry beef
and
vegetables.

Menu planning helps busy cooks prepare healthy meals that are a pleasure to eat. There is no doubt about it — preparing delicious meals takes much more time and effort than just popping convenience foods in the oven. Careful planning, however, will help to relieve the strain.

Whether on a daily basis or for a dinner party meant to impress, menu planning focuses the cook's attention on interesting and flavoursome food combinations that stimulate the appetite with a variety of colours and textures. It also helps streamline the time-consuming chores of shopping and food preparation, and keeps costs within the budget by preventing expensive impulse buying.

A well-balanced meal should contain a combination of textures and colours without all the courses being heavy or containing an over-abundance of one

ingredient. Eggs are versatile and it is very easy to use too many in one meal without spending some time menu planning. It wouldn't be very satisfying, for example, to eat a three course meal of eggs mayonnaise, French onion tart and a chilled lemon soufflé. By writing down the menu and looking at the list of ingredients, the repetition of eggs would have immediately become obvious and some of the dishes changed.

A much better planned menu for an informal dinner with friends would be kipper pâté, French onion flan with a fresh herb and lettuce salad dressed with a light oil and vinegar dressing and a fresh fruit salad. This menu balances meat and fish with a colourful seasonal fruit salad and uses crisp lettuce to provide extra texture. The whole meal is not too rich or too heavy.

A useful first step to menu planning is to decide on the main course. A heavy dish, such as lasagne, for example, should be preceeded by a light starter and followed by light dessert. A light main course, such as roast chicken, however, gives the cook more flexibility.

Steamed or grilled fish also make delicious main courses.

After the main course and its accompaniments are decided, plan the starter and dessert. Time is one of the important factors to consider when planning the starter. Individual cheese soufflés are always an impressive start to a dinner party, but the cook has to be confident all guests will arrive on time. Soufflés do not wait for anyone.

Select a starter to complement the main course that is to follow. Do not, for example, serve salad Niçoise with anchovies and hot garlic bread before a main course of poached sole with boiled new potatoes. The strong flavours of the anchovies and garlic will overpower the subtle flavours of the main course.

Think carefully when planning the dessert. This course is a chance for the cook to show off his or her culinary talents with extra special rich and fancy confections. Unfortunately, if the impressive dessert is served after two heavy and rich courses it will not be appreciated and a lot of effort — and expense — will have been wasted. Simple slices of fresh fruit with a liqueur spooned over the top is often considered just as impressive and appreciated even more than a rich chocolate and hazelnut gâteau with lashings of whipped cream, for example. If, however, the preceeding courses have been simple and without lots of rich butter or cream sauces, it could be the time to pull out all the stops with a Black Forest gâteau.

For special occasions, a cheeseboard and fresh fruit are often served. Think about complementary flavours. For a

cheeseboard, it is better to provide varied small selections of several cheeses

rather than a large amount of a single type of cheese.

The value of seasonal fruits and vegetables for successful menu planning can not be overstated. Because fruits and vegetables are most abundant when they are in season, they are also at their

cheapest — an important consideration for budget stretching. They also provide an endless variety of colours and textures to stimulate the appetite.

Red cabbages, carrots, aubergines, beetroots and fresh young garden peas are among the many vegetables with rich natural colours which should be exploited as much as possible when

menu planning. Slices of roast chicken, for example, look much more appetizing when served with ratatouille, a tasty combination of peppers, aubergines and courgettes, or dark green broccoli spears. Even traditional roast beef and roast potatoes are enhanced by lightly glazed bright orange carrots and steamed green beans flavoured with finely grated lemon zest.

Fresh fruit salad using a variety of seasonal fruits is not only delicious and healthy, but also provides a colourful dish to round off a meal. Brightly coloured pieces of fresh fruit also enhance the appeal of a simple dessert like ice cream or sorbet. When there is a glut of fruit, purée some and freeze for making flavoursome sauces for brightening winter meals.

Constrasting textures also play an important role in improving a meal. Only very young children or very old adults will appreciate a soft, mushy meal from start to finish. Steam vegetables rather than boil to retain some of the natural texture — as well as valuable vitamins — and serve crispy lettuce and crunchy celery and other vegetables in salads. It is good for digestion and makes the meal more interesting. Vegetable crudités with a cream dip is a

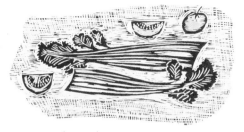

colourful and healthy start to a meal. It also has the advantage of preserving the vital nutrients that can be lost during cooking.

On pages 38-39 are four examples of well-planned menus. Each is nutritionally well balanced, as well as containing an appetizing combination of ingredients, colours and textures.

NUTRITIONAL MENU PLANNING

The most important benefit from planning well-balanced menus is good health. For the human body to remain healthy and properly functioning, it depends on the nutrients contained in foods — proteins, carbohydrates, fats, vitamins and minerals. Nutritional menu planning, therefore, concentrates on ingredient selection and preparation methods. The emphasis should be on fresh fruits and vegetables, and eliminating excessive fats, sugars and over-refined foods.

The value of natural, fresh foods is enormous. Almost all preserved, canned or refined products have already lost most, if not all, of the natural goodness by the time they reach the consumer.

A good menu should provide fibre, carbohydrates, proteins, vitamins and trace elements. Traditional meals have usually included large quantities of milk, cheese, butter and sugar. While acceptable in small quantities, it is important to plan menus that do not include these ingredients as staples.

Bad preparation methods can destroy the nutritional goodness of even the freshest foods. When planning menus, be sure to include dishes that are cooked in a healthy way.

Frying is one of the worst ways to cook foods, from a health point of view. Too much fat is not good for the body and excessive amounts of cholesterol has been linked to heart disease. It is far healthier — and less fattening — to grill meat or fish on a rack.

Other tips include roasting meat in a covered casserole to preserve the trace elements it contains and to steam vegetables to preserve the nutrients.

SUCCESS FOR PLANNING

Menu planning is unique for each cook and it is important to adopt an approach suitable to your lifestyle. Important factors to consider are: How many people are the meals for? Will everyone be eating at once or will mealtimes be staggered? Is the planning for three daily meals for a week or one special dinner party? Any special diets? What is the budget? Here are some helpful tips for successful menu planning:

● Write down the menus.
This allows you to quickly eliminate duplicated dishes or ingredients. Making a list also helps stop last-minute mental changes to the menus that throw out preparation timing and add expensive ingredients.

● Make a shopping list.
Nothing is more fustrating than not having all the ingredients at hand when you are ready to cook. A comprehensive shopping list means you won't forget vital ingredients and helps control costly impulse buying. It also means you buy the correct quantity of all ingredients.

● Make the most of leftovers.
It is economical and practical to plan menus that use up leftovers. Sunday's joint, for example, is ideal to use for sandwiches on Monday or as the basis of a hearty beef and vegetable soup. Leftover chicken can be used for a lunchtime salad or as a filling pie.

● Read new recipes in advance.
If you have never used a recipe before, read through it several days before so you will know how much time is required for preparation. It might be necessary to soak dried beans overnight, for example, or to marinate meat for several hours. An extra-special dish may depend on flavourful homemade stock for a perfect result, and you will have to allow extra time to make the stock.

Reading through the recipe also means you will be familiar with any tricky techniques. If you are a new cook, you will want to make certain you are not over-extending yourself.

● Make the most of all ingredients.
If you are making a meringue for dessert in one meal, plan a salad in another meal so you can use up the leftover egg yolks in mayonnaise or a salad dressing. Small amounts of leftover meat and bones are ideal for using to make stocks and soups.

● Plan well in advance.
Taking extra care and not doing things at the last minute means your meal will be perfect. Plan the menu so one or two courses can be made in advance — allowing you to enjoy the meal as much as the guests. It is also wise to plan courses that will not end up inedible if some guests arrive late. Flat tyres have foiled more otherwise successful dinner parties than flat soufflés!

Be sure to ask guests in advance if there are any foods they do not, or can not, eat. It would be a shame to go to the trouble and expense of preparing a Beef Wellington, then realise when you sit down that half the guests are vegetarians. Also, for medical reasons, many people have special diet requirements.

● Plan for the unexpected.
A well-stocked store cupboard is the best way to cope with unexpected guests or a sudden change in plans. If you have a supply of canned soups, dried pasta, canned fish, seasonings and herbs and longlife milk you should be able to cope with any unplanned situation.

LUNCH

This bean, mushroom and Stilton salad, baked salmon trout with new potatoes and poached pears with cinnamon cream combines textures to make a healthy meal. The raw starter aids digestion and the main course provides carbohydrates and proteins.

DINNER PARTY

This impressive party menu of consommé, roasted rack of lamb with scalloped potatoes and braised red cabbage and a raspberry and cream filled hazelnut meringue is well planned with a light starter to balance the richness of the dessert.

FAMILY SUPPER

This winter family supper of creamy leek soup, chicken and mushroom casserole with jacket potatoes and steamed carrots and baked apples with custard makes the most of seasonal ingredients for a healthy and economical meal.

VEGETARIAN MEAL

An appetizing combination of colour and textures highlights this delicious and nutritional vegetarian meal, consisting of an avocado, walnut and celery salad, ricotta and spinach stuffed pancakes with ratatouille and crème caramel.

Informal setting

TABLE SETTING

The style you use in laying a table will set the tone for the meal to follow. Before the guests taste the first bite of food, they will already be seated around the table. Glistening cut glass, polished silver, fine china, starched linen and soft candlelight indicates the start of an elegant and sophisticated meal. On the other hand, a less formal arrangement with everyday cutlery and crockery sets the mood for an informal evening.

With the growing emphasis on casual entertaining, many of the traditional rigid rules of 'proper' table settings are being laid aside. Use your common sense and arrange the table so it reflects your style of entertaining. Always remember that the table decorations are of secondary importance to well-prepared food and interesting company. They should complement the meal, add atmosphere and supplement the behind-the-scenes preparations.

INFORMAL DINNERS

Casual entertaining requires much less preparation than formal dinners, but some of the basic rules still apply — forks are placed to the left of the plates, with knives and spoons on the right. Generally, an informal meal with friends is more likely to have only two or three courses, and therefore requires fewer pieces of china and cutlery.

It is still just as important, however, to make the table look as attractive as possible. When guests sit down at a carefully prepared table, it makes them feel welcome and they appreciate all the effort that has been made. For special effects, add a small arrangement of flowers and brightly coloured napkins. Paper napkins are acceptable for casual meals, and there are many with decorative patterns.

FORMAL DINNERS

Laying the table for a formal dinner requires time and concentration. In fact, it is a good idea to draw a sketch of a place-setting so you will have a guide to follow. Also, a four-course formal dinner for six persons requires a lot of knives, forks, spoons and china, so you should check your inventory in advance to avoid being caught short.

If the table has a beautiful polished surface, use heat-resistant placemats. Otherwise, use a full-size tablecloth or cloth placemats with matching napkins — paper napkins are unacceptable for a formal dinner. White linen is traditional, but it is acceptable to use a soft colour if it co-ordinates with your china. If the dinner is to be centred around a specific theme, coloured table linen can help capture the atmosphere.

It can be daunting to sit down to a formally laid table with many pieces of cutlery on both sides of the plate. If the table has been correctly laid, however, everything should be arranged so the diner starts with the pieces on the outside and progresses inwards with each course. This is where a sketch can

help get the arrangement correct so there are not any awkward moments during the meal.

Forks are arranged on the left of the plate, and spoons and knives to the right, with the knife blades pointing inwards towards the plate. Cutlery for the dessert course is arranged next to the plate on the inside, above the plate, or brought to the table with the dessert if a quick wash-up is necessary. If a spoon and fork are used for the dessert and arranged above the plate, the spoon is on top pointing left and the fork is pointing right.

Rules governing the positioning of glasses are slightly less rigid. If only one wine is being served throughout the meal, place the glass directly above the tip of the dinner knife. If the meal will include both red and white wines, there should be a separate glass for each. The most logical positioning is in the order of their use, from right to left. If other glasses are to be used, such as a port glass or a water goblet, they may be arranged in a triangle or a diagonal line over the cutlery on the right. If water

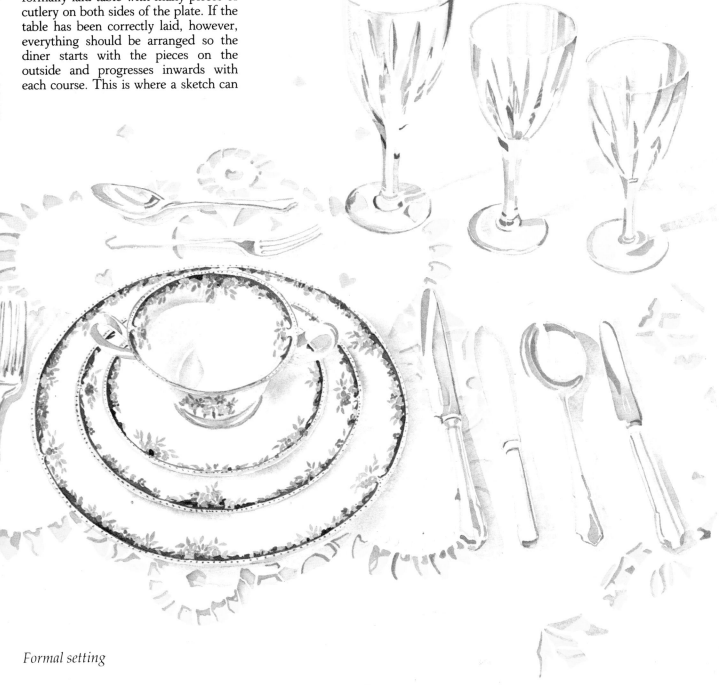

Formal setting

goblet are used, place a filled water jug on the table.

Beautiful matching china can add much to the overall effect of a table setting. For formal dinners, it is necessary to have china for several courses as well as china or silver serving bowls and platters. As a minimum, a formal setting requires a medium-sized plate for the first course or a soup plate or bowl with a lining plate, a dinner plate, and a medium-sized plate for dessert. Depending on the menu and size of the table, the place-setting may also include a butter plate, a crescent-shaped salad plate and another medium-sized plate for cheese and/or fruit.

The butter plate and crescent-shaped plates are placed to the left of the place-setting and put out when the table is laid. Plates for the main courses are added and removed before and after each course, although if the first course is cold it can be in position when the guests are seated.

Ideally the table setting should also include a salt cellar and pepper shaker for each two diners as well as small pots of mustard, if it is being used. Highly starched linen napkins can be folded into decorative shapes or simply laid across the butter plates.

Informal Place-setting

Formal Place-setting

Outdoor Buffet

Indoor Buffet

BUFFET DINNERS

The key to a successful buffet is organization, and the table setting and foods must be selected and arranged with the guests in mind. Whether the guests are serving themselves or being served by staff, they will be walking along a table to collect their food. It is important, therefore, to have the plates and required cutlery at the beginning of the buffet so each guest can take what they will need. It is a good idea to make a small parcel of the cutlery in a napkin so there is no chance of someone getting to the end of the table and realizing they have forgotten their fork. It causes confusion and delays the serving if guests have to double back on a buffet. If, however, there is a wide selection of foods that would require different pieces of cutlery, place the cutlery at the end of the buffet table so that the guests can make their selection after they have selected their food.

One of the advantages of a buffet is that it requires fewer pieces of china and cutlery than a sit-down dinner, since there is usually only the main and dessert courses. If the guests will sit down to eat after collecting their food, the cutlery can be arranged on the tables.

There are three basic plans for buffet meals, all of which involve using a long serving table. If staff are serving, they stand on one side of the table and the guests walk along the opposite side of the table, indicating what dishes they would like to eat. Alternatively, if guests are serving themselves, they can walk along one side of the table selecting the amount of each dish they want. If there are lots of people to be served, it is a good idea to arrange double serving dishes of each dish and let the guests help themselves from either side of the table. This is particularly useful if there is hot food and it is essential to get everyone served as quickly as possible.

When all the guests have been served and helped themselves to seconds, the serving table is cleared and the dessert course is put out with the required cutlery. Guests follow the same procedure for serving themselves. After dessert, coffee can be put out and the guests can again help themselves. It is a good idea to have several pots on a hot tray or special gas burners so everyone has a hot cup.

Floral Centrepiece

CENTREPIECES

Attractive centrepieces are often the focal point of a table setting and can be composed of flowers or fresh fruit.

The table dictates the shape and size of the centrepiece. For rectangular tables, use oval centrepieces, and for round tables, round arrangements are the most suitable. The most important consideration in designing a centrepiece, however, is the size of the table. In most instances there still has to be enough room for salt cellars, pepper shakers and sauceboats along with vegetable dishes. It is also important to make the centrepiece low enough not to block cross-table conversations.

For best results when using fresh flowers, use shallow containers with a piece of sponge that is about 1 inch/2.5 cm taller than the top of the container and soak it in water until it is saturated. To help keep the freshness of the flowers, give each stem a good long drink of water before making the arrangement. If the flowers begin looking a bit tired on the day, revive them by mixing 1 teaspoon of caster sugar in 1 pint/600 ml water and add this to the container.

A luscious fresh fruit arrangement, besides being an attractive centrepiece, also has the advantage of being served as a fruit course at the end of the meal rather than a rich dessert. To make a fruit arrangement, use only the freshest looking fruit, and include as much variety as is available. Use a shallow bowl so all the bright colours are visible.

If the table will be too crowded with a centrepiece, consider small arrangements for each guest. A single blossom floating in a fingerbowl is a simple and elegant example.

Individual Centrepiece

GREAT BRITISH COOKERY YEAR

The calendar is filled with traditional holidays and celebrations, and food plays an important part in the festivities. With mouthwatering recipes using seasonal ingredients, you can enjoy the best of British all through the year.

NEW YEAR

To mark the beginning of another year, New Year's Day is traditionally celebrated with rites expressing joy over the rejuvenation of life. It is one of the oldest and most universally-observed festivals. There are records of new year celebrations in Mesopotamia as long ago as 2,000 BC.

The new year, however, has not always begun on 1 January. In the early Mesopotamian celebrations, the year began with the new moon nearest the spring equinox. Until the fifth century BC, the Greeks began their calendar on the winter solstice, 21 December. Ancient Romans began the year on 1 March until 154 BC when the official date was changed to 1 January.

In Anglo-Saxon England, New Year's Day was observed on 25 December, until William the Conqueror changed the official start of the year to 1 January. Then, however, England fell in line with the other European Christian countries and started the year on 25 March. It wasn't until 1582 that 1 January was adopted as the start of the year by all Roman Catholic countries. Scotland followed in 1600 and England in 1752.

January is named after Janus, the double-faced Roman god. Janus symbolically captures the spirit of the new year with one head looking back over the past 12 months and the other looking to the future.

In rural England, each county has traditionally had local sayings and superstitions for ridding the houses of evil and starting the new year afresh. In Lancashire and Lincolnshire, for example, it was unlucky to say 'to give away a light from the house'. Light as a symbol plays an important part in ancient end-of-year rituals. Lighting of the yule-log is one such tradition. This log was kept burning throughout Christmas with one small section set aside to start the first kindling of new year's fire. To give away a light implied bad luck throughout the following year.

Elsewhere it was thought bad luck to take anything out of the house before first bringing something else in. Bringing in something green meant plenty of bread for the year, but to bring in bad news meant that disaster was sure to follow, according to the superstition.

To pay out money on the 1st January in Cornwall was thought to mean you would be paying out all year. Washing on New Year's Day would 'wash a friend away', while sweeping towards the door instead of the hearth was thought to take every bit of luck from the house, according to other folklore.

The bleak, icy weather in January is not conducive to growing and only the hardiest of vegetables manage to survive in the hard, frosty ground. Root vegetables such as kohlrabi, parsnips, swedes, turnips, carrots, scorzoneras and Jerusalem artichokes provide some seasonal variety. Also available are rhubarb, mange tout, leeks and spinach.

The game season is drawing to a close, so it is best to use the birds and hares that are available now for casseroling. Because the demand for turkey has dropped off after the Christmas holidays, it is an economical buy at this time of the year.

The fishmongers' stalls should be full with coley, sole and mackerel.

As the first of the Seville oranges and limes appear it is time to think about jam and marmalade making.

NEW YEAR'S DAY BRUNCH

Smoked Salmon Soufflé

Blue Cheese and Onion Tart

Hot Chicken Liver Salad

Smoked Salmon Soufflé
SERVES 8
9 fl oz/250 ml milk
1 bay leaf
1 onion, thinly sliced
6 black peppercorns
2 parsley stalks (optional)
7 oz/200 g fresh salmon
2 tablespoons butter
1 tablespoon plain flour
4 tablespoons double cream
salt
cayenne pepper, to taste
grated nutmeg, to taste
½ lb/225 g smoked salmon
4 egg yolks
6 egg whites
extra butter for greasing the soufflé dish

1 Put the milk, bay leaf, half the onion,

Smoked Salmon Soufflé

form, then beat in ½ teaspoon salt. Stir one-quarter of the egg whites into the béchamel sauce, then gently fold in the remaining egg whites.

8 Pour the mixture into the prepared soufflé dish and cook for 12-15 minutes or until the soufflé is well risen and browned. Serve at once.

Blue Cheese and Onion Tart
SERVES 8
1 tablespoon butter
1 lb/450 g onions, sliced
salt and pepper
2 eggs
2 fl oz/50 ml milk
7 fl oz/200 ml double cream
grated nutmeg
7 oz/200 g blue cheese
Pastry
7 oz/200 g flour
¾ teaspoon salt
1 egg
4 oz/100 g butter, diced

1 To make the pastry, sift the flour and salt into a bowl. Make a well in the centre and add 2 tablespoons cold water, then the egg and butter.
2 Using your fingertips, mix all the ingredients together with 2-3 tables-

peppercorns and parsley stalks into a saucepan. Bring to the boil, then remove the pan from the heat, cover and leave for 15 minutes to infuse.
2 Meanwhile, heat the oven to 220C/ 425/Gas 7. Grease a 3 pint/1.7 litre soufflé dish.
3 Return the pan to the heat and add the fresh salmon. Cook over medium heat for 2-3 minutes or until the salmon flakes easily. Remove the salmon with a slotted spoon and reserve.
4 Finely chop the remaining onion. Melt the butter in a heavy-based saucepan and add the onion, cooking until it is soft but not browned. Stir in the flour and whisk to make a smooth roux. Cook, stirring constantly, to prevent browning. Strain in the infused milk, whisking constantly, until the liquid boils and thickens. Add the cream and season with salt, cayenne pepper and nutmeg, then simmer on low heat for 2-3 minutes. Dot the surface with butter to prevent a skin forming and set aside.
5 Purée the cooked salmon and smoked salmon and set aside.
6 Return the cooled sauce to the heat until tepid. Whisk in the egg yolks, then stir in the salmon purée and season.
7 Whisk the egg whites until stiff peaks

Blue Cheese and Onion Tart

Hot Chicken Liver Salad

poons cold water, until the mixture resembles large crumbs. If it is too dry, add another tablespoon of cold water.

3 Knead the dough on a lightly floured surface until smooth and pliable. Form into a ball, wrap in cling film and rest in the refrigerator for 30 minutes.

4 Meanwhile, heat the oven to 200C/400F/Gas 6.

5 Use the pastry to line a 9 inch/23 cm quiche ring. Bake blind for 7 minutes. Remove the baking beans and cook for a further 8 minutes. Lower the oven temperature to 180C/350F/Gas 4.

6 Meanwhile, to make the filling, melt the butter in a large frying pan and add the onions. Season, cover and cook over medium heat, stirring occasionally, for about 15 minutes or until the onions are soft but not browned. Remove from the heat and cool slightly.

7 Place the eggs, milk, cream, seasoning and nutmeg in a bowl and whisk

until all are thoroughly combined.

8 Remove the onions from the frying pan with a slotted spoon and spread evenly over the pastry base, then crumble over the cheese. Pour in the cream mixture. Bake for 20-30 minutes or until the tart is firm in the centre and golden.

Hot Chicken Liver Salad

SERVES 8

2 tablespoons vegetable oil

1 tablespoon butter

2 cloves garlic, crushed

1½ lb/675 g chicken livers, trimmed

salt and pepper

2 heads lettuce, washed and drained

6 hard-boiled eggs

2 tablespoons white wine vinegar

French Dressing

3 tablespoons red wine vinegar

6 tablespoons olive oil

1 tablespoon Dijon mustard

salt and pepper

1 To make the French dressing, place all the dressing ingredients in a screw-top jar. Secure the lid and shake until well mixed. Set aside.

2 Place the oil and butter in a heavy-based frying pan over medium heat. When hot, add the garlic and cook until soft. Add the chicken livers, season and sauté, stirring occasionally, for about 5 minutes.

3 Meanwhile, arrange the lettuce on a large serving platter. Cut the eggs into wedges and arrange in the centre and round the edge.

4 When the chicken livers are cooked, pour in the vinegar, stirring the bottom to scrape up any sediment. Spoon the chicken livers on to the lettuce and pour over the cooking juices. Serve with the French dressing to spoon over the salad.

Note Alternatively, serve the sautéed chicken livers with just trimmed spring onions and hard-boiled eggs.

BURNS' NIGHT

The 25th January is one of the most important events on the Scottish calendar. It is the birth date of Robert Burns, the Scottish poet born in 1759. In Scotland, and throughout the world wherever there is a group of Scots, a celebration is likely to take place. This tradition was started by the Burns' Club, which was founded in 1802 in Renfrew shortly after Burns' death. There are now 700 clubs world-wide.

Burn's poetry is recited and haggis, a sheep's stomach filled with minced heart, liver and lights (lungs) mixed with oatmeal and spices, is eaten. 'Wi' a swingin' o' kilts and a playin' o' bagpipes', the haggis is ceremoniously carried into the room by a chef dressed in his whites and flanked by two waiters in tails.

Before cutting the haggis in the ceremonial fashion, Burns's *Address to a Haggis* is recited.

Fair fa' your honest, sonsie face,
Great chieftain o' the puddin'-race!
Aboon them a' ye tak your place,
    Painch, tripe or thairm:
Weel are ye wordy of a grace
    As lang's my arm.

The groaning trencher there ye fill,
Your hurdies like a distant hill,
Your pin wad help to mend a mill
    In time o'need,
While thro' your pores the dews distil
    Like amber bead.

His knife see rustic Labour dight,
An' cut you up wi' ready slight,
Trenching your gushing entrails bright,
    Like onie ditch;
And then, O what a glorious sight,
    Warm-reekin, rich!

Then, horn for horn, they stretch an' strive:
Deil tak the hindmost, on they drive,
Till a' their weel-swall'd kytes belyve
    Are bent like drums;
Then auld Guidman, maist like to rive,
    "Bethankit!" hums.

Is there that owre his French *ragout,*
Or *olio* that was staw a sow,
Or *fricassee* was mak her spew
    Wi' perfect sconner,
Looks down wi' sneering, scornfu' view
    On sic a dinner?

Poor devil! see him owre his trash,
As feckless as a wither'd rash,
His spindle shank a guid whip-lash,
    His nieve a nit;
Thro' bloody flood or field to dash,
    O how unfit!

But mark the Rustic, haggis-fed,
The trembling earth resounds his tread,
Clap in his walie nieve a blade,
    He'll make it whissle;
An legs an' arms, an' heads will sned,
    Like taps o' thrissle.

Ye Pow'rs, wha mak mankind your care,
And dish them out their bill o' fare,
Auld Scotland wants nae skinking ware
    That jaups in luggies;
But, if ye wish her gratefu' prayer,
    Gie her a Haggis!

ROBERT BURNS

Haggis

SERVES 6-8

9 oz/250 g sheep's liver
4 oz/100 g sheep's heart
4 oz/100 g lamb's sweetbreads
9 oz/250 g rolled oats
9 oz/250 g pork back fat
7 oz/200 g onions
2 teaspoons salt
¾ teaspoon pepper
½ teaspoon allspice
4 fl oz/125 ml Drambuie
1 piece caul fat (approximately a 12-inch/ 30.5 cm square with no holes)

1 Soak the liver, heart and sweetbreads in cold water overnight, changing the water 3 or 4 times.

2 Lay the rolled oats on a large baking tray and place under a hot grill. Cook for a few minutes, stirring with a long-handled wooden spoon, until lightly toasted.

3 Finely mince the liver, heart, sweetbreads, pork fat and onions in a food processor or use a hand mincer.

4 Add the seasonings, Drambuie and oats to the minced mixture and mix well. Cover with cling film and refrigerate for 12-24 hours to let the flavours develop and blend together.

5 Rinse the caul fat well under cold running water. Drain and spread it out on a clean working surface. Patch holes with any excess caul. Use to line a large mixing bowl. Butter and lightly flour the inside of a piece of muslin large enough to cover the haggis.

6 Place the minced mixture into the centre of the caul, then fold it over, covering the mixture. Lift the haggis out of the bowl and place it in the centre of the muslin. Gather up the corners and tie tightly with string, leaving room for the haggis to expand.

7 Half fill a large saucepan, just large enough to hold the haggis, with water. Bring to the boil, then lower the haggis in. Cover the pan and simmer gently for 2½ hours, topping up with boiling water from time to time.

8 Remove the haggis from the liquid and drain well. Cut away the cloth and place in a warmed serving dish. Serve with bashed neeps (puréed swedes) and Scotch whisky.

Note Haggis is traditionally made from a sheep's pluck (the heart, liver and lungs), which is blanched, minced and boiled in the stomach. As these ingredients are not sold at all butcher's shops, this recipe has been adapted using more readily available ingredients.

Haggis

ST. VALENTINE'S DAY

St. Valentine's Day is as significant to the early arrival of spring as the buds on the trees and bluebells in the forest. It is the day for love, for exchanging anonymous greeting cards and sending small gifts.

These customs are thought to have originated from an ancient Roman festival connected with the mating season of birds each spring.

Like many other ancient festivals, however, there are several vague and obscure versions of the origin. The beginnings have also been linked with Lupercalia, a Roman feast annually held in February, when men and maidens drew lots for partners. This custom of choosing a valentine was originated by the Roman priest, Valentine, who was martyred on 14th February AD 271.

Celebrations of love, love potions and food have been acknowledged on the anniversary of St. Valentine's death throughout the centuries. Henry VIII, for example, believed rhubarb was an erotic food to eat, Casanova reputedly ate 50 oysters for breakfast and Aristotle was thought to believe the best aphrodisiac for St. Valentine's Day was fasting.

In the Middle Ages, local villagers followed certain traditions. Men and women exchanged love tokens, such as the love knot. This was a small metal pin shaped like a figure 8 on its side and worn over the heart to represent eternal love.

Another gesture was to wear a love sleeve. In the 15th and 16th centuries clothes were made with detachable sleeves. It was, however, also fashionable to wear distinctive sleeves as an individual mark. On St. Valentine's Day, lovers swapped sleeves and wore them throughout the day as a sign of loyalty.

In the evening, the festivities continued with a large feast for villagers. The village hall was decorated with valentine lights (hollowed turnips with a face cut through to the centre and a lit candle inside) and bowls of rosewater scented with crushed herbs. Tables were decorated and between each two settings rested a platter of bread tinted and spiced with saffron.

Guests arrived to the sound of valentine melodies, or imitated bird songs, intended to create a romantic mood. Once seated, everyone drew a name from a bag and this person became their valentine for the year.

After guests reseated themselves next to their new partner, a St. Valentine's Day cup was placed on the high table in front of the distinguished guests. This cup symbolized the spirit of love and a toast was made to love before the feasting and celebrations commenced.

A spectacular array of foods, each thought to stimulate affections, was served. Every dish of meat, fish, vegetables and seed fruit, was carried into the hall to a fanfare of trumpets. Quail, sparrow and geese eggs, considered symbolic to the day, were mixed with almonds and served as omelettes.

Dishes were painstakingly prepared and presented, especially the peacock, which was the highlight of the feast. The bird was skinned and roasted, then the feathered skin was replaced and sewn on. Its beak was painted with gold leaf and a wad of camphor-soaked cotton was set ablaze in its mouth so it appeared to breathe fire. Considered too important for a servant to carry in, the peacock was presented by the two most distinguished female guests.

As the garden gradually comes to life after the winter frosts, gardeners can plant shallots, lettuce, radishes, broad beans and garlic, which will be ready later in the summer. Root vegetables, however, are still predominant on market stalls with a variety of produce (celeriac, endives, celery and avocados) imported from overseas.

The following Valentine's Day menu is not quite as elaborate as on ancient St. Valentine's Day feasts, however, it is ideal for a romantic dinner for two. At this time of the year the selection of vegetables and fruit does not include the wide range you can find during summer, but it is still possible to cook an exciting and attractive meal.

ST. VALENTINE'S DAY DINNER

Moules Marinière
or
Avocado and Crab Salad

Chicken Breasts with Sweet Pepper Sauce

Potato Balls

Chilled Lemon and Pistachio Soufflé
or
Clementines in Cointreau Syrup

Without exception, all these dishes can be prepared in advance, so if the meal is well planned, there should be a minimum of work required on the night. The mussels can be cleaned, left in the pan and cooked 2 minutes before eating. Prepare the avocado salad the afternoon before the meal, making sure it is well coated with lemon dressing so it doesn't turn black, then assemble it one hour before the meal. The potato balls can either be prepared to the cooking stage or cooked before dinner and kept in a warm oven. Both desserts are best made well in advance.

Not only is this meal decorative and appetizing, but the combined dishes are very light so you do not feel too full and bloated afterwards.

Avocado and Crab Salad   Moules Marinière

Moules Marinière

SERVES 2

3 pints/1.7 litres mussels
1 tablespoon butter
1 tablespoon finely chopped onion or shallot
4 fl oz/125 ml dry white wine
1 tablespoon chopped fresh parsley
freshly ground black pepper
French bread, to serve

1 Clean the mussels under cold running water and scrape off any barnacles and the 'beard'. Discard any open shells.
2 Melt the butter in a large, flameproof dish, then add the onion and sauté until soft but not browned. Add the mussels, wine, parsley and pepper. Stir once, cover the pan and increase the heat.
3 Cook for 1-2 minutes, until all the shells have opened. If the mussels on top have not opened, stir once more and cook for another minute. Discard any mussels which have not opened.
4 Eat the mussels directly from the serving dish or transfer to a plate with the juices. Serve with French bread.

Avocado and Crab Salad

SERVES 2

1 ripe avocado
3 oz/75 g cooked crabmeat, flaked
¼ small cucumber, peeled, deseeded and diced
1 teaspoon finely chopped fines herbes (parsley, tarragon, chives and chervil) (optional)

Lemon Dressing
2 tablespoons lemon juice
4 fl oz/125 ml olive or vegetable oil
1 teaspoon Dijon mustard
salt and pepper

1 Cut the avocado in half and remove

the seed. Peel and finely slice each half and place in a small dish.
2 Mix all the dressing ingredients together and pour over enough dressing to coat the avocado slices on both sides, reserving 2 tablespoons. Cover the advocado with cling film and chill until required.
3 Mix together the crabmeat, cucumber, tomato and fines herbes. Season to taste. Spoon over the remaining dressing, and gently stir to mix. Cover the dish with cling film and chill.
4 Drain the avocado and carefully arrange the slices in a fan in the middle of a plate and add the crab salad. Cover again with cling film and chill for up to 1 hour.

Chicken Breasts with Sweet Pepper Sauce

SERVES 2

1 large red pepper
1 small green pepper
2 skinless chicken breasts, 5-6 oz/150-180 g each
salt and pepper
1 tablespoon unsalted butter
1 tablespoon dry sherry
½ chicken stock cube dissolved in 2 tablespoons water
4 fl oz/125 ml double cream
vegetable oil for brushing

1 Heat the grill to high.
2 Cut the tops and bottoms off the peppers, then slice vertically into 2 or 3 pieces, trimming the white pith.
3 Flatten the pepper pieces and brush the skin side with the vegetable oil. Cook under the grill until the skin

blisters, then peel off the skin. It may be necessary to scrape the skin off with a sharp knife.
4 Slice the peppers into strips. Use an aspic cutter to cut out heart shapes from the green pepper and about half the red pepper. Set aside for garnish, reserving the remaining red pepper for the sauce. Use any remaining green pepper in a salad or another dish.
5 Place the chicken breasts between 2 sheets of cling film and flatten with a mallet or rolling pin until the meat is about ⅓ inch/1 cm thick. Season.
6 Melt half the butter in a frying pan over medium heat and, when foaming, add the chicken breasts. Cook gently, for about 8 minutes, turning once, until cooked through but not brown. Remove and keep warm.
7 Pour the excess fat from the pan. Add the sherry and dissolved stock cube and stir to scrape up any sediment in the bottom of the pan. Add the cream and reserved sliced red pepper.
8 Bring the sauce to the boil, then purée in a blender or food processor until smooth and well blended.
9 Strain the sauce through a fine sieve into the rinsed-out pan. Taste and adjust the seasoning, if necessary. Return the sauce to the boil and cook until slightly reduced.
10 Remove from the heat and whisk in the remaining butter. Place the chicken breasts on a warmed serving plate. Spoon the sauce evenly over the chicken and the base of the plate, then sprinkle over the reserved red and green pepper heart shapes. Serve at once.

Potato Balls

SERVES 2

3-4 potatoes, peeled
1 oz/25 g butter
2 tablespoons vegetable oil
salt and pepper
finely chopped fresh parsley

1 Using a melon baller, cut out as many potato balls as possible. If you do not have a melon baller, cut the potatoes into ½ inch/1.2 cm dice. Place into a bowl of cold water until ready to cook.
2 Place the potato balls into a saucepan. Cover with cold water and bring to the boil. Cook until tender but still holding their shape, then drain.
3 Heat the butter and oil in a frying pan and sauté the potato balls until golden on all sides. Season to taste with salt and pepper and sprinkle with the chopped parsley. Toss gently and serve.

Chicken Breasts with Sweet Pepper Sauce   Potato Balls

lightly whipped cream. Do not overheat. Remove from the heat and leave to cool.
4 Whisk the egg whites with the remaining 2 oz/50 g sugar until stiff peaks form. Lightly fold the whipped cream into the cooled egg yolk mixture.
5 Spoon the egg whites on top and use a large metal spoon to gently fold in. Immediately spoon the mixture into the prepared ramekins, then chill for 2-3 hours or until set. Carefully peel off the foil collar. Press the chopped pistachio nuts around the sides and chill.

Clementines in Cointreau Syrup
SERVES 2
3 clementines
2 tablespoons sugar
2 tablespoons Cointreau

1 Using a potato peeler, pare the zest from the clementines and cut into fine shreds. Reserve. Peel the clementines and separate into segments, cutting away as much white pith as possible. Place in a small serving dish.
2 Put the shredded zest into a small saucepan with the sugar and just enough water to cover. Bring to the boil, reduce the heat and simmer until 1 tablespoon of liquid remains in the pan. Remove and add the Cointreau. Cool.
3 When cool, pour the syrup over the clementine segments and chill for at least 3 hours, stirring once or twice.

Chilled Lemon and Pistachio Soufflé
SERVES 2
juice and finely grated zest of 2 lemons
1 teaspoon gelatine
3 eggs, separated
6 oz/150 g sugar
3½ fl oz/90 ml double cream, whipped
4 oz/100 g pistachio nuts, chopped, to garnish
unsalted butter for greasing the foil collar

1 Butter two ¼ pint/150 ml ramekins. Wrap an aluminium foil collar 1 inch/2.5 cm taller than the ramekin round each and secure with string. Butter the foil well and chill until required.
2 Heat the lemon juice in a small saucepan and sprinkle over the gelatine, then stir until dissolved. Remove from the heat.
3 Place the egg yolks, dissolved gelatine, lemon zest and 4 oz/100 g of the sugar in a heatproof dish. Whisk until thoroughly blended, then place the bowl over a saucepan of simmering water, without the base of the bowl touching the water. Continue whisking until the mixture thickens to the consistency of

Lemon and Pistachio Soufflé   Clementines in Cointreau

SHROVE TUESDAY

Traditionally, on Shrove Tuesday morning, bells tolled from church belfries throughout the land in ancient Britain. It was the one day of the year when a villager could have the honour of being the bell-ringer and the bell would ring out loudly to convey several messages to the awaiting local people.

The bell signified the start of holiday festivities, time to close shops and down tools. Pancake batter was immediately poured into the skillets and the family changed into their best clothes in readiness for church.

Shrove Tuesday derives its name from the Catholic church, since it was the day set aside for shriving one's sins. For villagers, it became thought of as the time for the last fling before the lean weeks of Lent.

Because fasting was to begin the next day on Ash Wednesday, all produce forbidden during the following six weeks, such as milk, eggs, lard and meat, was used up in a pre-fast feast of pancakes.

Local fairs were held throughout the country, and fraise, or fritters, as they were called, could be bought from stalls. Pancakes were also popular fare to serve because they were quick to prepare and easily eaten.

A local pancake race was the highlight of the celebrations held in Olney, Buckinghamshire. It is said to have started in the 15th century when a housewife, late for church, ran to the service dressed in an apron and carrying a skillet with a partially cooked pancake.

This race, for women only, is still held each year, with contestants required to dress in an apron and scarf. A bell rings at 11.30 a.m. and the contestants start cooking their pancakes. At the sound of a second bell, the women line up at the starting line, and on the third bell they run the 415 yard/380 metre course from the square to the church door. Each must toss her pancake in the air three times and serve the pancake to the bell-ringer when she arrives.

This tradition has been adopted by the American town Liberal, Kansas, and a friendly rivalry exists between the two towns. In Liberal, the pancake festival lasts for three or four days with the race, a Miss Flipper beauty contest and a pancake-making competition. Liberal also holds a record for the largest pancake ever made.

Traditionally, pancakes are eaten rolled up and sprinkled with lemon juice and sugar. In some counties they are stacked one on top of the other like a cake and filled with bacon, tomatoes and cheese.

Today, pancakes are served throughout the year as a versatile and satisfying meal. They are as delicious as a savoury course with a substantial filling as they are a dessert, filled with sautéed apples and syrup.

Pancake Batter

MAKES 28 PANCAKES
7 oz/200 g plain flour
4 large eggs
1 teaspoon salt
13 fl oz/375 milk
4 oz/100 g butter, melted
vegetable oil for cooking

1 Sift the flour into a bowl and make a well in the centre. Whisk the eggs and salt together with half the milk, then pour into the well. Gradually incorporate the flour and whisk until the batter is smooth. Add half the remaining milk and the melted butter. Cover the bowl with a tea towel and leave the batter to rest for 2 hours.

2 Just before cooking, add enough of the remaining milk to the batter so it is the consistency of thin cream. Heat a 7 inch/18 cm crêpe pan or frying pan and brush the base with a little oil. When the pan is hot, pour in 3-4 tablespoons of batter, rotating the pan so the batter

Bolognese Filling

SERVES 4-6

2 tablespoons olive oil
1 onion, finely chopped
2 carrots, finely diced
salt and pepper
2 cloves garlic, crushed
2 rashers bacon, finely diced (optional)
1 lb/450 g lean minced beef
2 lb/1 kg ripe tomatoes, peeled, deseeded and
  diced, or 2 × 14 oz/400 g cans peeled
  tomatoes
1 bouquet garni
1 tablespoon tomato purée
¼ pint/150 ml dry red wine
½ lb/225 g cheese, grated
8-12 prepared pancakes

1 Heat the olive oil in a heavy-based saucepan, then add the onion, carrots and seasoning. Cook about 3 minutes, until the onion is soft but not brown, then add the garlic and bacon.
2 Add the minced beef and cook, stirring frequently, until browned. Add the tomatoes, bouquet garni, tomato purée and red wine. Cook, uncovered, for 45 minutes or until the sauce has reduced and thickened. Season and add more tomato purée, if wished. Discard the bouquet garni.
3 Heat the grill to high.
4 Spoon the filling on to the pancakes, roll up and place in a shallow ovenproof serving dish, join side down. Sprinkle over the cheese and cook under the grill until the cheese is melted and bubbling.

thinly covers the base. Pour any excess batter back into the bowl.
3 Cook over high heat for about 20 seconds or until the pancake is lightly browned. Turn over and cook the other side until brown, about 10 seconds.
4 Stack the pancakes on to a buttered plate, layering with greaseproof paper and keep warm while cooking the remainder. Continue cooking, brushing the pan with oil only when the pancakes begin to stick.

Pancake Variations

• Add 1 tablespoon Cointreau or Grand Marnier to the batter and serve the pancakes filled with fruit and whipped cream.
• Fill hot pancakes with cottage cheese and prawns, then roll up and serve.
• Make a white sauce and add sautéed mushrooms and sweetcorn. Use to fill the pancakes, sprinkle with finely grated cheese and brown under the grill. Other fillings can also be combined in the sauce.

Pancakes with Bolognese Filling

ST. PATRICK'S DAY

On 17th March, Irish people throughout the world celebrate the feast day of their patron saint, St. Patrick. Big parades are held, the largest in Dublin, the country's capital. The Irish proudly turn out 'wearing the green'.

St. Patrick was born in Wales about AD 389, the son of a deacon and landowner. One day, Succat, as he was named, was captured by pirates and taken to Ireland. There he was sold to a minor chief and spent six years of great hardship working as a herdsman. He managed to escape and, after being held captive in England, he made his way back to Wales.

In one of several significant dreams he had during his lifetime, he was called by the 'voice of Ireland' to return as a missionary. He first set out for France and studied in a monastery near Paris, then he went to Ireland in AD 432. Ordained as a bishop, he was known as Patricius, the Latin word for 'noble'.

At the time, Ireland was a hostile country full of warring Celts who lived in tribal groups, ruled by five provincial kings. Patrick's overwhelming acceptance in Ireland as a missionary was largely due to his knowledge of the tribal system and its laws.

Patricius, or Patrick in Ireland, first endeavoured to convert the Irish King Laoghaire. Although he failed in this mission, he secured Laoghaire's permission to continue his work as a missionary.

By the end of the 5th century, Ireland had been converted to a Christian nation. In his 26 years as a missionary, Patrick and his disciples had visited all the towns, from large cities to isolated villages of only several households.

In his teachings, Patrick used the shamrock to illustrate the concept of the Holy Trinity. He showed the trifoliate leaf as a representation of the Father, Son and Holy Ghost — three persons in one God.

During his missionary work, Patrick returned to the home of Milchu, his taskmaster during his six years' imprisonment. When Milchu heard Patrick was coming to convert him, he burned down the house with himself inside, rather than having to face Patrick again.

On 17th March, Patrick died in Saul and villages and towns throughout the country wanted the honour of burying him. According to legend, his corpse was placed on a cart drawn by two cows and set free to wander. Wherever it stopped would be his burial place. The cart came to a halt a few miles from Saul in Downpatrick, and it is said that is where he was buried.

A granite boulder inscribed with his name and a cross marks the site.

Irish Stew, a classic Irish dish, is often eaten on St. Patrick's Day. It is essential to use good meat and stock to make this dish properly. Kid was once used, but nowadays lamb and mutton are more popular and readily available.

One way of preparing this dish is to make layers of sliced potato, onion and meat in a large casserole, then cook gently until potatoes at the bottom dissolve, absorbing the rich meat juices and stock. This recipe for Irish Stew is a slightly different interpretation. The potatoes are first mashed and then simmered with the meat, thus absorbing the delicious juices.

Traditional Irish Stew

SERVES 6-8

10 lb/4.5 kg middle neck of lamb, chined and
  cut into double chops (bones reserved)

2 onions, peeled

1 leek, trimmed

1 stalk celery, trimmed

bouquet garni of parsley stalks, thyme and
  rosemary

1 bay leaf

6 black peppercorns

salt and pepper

3 lb/1.4 kg potatoes, peeled and cut
  into dice

4 fl oz/100 ml single cream

2 lb/900 g button onions, peeled

1 The day before, place the chops in enough cold water to cover and leave in the refrigerator overnight, changing the water 2 or 3 times.

2 Meanwhile, put the bones and trimmings into a large saucepan or stockpot and cover with cold water. Bring to the boil and skim the surface. Simmer for 30 minutes, skimming the surface as necessary.

3 Add the onions, leek, celery, bouquet garni, bay leaf and peppercorns, and simmer for another 3 hours, skimming occasionally.

4 Strain the stock, then return it to the rinsed-out pan and boil rapidly until the liquid has reduced to 1¾ pints/1 litre. Reserve.

5 Drain the chops and season. Place in a flameproof casserole with the reserved stock. Bring to the boil and skim the surface. Lower the heat and simmer for 15 minutes, skimming occasionally.

6 Add the potatoes and simmer for 30 minutes or until cooked. Remove the potatoes from the casserole with a slotted spoon and mash with the cream.

7 Meanwhile, add the button onions to the stew and cook for about 15 minutes or until tender. Return the mashed potatoes to the pan and stir. Adjust the seasoning and serve.

Traditional Irish Stew

MOTHERING SUNDAY

The tradition of Mothering Sunday is believed to have its origins 400 years ago when, on the fourth Sunday of Lent, parishioners left the small village chapels and walked miles in order to attend the mother church of the district, bringing offerings, prayers and thanks. The custom of honouring all mothers sprang from this.

This occasion provided a welcome break from the Lenten fast, and all children who were working on farms away from home were given the day off to spend it with their mother. On their way to the church they would collect bunches of wild flowers or trinkets for her. The girls, usually in service away from home, also made simnel cake, a cake now associated with Easter.

Traditionally, the young family members met at the church and gifts were offered at the altar to show love and gratitude to their mothers. After the service all the youngsters returned home for a meal of lamb or veal with a fig pie or plum pudding to finish. Adults drank mulled ale and the children enjoyed frumenty, a drink of wheat grains boiled in milk with sugar and spices.

The ancient Greeks and Romans also acknowledged their mothers. The Greeks held a festival for Cybele, the mother of gods, and the Romans also celebrated with rites in honour of divine motherhood.

Fruit Scones   Eccles Cakes

Eccles Cakes

MAKES 12

*9 oz/250 g puff or rough puff pastry, defrosted
if frozen*
1 egg white, beaten
1 tablespoon caster sugar

Filling

1 oz/25 g butter, softened
1 oz/25 g mixed candied peel
1 oz/25 g demerara sugar
4 oz/100 g currants

1 Heat the oven to 220C/425F/Gas 7.
Lightly grease a baking sheet.
2 In a bowl, combine all the filling
ingredients and mix well. Set aside.
3 Roll out the pastry on a lightly
floured surface, to a ⅛ inch/3 mm
thickness. Using a 3 inch/7.5 cm cutter,
stamp out 12 rounds.
4 Place about 1 teaspoon filling in the
centre of each round. Bring the sides of
the rounds up over the filling and press
them well together to form small bun-
dles. Turn over and roll out gently until
you can see the fruit, then make 3
incisions in the pastry.
5 Brush with the egg white and sprinkle
over the caster sugar. Place the rounds
on to the prepared baking sheet. Bake
for 20 minutes or until the pastry is
golden.
6 Cool on a wire rack.

Fruit Scones

MAKES 12

7 oz/200 g self-raising flour
½ teaspoon salt
2 oz/50 g butter, diced
4 oz/100 g sultanas or raisins
about 4 fl oz/125 ml milk
extra milk, to glaze
butter for greasing

1 Heat the oven to 220C/425F/Gas 7.
Lightly grease a baking tray.
2 Sift the flour and salt into a bowl.
Add the butter and rub it in lightly until
the mixture resembles fine breadcrumbs. Add the sultanas.
3 Pour in half the milk and quickly mix
with a knife, gradually adding enough of
the remaining milk to make a firm ball.
4 Turn out the dough on to a lightly
floured surface and knead until smooth.
Roll out to a round 1 inch/2.5 cm thick.
Using a 2 inch/5 cm pastry cutter, cut
out 12 rounds, re-rolling the trimmings
until all are used.
5 Brush the surface with milk and place
on a greased baking tray. Bake for 10-15
minutes, until well risen and lightly
browned. Cool on a wire rack.

Rich Chocolate Cake

Rich Chocolate Cake

SERVES 4-6

4 oz/100 g plain chocolate
4 oz/100 g butter, softened
3 oz/75 g caster sugar
3 eggs, separated, plus 1 extra egg white
4 oz/100 g ground almonds
2 oz/50 g self-raising flour
1 egg white
whipped cream for decorating
crystallized violet leaves for decorating

Icing

3 oz/75 g plain chocolate
3 oz/75 g icing sugar
1 egg white
½ tablespoon butter, softened

1 Heat the oven to 180C/350F/Gas 4.
Butter and flour a round cake pan 7½
inches/19 cm across and 1 inch/2.5 cm
deep or a 9 inch/23 cm gugelhopf
mould.
2 Place the chocolate in a bowl placed
over a pan of simmering water and stir
until melted.
3 Beat together the butter and half the
sugar until light and creamy, then beat
in the egg yolks, one at a time, beating

well after each addition.
4 Add the chocolate and mix well. Sift
the almonds and flour over the surface
and gently fold in.
5 Whisk together the 4 egg whites with
the remaining sugar until stiff peaks
form. Gently fold into the batter.
6 Spoon the batter into the prepared
cake pan and bake for 30-35 minutes.
When cooked the centre should be
raised but still soft. Turn out the cake
immediately and cool on a wire rack.
7 To make the icing, melt the chocolate
in a bowl over a saucepan of simmering
water.
8 Beat the sugar and egg white
together, then add the chocolate. Add
the butter and beat well.
9 Spoon the icing over the cake. Pipe
rosettes of whipped cream round the
top and decorate with crystallized
violets, if desired.
Note If made in a plain round cake pan,
this luscious cake can be cut in half
horizontally and filled with additional
whipped cream. For an extra special
touch, add a little fruit-flavoured liqueur
to the cream before whipping.

GOOD FRIDAY

Good Friday comes this month; the old woman runs
With one a penny, two a penny 'hot cross buns',
Whose virtue is it you believe what's said,
They'll not grow mouldy like the common bread.

POOR ROBIN'S ALMANACK (1733)

Good Friday is the anniversary of Christ's crucifixion and a solemn occasion in the Christian calendar. It is thought that hot cross buns were introduced into England by the Romans who, like the Greeks, used similar cakes for festivals. These buns have pre-Christian origins and the symbols can be interpreted in several ways. Some say the circular shape of the bun represents the moon and the cross symbolises the quarters, while others claim the bun is the shape of the sun and the cross divides it into the four seasons. The cross on the bun has come to symbolize Christ's cross.

There are many folk beliefs attached to Good Friday; one is that baking is a good thing to do on this day. This has sprung from the legend told about Christ travelling to Golgotha. According to the legend, he stopped to rest at one woman's cottage who was washing. Not wanting to encourage him to stop, the woman threw washing suds over him and sent him on his way. Christ picked up his cross and went on to the next cottage where a woman was baking. She gave him a seat and offered him bread and water. From this tale has arisen the superstition that women who wash on Good Friday are cursed and those who bake are blessed.

Once made, the buns were hung in the doorway as a charm against evil. Villagers believed the buns had special medicinal properties because they would last for a year without becoming mouldy. In the Widow's Son, a London public house, it is now traditional for the first fresh hot cross bun of Easter to be placed in a hanging basket from the ceiling by a young sailor. This started 160 years ago when the tenant of the public house, a widow, saved a hot cross bun for her son's return home from sea. The young sailor did not return, but the widow refused to give up hope and kept the bun he had asked her to save. Each year for the rest of her life, she made a bun for him and hung it in a basket hanging from the ceiling. The succeeding tenants have retained this custom.

Hot Cross Buns
MAKES 24

2¼ lb/1 kg strong white flour
1 tablespoon salt
2 teaspoons allspice
4 oz/100 g sugar
4 oz/100 g chilled unsalted butter, cut into
    small dice
4 eggs
2 oz/50 g fresh yeast dissolved in
    ½ pint/275 ml warm milk and set
    aside until frothy
6 ½ oz/180 g currants
3 ½ oz/90 g candied mixed peel
1 egg, beaten, to glaze
extra butter for greasing baking sheet

Decoration
4 tablespoons plain flour
2 tablespoons milk

1 Sift the flour, salt, allspice and sugar into a bowl. Rub in the butter until the mixture resembles fine crumbs, then make a well in the centre.

2 Mix the eggs and the yeast mixture together and pour into the well. Gradually work the liquid into the flour, adding more milk if the mixture is too dry. Mix the dough until it forms a firm ball.

3 Turn out the dough on to a floured surface and knead until the dough is elastic. Form into a round ball and place in a buttered bowl. Cover with a tea towel and leave in a warm place for 20-30 minutes or until the dough starts to rise.

4 Lightly grease a baking sheet. Return the dough to the work surface and knead in the dried fruit and peel. Shape the dough into 24 small round balls and place them on the prepared baking sheet, leaving enough room for them to rise.

5 Cover and leave in a warm place 20-30 minutes, until the buns start to rise. Brush the tops lightly with the beaten egg.

6 To make the decoration, whisk the flour and milk together in a bowl until it is of piping consistency. Fill a small piping bag and pipe a cross on the top of each bun. Cover again with the tea towel and leave until the buns have doubled in size.

7 Heat the oven to 200C/400F/Gas 6 and place the shelf in the centre.

8 Brush with egg again and immediately place in the oven. Bake for 20-25 minutes or until the buns have risen and are golden.

9 Cool on a wire rack. Serve toasted and buttered.

Hot Cross Buns

EASTER

Named after Eostre, the Roman goddess of the dawn and spring, Easter has always been a time of great joy and festivities heralding the arrival of spring. After Christianity swept England, Easter became a Christian celebration to commemorate the resurrection of Christ and the end of the Lenten fast. Eggs are an ancient symbol of life and play a prominent part in Easter and its celebrations.

Decorating Easter eggs has traditionally involved detailed work. In ancient Britain an intricate pattern was drawn on to the shell with wax, then the egg was wrapped in onion skins and boiled. When cold, the skin was removed, leaving the waxed pattern white and the egg a reddish brown. Red was the most popular colour, but a variety of vegetable and flower dyes were used to create other colours.

Each Easter, peasants made a payment of eggs to their overlords and it is thought giving eggs as gifts came from this custom. These hard-boiled eggs, known as pace eggs, were given to friends or hidden in the garden for the children to find. Adults also played Easter games. Two teams competed by rolling eggs over a piece of carpet in a straight line and then manoeuvred them through a set of wickets without, hopefully, cracking the pace eggs.

In medieval times, large banquets were held. Minstrels welcomed guests with lively music and then attention was drawn to a large glass bowl on the high table, filled to the brim with painted and decorated eggs. The tapered end of each egg was bordered with lace and decorated with embroidery or glass jewels. Some eggs were painted with each guest's family crest. Throughout the evening, these pace eggs were given to the performers as gifts.

Dishes traditionally served during Easter reflect the arrival of the new season and the renewal of life and fertility. Lamb, symbolizing sacrifice, eggs, symbolizing the renewal of life, and almonds, the first blossoming tree in season, were the main ingredients served at the feast. Apple fritters and tansy cake, made with sharp tasting herbs, were also served.

Morris Dancers, very popular during the 16th century, were often invited to dance at the banquets. They dressed in flowing scarves, dark tights and tunics and wore wooden clogs. Bells attached to bands were worn round their ankles. The tapping steps and ringing bells were meant to arouse the slumbering spirits in the fields and the dancers' leaping was a reminder to the spirits to allow grain to grow high, flocks to multiply and people to prosper.

During Easter a play called the Deluge, a story about Noah's ark, was played from a moveable stage called a pageant wagon. This and other miracle plays were used to dramatize popular Bible stories. The authors and actors of the tales were the town craftsmen, whose work was applicable to the story. The Deluge, for example, was played by the town's water carriers. The play depicted the Easter themes of rebirth, renewal after death and resurrection of life in a finer form.

As well as being a delicious and satisfying meal for an Easter family lunch, this menu could be served on other special occasions. It includes foods traditionally eaten at Easter — lamb, eggs and almonds. The remaining dishes have been selected from foods in season and reflect the increased variety of produce now available.

Alternative suggestions using seasonal fruit and vegetables are cream of carrot soup, a tomato and basil salad, steamed asparagus, pears poached in red wine and gooseberry fool.

EASTER LUNCH

Broccoli and Hollandaise Sauce
or
Sardines in Puff Pastry

Roast Lamb with Garlic and Parsley Crumb Topping

Baked Tomatoes and Courgettes

Potatoes in Cream

Almond Cake

Broccoli and Hollandaise Sauce
SERVES 6-8
2 ½ lb/1.1 kg broccoli
salt and pepper
Hollandaise Sauce
6 egg yolks
3 tablespoons dry white wine
salt and cayenne pepper
14 oz/400 g clarified butter, warmed
juice of 1 lemon

1 In a bowl, whisk the yolks, 3 tablespoons warm water, the wine, a pinch of salt and cayenne pepper together. Place the bowl over a pan of simmering water and whisk constantly until light and fluffy. Do not allow the water to boil or overheat the mixture because it will curdle.

2 Continue whisking on and off the heat until the mixture is the consistency of lightly whipped cream. Immediately
continued on page 66

remove from the heat and gradually whisk in the clarified butter, discarding any milky sediment.

3 When all the butter has been incorporated, adjust the seasoning and add lemon juice to taste. Remove the bowl and pan from the heat and reserve in a warm place. The Hollandaise Sauce should be served tepid, not hot.

4 Blanch the broccoli in boiling salted water until just tender. Drain well and place in a warmed serving dish. Season lightly. Serve with Hollandaise Sauce.

Sardines in Puff Pastry

SERVES 6-8

4 oz/100 g unsalted butter
1 tablespoon finely chopped shallots or onion
3 × 4 oz/125 g tins sardines in oil, drained
1 teaspoon prepared whole-grain mustard
1 teaspoon Worcestershire sauce
pepper
6 large spinach leaves, blanched
9 oz/250 g puff pastry, defrosted if frozen
1 egg, beaten, to glaze
lemon wedges for garnish

1 Melt the butter in a saucepan, then add the shallots. Cook, stirring occasionally, until softened but not browned. Leave to cool.

2 Scrape as much black skin and bone off the sardines as possible, then add them to the shallots. Add the mustard and Worcestershire sauce and mix well.

Season to taste with pepper.

3 While soft, spread the mixture on to a baking sheet and shape into a neat 3 × 8 inch/7.5 × 20 cm rectangle with a palette knife. Chill until firm.

4 Carefully remove the sardine mix from the tray and wrap the spinach leaves round it until covered.

5 Roll out half the puff pastry to a rectangle a little larger than the sardine mix, leaving a 1 inch/2.5 cm border all round. Place the sardines on top. Brush the border with the beaten egg. Roll out the remaining pastry to the same size and use to cover the sardines. Press the edges to seal. Use any leftover pastry to make decorative leaves. Brush the top of the pastry with the egg, then chill for 1 hour. Reserve the remaining egg.

6 Heat the oven to 200C/400F/Gas 6.

7 Just before cooking, brush the pastry with egg once more. Bake for 20-30 minutes or until the pastry is golden. Serve warm garnished with lemon.

Baked Tomatoes and Courgettes

SERVES 6-8

2 tablespoons butter
2 onions, thinly sliced
salt and pepper
6 tomatoes, thinly sliced
4 courgettes, thinly sliced

1 Heat the oven to 200C/400F/Gas 6.

2 Melt half the butter in a frying pan,

then add the onion and season to taste. Cook, stirring occasionally, until soft and golden brown. Spread the onion over the base of an ovenproof serving dish.

3 Arrange the tomato and courgette slices on top of the onion in alternate rows. Season well. Melt the remaining butter and use to brush the surface.

4 Cook for 15-20 minutes or until the courgettes are tender.

Note This dish can be cooked up to 1 hour ahead and kept warm in a low oven. Reheat under the grill.

Potatoes in Cream

SERVES 6-8

½ pint/275 ml milk
½ pint/275 ml double cream
3-4 cloves garlic, crushed
salt and pepper
8 large potatoes, peeled and cut into thin slices
4 oz/100 g Gruyère or Cheddar cheese, grated

1 Heat the oven to 200C/400F/Gas 6.

2 Put the milk, cream and garlic into a saucepan and bring to the boil. Season to taste, then add the potatoes and mix well. Return the liquid to the boil, then spoon the potatoes into an ovenproof serving dish. Sprinkle over the cheese.

3 Place the dish in a roasting pan and pour in enough boiling water to come three-quarters of the way up the sides of the dish. Cook for about 45 minutes.

4 The potatoes are cooked when a skewer or fork pierces the potatoes easily and the top is golden brown. If the top is browning too quickly, cover it with aluminium foil.

Note This dish can be cooked up to 1 hour ahead and kept in a low oven.

Roast Lamb with Garlic and Parsley Crumb Topping

SERVES 6-8

4 whole best ends of lamb, oven ready
Marinade
½ pint/275 ml vegetable oil
3 cloves garlic, halved
2 bay leaves
6 parsley stalks (optional)
thyme and rosemary sprigs
6 black peppercorns
Crumb Topping
4 oz/100 g butter
5 oz/150 g dried breadcrumbs
6 cloves garlic, crushed
1 tablespoon chopped fresh parsley
salt and pepper

1 Two days before cooking, place all the marinade ingredients into a large

Broccoli and Hollandaise Sauce   Sardines in Puff Pastry

Roast Lamb with Garlic and Parlsey Crumb Topping and vegetables

shallow dish and add the lamb. Marinate for 2 days, turning the meat twice a day, spooning the marinade over.

2 To make the crumb topping, place the butter in a large frying pan and heat until it begins to froth. Add the breadcrumbs and stir into the butter. Add the garlic and cook over medium heat, stirring constantly, until the crumbs are light golden brown. Pour into a sieve placed over a bowl and leave to drain. When cooked, place in a bowl and mix in the chopped parsley and season to taste. Reserve.

3 Heat the oven to 250C/500F/Gas 10 and place a roasting pan in the oven to warm.

4 Remove the lamb from the marinade and pat dry with kitchen paper. Strain in enough oil from the marinade to cover the base of the roasting pan. Arrange the lamb so the bones are standing upwards, then brown in the oven for 10

minutes to seal. Turn the lamb so it is skin side down and continue cooking for 5-10 minutes for medium rare or 10 minutes more for well done.

5 Transfer the lamb to a warmed serving dish and rest in a warm place for 5 minutes. Press the crumb mixture on to the meat so it is well covered. Place under a preheated high grill and cook until the crumbs begin to brown. Carve the lamb into individual cutlets.

Almond Cake

SERVES 6-8

1 oz/25 g slivered almonds
4 eggs, separated
4 oz/100 g caster sugar
5 oz/150 g ground almonds
1 tablespoon Cointreau or kirsch
2 oz/50 g self-raising flour, sifted
2 oz/50 g warm melted butter
1 tablespoon softened butter for greasing
icing sugar, to decorate

1 Heat the oven to 180C/350F/Gas 4. Lightly butter an 8 inch/20 cm round cake pan, then chill in the freezer for 5 minutes. Butter the pan again, then press the slivered almonds round the sides and bottom of the pan. Leave in the refrigerator to chill until it is required.

2 Meanwhile, beat the egg yolks with half the sugar until pale and fluffy. Add the ground almonds, liqueur, flour and melted butter.

3 In another bowl, beat the egg whites with the remaining sugar until stiff peaks form. Lightly fold into the almond mixture. Pour into the chilled cake pan.

4 Bake the cake for about 30 minutes or until a skewer or fork inserted into the centre comes out clean. Turn out on to a wire rack to cool, then lightly sprinkle the top of the cake with sifted icing sugar. Serve sliced.

MAY DAY

May Day is a celebration symbolizing the awakening of life and the arrival of spring. The customs, costumes, decorations, dances and food of the day's celebration are all directed towards the change of season.

These festivities originated from the Roman festival to Flora, goddess of flowers, and was held annually between 28th April and 3rd May. The cult of Flora was introduced to England by Belgic invaders at the end of the 1st century, as a pagan attempt to force spring to return to the world. Dancers stamped the ground to awaken it and May horns, loud May whistles and May bells were sounded to alert sleeping spirits in fields and forests that spring had arrived. These rituals were later adopted by the Catholic church.

To start the celebrations, children and teenagers made their way to the fields and forests to collect evergreen boughs and meadow flowers long before dawn. This greenery was called the 'may' and was woven into garlands and wreaths. Houses were decorated with greenery to announce spring's arrival.

A maypole was erected for the day in all villages. Some maypoles were as high as 30 yards/27.4 metres and had to be permanently anchored outside, but were only decorated on May Day. Garlands of leaves and flowers covered the maypole and brightly coloured ribbons were wound from bottom to top.

A Queen of the May was usually chosen for the day and she wore a gold crown with a single gold leaf on her forehead. She sat in the place of honour watching the juggling, magic tricks and games. The Queen decorated the winners and led the circle of dancers around the maypole.

Other competitions, such as leap jumping, archery, running races, ball throwing, hoop rolling and guessing the number of beans in the barrel, were all held on the village green. Each winner received a prize of bells attached to an ankle band. They would then dance around the maypole, jingling loudly, take off the bell band and place it on a hook on the maypole.

Backgammon, chess and billiards were also popular May Day games. Billiards or pool was also played with players using a table or a large outdoor court set up for teams.

An enormous feast was another important part of the day's festivities and all the food and drink was either green or coloured green. Trenchers, or green parsley bread slices, were served covered with a salad of lettuce, spinach, peas, endive, fennel and greengage plums, and washed down with cider.

Chicory and Orange Salad, Honey Glazed Chicken and Mushroom Tart

MAY DAY PICNIC

Chicory and Orange Salad

Honey Glazed Chicken

Tomato Salad

Mushroom Tart

Banana and Walnut Cake

With the warmer weather comes a drop in prices for the readily available hot-house vegetables. Good quality new potatoes, broad beans, tender Savoy cabbages, spring greens and carrots can now also be bought.

Supplies of fish continue to be plentiful and varied. River trout and sea or salmon trout are at their peak.

Chicory and Orange Salad
SERVES 8
2 heads chicory, leaves separated
1 orange, sliced
fresh dill for garnish
Dressing
1 tablespoon olive oil
3 tablespoons orange juice
salt and pepper

1 To make the dressing, place all the ingredients in a screw-top jar and shake.
2 Arrange the chicory leaves and orange slices in a shallow bowl. Garnish with the dill and cover with cling film until ready to serve. Shake the dressing and pour over just before serving.

Honey Glazed Chicken
SERVES 8
finely grated zest and juice of 1 orange
1 clove garlic, crushed
3 tablespoons honey mixed with 2 tablespoons whole-grain French mustard
salt and pepper
3 lb/1.4 kg chicken drumsticks
bunch watercress, to garnish

1 Heat the oven to 180C/350F/Gas 4.
2 Mix together the orange zest and juice, garlic and the honey and mustard.
3 Pour the orange-flavoured mixture over the chicken drumsticks and turn until they are completely covered.
4 Place the drumsticks in an ovenproof dish in a single layer and bake for about 30 minutes, turning the legs several times during cooking. The chicken is cooked when the juices run clear when pierced with a fork. Cool completely before packing and garnishing.

Tomato Salad
SERVES 8

1 ½ lb/750 g salad tomatoes, chopped or
*   quartered*
1 tablespoon finely chopped basil
salt and pepper

Dressing
1 tablespoon white wine vinegar
1 teaspoon Dijon mustard
salt and pepper
pinch of sugar
4 tablespoons olive oil

1 For the dressing, whisk the vinegar, mustard, seasoning and sugar in a small bowl. Add the olive oil, a little at a time, whisking continually, so the dressing thickens.

2 Put the tomatoes into a serving dish and sprinkle over the basil. Season with salt and pepper, then pour over the dressing. Cover with cling film and refrigerate until required.

Mushroom Tart
SERVES 8

2 tablespoons butter
2 shallots, finely chopped
12 oz/350 g button mushrooms, sliced
salt and pepper
1 teaspoon lemon juice (optional)
1 teaspoon dry sherry
grated nutmeg, to taste
2 eggs
3 fl oz/75 ml milk
1 egg yolk
9 fl oz/250 ml double cream

Pastry
9 oz/250 g plain flour
1 teaspoon salt
4 oz/100 g butter, diced
2 egg yolks

1 For the pastry, sift the flour and salt into a bowl. Make a well in the centre and add 1-2 tablespoons cold water and the butter. Using your fingertips, incorporate all the ingredients until the mixture resembles large crumbs. If it is too dry, add another tablespoon of water, little by little.

2 Turn the pastry on to a floured work surface. Knead the dough 2 or 3 times until it is smooth and pliable. Form into a ball, cover with cling film and refrigerate for 30 minutes.

3 Heat the oven to 200C/400F/Gas 6.

4 Use the pastry to line a lightly buttered 12 inch/30 cm quiche ring or ceramic flan dish. Blind bake for 7 minutes. Remove the baking beans and cook for a further 8 minutes.

5 Meanwhile, for the filling, place the butter in a large frying pan. When hot, add the shallots, mushrooms and seasoning, and sauté for 1 minute. Add the lemon juice and sauté for 1 minute more, or until the mushrooms are just cooked. Add the sherry and remove from the heat. Reserve.

6 Beat the remaining ingredients together, adding any juice from the mushrooms in the frying pan.

7 Using a slotted spoon, put the mushrooms into the base of the pastry, pour over the cream mixture and bake for 20-30 minutes or until firm in the middle. Cool before packing.

Banana and Walnut Cake
SERVES 8

4 oz/125 g unsalted butter
9 oz/250 g caster sugar
2 eggs
1 lb/450 g bananas
3 fl oz/75 ml milk
12 oz/350 g self-raising flour
½ teaspoon salt
3 oz/75 g chopped walnuts
extra butter for serving

1 Lightly butter a 7½ x 4½ inch/19 x 11 cm loaf pan. Heat the oven to 180C/350F/Gas 4.

2 Cream the butter and sugar until pale and well blended. Whisk in the eggs, one at a time, beating well after each addition.

3 Mash the bananas and stir in the milk, then sift the flour and salt over the mixture. Add the nuts and fold in.

4 Pour the mixture into the prepared pan and cook for 1-1¼ hours or until risen and golden brown. Insert a skewer into the centre of the cake and if it comes out clean, the cake is cooked.

5 Leave the cake for 1 day to let the flavours develop, then serve sliced and spread with butter.

Banana and Walnut Cake

ROYAL ASCOT

In 1711, the first racing meeting was inaugurated on Ascot Common by Queen Anne. She drove from Windsor Castle with her courtiers and maids of honour to attend a day's sport, which had been organized at her command. Little attention was paid to horse racing or Ascot then, but the Duke of Cumberland, until his death in 1765, revived interest in Ascot races. It is said that over 40,000 people attended a race in Ascot in 1791. There was no grandstand, but on the common was a vast array of booths and tents. The Gold Cup was instituted in 1807, when Queen Charlotte attended Ascot. In 1907, during the running of the Gold Cup, the trophy was stolen from the display case at the back of the grandstand. It has never been recovered. Ascot's popularity with members of the Royal Family has come and gone, although Edward VII, then Prince of Wales, was far more enthusiastic than either of his parents. In a letter to his mother, he said '… it is an opportunity for the Royal Family to show themselves in public – which I am sure you desire – and after all Racing with all its faults still remains, I may say, a National Institution of the Country'.

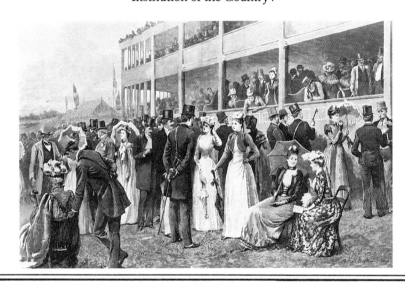

Lemon Asparagus Rolls
MAKES 24
2 oz/50 g butter, softened
finely grated zest and juice of 1 small lemon
pepper
12 slices brown bread, crusts removed
24 cooked asparagus tips

1 Beat together the butter and lemon zest with the juice to taste. Season.
2 Butter the bread, then lay 2 asparagus tips on each piece of bread, trimming the asparagus as necessary. Carefully roll up the bread, like a Swiss roll, completely encasing the asparagus. Press gently so the butter seals the rolls.
3 To serve, cut in half diagonally.

Crab and Cucumber Sandwiches
MAKES 24
12 slices brown or white bread
butter for spreading
4 oz/100 g crab pâté or dressed crab
½ cucumber, thinly sliced
salt and pepper

1 Spread the bread with the butter, then spread the crab pâté over 6 slices.
2 Top each of the pâté-covered slice with cucumber slices and season to taste. Top with the remaining bread, buttered side down, and press down.
3 Trim off the crusts and cut each sandwich into 4 triangles.

Ham and Gruyère Fingers
MAKES 24
6 oz/175 g puff pastry, defrosted if frozen
3 oz/75 g gruyère, thinly sliced
3 oz/75 g cooked ham, thinly sliced
whole-grain French mustard
1 egg, beaten, to glaze
flour for the work surface

1 Heat the oven to 220C/425F/Gas 7.
2 Roll out the pastry on a lightly floured work surface to make 4 rectangles about 12 x 3 inches/30 x 7.5 cm. Trim the edges.
3 Carefully arrange the cheese, then the ham along the length of 2 pieces of pastry. Spread mustard over the remaining pieces of pastry.
4 Brush the edges of the pastry with water. Place the pastry with the mustard, mustard side down, on top of the pastry with the ham and cheese. Seal the edges well and decoratively crimp.
5 Place the pastry on baking sheets and brush the surface with the beaten egg. Use a fork to make air vents.
6 Bake for 12-15 minutes, until crisp and golden. Cut into fingers and serve.

WIMBLEDON

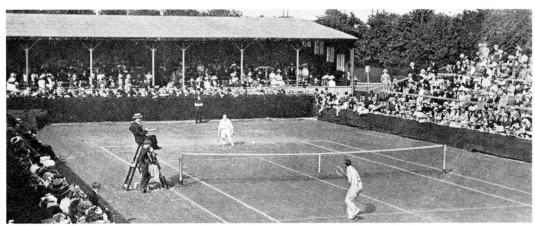

The championship, founded in 1877 by the All-England Lawn Tennis and Croquet Club, was first chronicled in *The Field* sports magazine:

"The All-England Lawn Tennis and Croquet Club, Wimbledon, propose to hold a lawn tennis meeting open to all amateurs, on Monday July 9th and following days. Entrance fee is 1 shilling. Two prizes will be given – one gold champion prize to the winner, one silver to the second player."

Twenty two male competitors played in the first championship which attracted 200 spectators for a week of sport, and champagne and strawberries on the lawn. Spencer Gore became the first Wimbledon champion.

By 1880, the championships had already expanded from its original garden party atmosphere into a serious, annual sporting event. In order to accommodate the increased entry of 60 competitors, more courts were built and admission was raised to half a crown.

In the early days of the competition, male players wore knickerbockers, black stockings, black gym shoes, stripped jerseys and pork-pie hats. Female competitors were just as encumbered in petticoats, trailing skirts and boaters. Playing clothes were gradually improved by 'radical' competitors, such as Mary Sutton from America, who declared that women would play in shorts. And, in 1905, she further scandilized the priggish Wimbledon authorities by rolling up her sleeves during play.

Nowadays, Wimbledon attracts 350,000 spectators a year, plus millions of followers through radio and television. Entry is now limited to 112 players, who come from 40 countries.

Strawberries and cream have remained entwined in the social customs of Wimbledon. Growers in the Home Counties endeavour to have crops at their peak during the championships where spectators consume approximately 1 ton of strawberries per day.

During this peak summer month the market stalls are tightly packed with salad vegetables, including spring onions, radishes, watercress, mange tout, globe artichokes and English tomatoes. Cauliflowers are also at their best during the summer months.

Lobster and salmon join the growing range of available seafood which now includes Dover sole, mullet, turbot, shrimps, hake, clams, cockles and brill.

Fresh fruit, such as raspberries, apricots, peaches, cherries and black-currants, also make their first appearance in July. However, no description of July's produce could be complete without mentioning strawberries, a fruit which is synonymous with England, afternoon tea and the Wimbledon Lawn Tennis Championships.

Strawberries and cream is a simple, yet always popular, July treat. Hull the berries and serve as soon as possible after picking.

AUGUST BANK HOLIDAY

In 1871, a Bank Holiday act was passed in Parliament. This was a special day nominated by parties required to negotiate papers, exempting them from the obligation of presentation and payment. This meant that banks and Government offices could close for the day. Before this bill was passed, the Bank of England used to close on more than forty saint's days. London's August Bank Holiday is still the day for the Hampstead Fair, originally a trading fair. Many other trading fairs coincide with bank holidays.

The long working days of summer and autumn were frequently broken by fair days. Fairs were often held on a saint's day and were enthusiastically welcomed by villagers as a market day and holiday. These days were possibly one of the few holidays allowed before working days were regulated with official breaks.

For the original bank holiday, market stalls were gaily dressed with small trinkets, pin cushions and ribbons. Edible presents, like gingerbread decorated with gilded leaves or studded with cloves, and fancy biscuits known as 'fairings' were also sold. It was the custom for sweethearts to buy 'favours' from the stalls for each other.

Swansea market was first erected in 1652 to sell corn, fish and vegetables. The following account was made in 1880 by the American consul to Cardiff. 'A constant procession of market women setting toward market town. They are of every age and of varying conditions, and they bear to market all sorts of farm produce, as well as shellfish, which they have gathered by the sea'.

Trading fairs held throughout the country in August include:

Horse Fair in Lincolnshire. This has been held since the 13th century and is always well attended. Gypsies gallop their horses through the street to show prospective buyers and then confirm the sale with a traditional gypsy hand slap.

Cranham, Gloucestershire. Held on the second Monday in August, this was largely a social occasion. Deer were roasted over a spit and served to villagers. After lunch a tug of war was held between local teams, with the losing team being pulled into the stream in the middle.

Horse Fair in Lee Gap, Yorkshire. This fair is over 800 years old and is the most popular in Yorkshire. It is a favourite with the gypsies who turn up in large numbers to do business.

Spare-Ribs
SERVES 8
4 lb/1.8 kg pork spare-ribs
Marinade
2 tablespoons soy sauce
1 tablespoon dry sherry
2 cloves garlic, crushed
1 tablespoon tomato ketchup
1 teaspoon sesame oil
½ tablespoon honey
salt and pepper
2 tablespoons vegetable oil

3 Place on a dish, cover with cling film and chill until required.
4 Prepare the barbecue. When the coals are ready, season the banana rolls with pepper and barbecue on the grill until the bacon is cooked. Serve hot.
Note This dish can also be cooked under a high grill.

Aïoli and Crudités
SERVES 8
12 cloves garlic, peeled
½ teaspoon salt
pinch cayenne pepper
2 egg yolks, at room temperature
14 fl oz/400 ml olive oil, at room temperature
juice of 2 lemons
fresh carrots, peppers, celery, courgettes,
  cucumber and mushrooms, to serve

1 Place the garlic, salt, cayenne pepper and egg yolks into a blender or food processor and blend until smooth. With the motor still running, add half of the olive oil in a thin steady stream through the opening in the lid. Add the lemon juice and continue blending, adding the remaining oil.
2 Taste and add more seasoning and juice, if necessary. If the aïoli is very thick, thin it down with 1-2 teaspoons warm water. Pour the aïoli into a serving dish, cover and chill until required.
3 Scrape the carrots and cut into strips. Deseed, core and slice the peppers into strips. Cut the courgettes and cucumbers into bite-sized chunks and trim the mushrooms. Serve with the aïoli as dippers.

Seafood Skewers
SERVES 8
14 oz/400 g firm white fish fillets, such as brill,
  turbot or monkfish
14 oz/400 g salmon fillet
14 oz/400 g scallops, shelled, cleaned and
  defrosted if frozen
14 oz/400 g Dublin Bay prawns or scampi,
  shelled, deveined and defrosted if frozen
sea salt
fresh ground white pepper
3 tablespoons butter, melted
Marinade
4 fl oz/125 ml vegetable oil
4 fl oz/125 ml olive oil
2 tablespoons chopped fresh herbs, such as
  chervil, chives, tarragon or parsley
juice of 1 lemon
small bulb fennel, thinly sliced

1 Cut the white fish and salmon into 16 equal-sized pieces. Thread alternate

1 Combine all the marinade ingredients together in a large shallow dish. Add the spare-ribs and turn until well coated.
2 Cover the dish with cling film and marinate in the refrigerator for 24 hours, turning the ribs occasionally and spooning over the marinade.
3 To cook, prepare the barbecue. When the coals are ready, barbecue the spare-ribs on a lightly oiled grill for 15-20 minutes, turning once and basting frequently.

Bacon Wrapped Bananas
SERVES 8
4 ripe bananas
juice of ½ lemon
4 oz/100 g bacon rashers, rinds removed
pepper

1 Cut the bananas into 1 inch/2.5 cm slices. Sprinkle over the lemon juice.
2 Cut each bacon rasher into quarters and warp each piece around a slice of banana. Secure with a cocktail stick.

pieces of fish and shellfish on to 8 long wooden satay sticks or skewers, fitting them closely together. Place a piece of firm white fish at the end of each skewer. Arrange the skewers in a single layer on the base of a large, shallow dish.

2 Mix together all the marinade ingredients. Pour the marinade over the skewers and add the fennel slices. Cover with cling film and refrigerate for up to 8 hours, carefully turning the skewers occasionally so all the pieces of fish are well-coated with marinade.

3 To cook, prepare the barbecue. When the coals are ready, remove the skewers from the marinade and drain. Sprinkle with the salt and pepper. Cook on a lightly oiled grill, giving a quarter turn every 5 minutes and basting with the butter. Cook for about 20 minutes or until the white fish flakes easily when tested with a fork.

Note These delicious Seafood Skewers can also be cooked under a hot grill.

Seafood Skewers

Fruit Kebabs with Yoghurt Sauce

SERVES 8

1 grapefruit, peeled and cut into chunks
1 orange, peeled and cut into chunks
1 pear, peeled, cored and cut into chunks
1 apple, peeled, cored and cut into chunks
4 kiwi fruit, peeled and halved
2 bananas, peeled and each cut into 4 pieces
16 large red grapes
1 small pineapple, cut into 16 chunks
juice of 2 lemons
1 pint/600 ml Greek yoghurt
1 tablespoon desiccated coconut
grated nutmeg, to taste
2 oz/50 g butter
2 tablespoons honey

1 Thread the fruit on to 8 long wooden satay sticks or skewers, beginning and ending with a piece of firm fruit, such as apple or pear. Brush with lemon juice, then cover and chill until required.

2 In a bowl, combine the yoghurt, coconut and nutmeg. Cover with cling film and chill until required.

3 Melt the butter in a pan over low heat, then stir in the honey. Reserve at room temperature.

4 To cook, prepare the barbecue. When the coals are ready, brush the fruit generously with the honey and butter glaze. Place on the grill and cook, turning 2 or 3 times and basting with the remaining glaze. Cook for 15 minutes or until the fruit is glazed and golden. Cool slightly, then serve with the yoghurt sauce.

Fruit Kebabs with Yoghurt Sauce

HARVEST FESTIVAL

Harvest festivals have been an occasion of rejoicing since earliest times. It is a non-religious holiday, intended to celebrate the fruits of the earth and a time to give thanks for the year's crops.

It has also been the occasion for many unusual customs having to do with a belief in the corn spirit or corn mother. In Northumberland, an image formed of a wheat sheaf and dressed in white frock and coloured ribbons was hoisted on a pole. This was the 'kern baby' or harvest queen, and was set up in a prominent place during the festival.

Today, most churches have harvest festival celebrations, although the connection with the church did not come about until 1834. The churches are decorated with fruits and ·flowers.

Granary Rolls

As fruit and vegetables are available in large quantities at low prices, the mild September days are ideal for making pickles and preserves. Greengages, plums, gooseberries, damsons and redcurrants are best for jams, jellies and pies, while cauliflowers, peas, beetroots, courgettes and onions can be used for pickles and chutneys. Tomatoes are also good for chutney but are equally delicious as a sauce which can be bottled and used during winter.

Granary Rolls
MAKES 12
1½ lb/700 g granary flour
2 teaspoons salt
1 oz/25 g vegetable fat
1 oz/25 g fresh yeast
1 tablespoon black treacle
vegetable oil for greasing.

1 In a large bowl, combine the flour and salt, then rub in the vegetable fat.
2 Mix the yeast with about ¼ pint/ 150 ml lukewarm water and set aside for 10-15 minutes, until frothy. Mix the treacle with ½ pint/275 ml lukewarm water.
3 Add the liquid ingredients to the dry ingredients and mix well. Knead for about 10 minutes, until smooth.
4 Place the dough in a large well oiled bowl, cover with oiled cling film and leave to rise in a warm place for 30-45 minutes, until doubled in size.
5 Knead the dough on a lightly floured work surface, then divide into 12 equal portions. Shape into individual plaits, round baps or cottage loaves.
6 Place the rolls on lightly greased baking sheets, cover with oiled cling film and leave in a warm place for 15-20 minutes, until doubled in size.
7 Meanwhile, heat the oven to 230C/ 450F/Gas 8.
8 Bake the rolls for 10-15 minutes, until golden brown. When the rolls are cooked, they will sound hollow when tapped on the bottom. Leave to cool on a wire rack.

HALLOWE'EN

Held on 31st October, the eve of All Saints' Day, Hallowe'en is thought to have originated from an ancient Druidic festival. Centuries ago the night was marked by the lighting of bonfires, or *bone fires*, so called because the bones of close relatives were burned.

The fires were to honour the Sun God and give thanks for the harvest. It was also believed, however, that on this night ghosts, witches and restless spirits walked abroad. Connected with this is another Druidic belief that Samhain, the Lord of Death, called together all the evil spirits who had been condemned to live in the bodies of animals. Celtic New Year was held the following day on 1st November.

From these ancient and somewhat gruesome beliefs and rituals more charming and light-hearted customs have developed that are followed today. Hallowe'en is now known as the night for tricks, parties and games, such as apple bobbing. A large bonfire burns throughout the night and lanterns carved from pumpkins are carried by children parading through villages. It is also the night for practical jokes, when cabbages and turnips are hung above neighbours' doors. This stems from the custom known in Munster and Connaught, both in Ireland, as 'battering away the hunger'.

Many traditional Irish dishes are associated with Hallowe'en, such as barn brack, colcannon (boiled and mashed potatoes and cabbages) and Boxty cake or bread. Boxty is made from equal quantities of grated raw potato and cooked potato. This is stirred into hot milk and cooked until firm. The mixture is then put into a warm dish and melted butter is poured into a well in the centre. A wedding ring is mixed in the ingredients and, according to custom, whoever finds it will be married within the year.

In Scotland, a rich fruit cake iced in black and orange, the colours of Hallowe'en, was traditionally baked on 31st October.

Irish and Scottish immigrants introduced Hallowe'en customs to America, where they are still followed.

Toffee Apples
SERVES 8

8 sweet dessert apples
½ lb/225 g caster sugar
2 oz/50 g unsalted butter
1 tablespoon golden syrup
1 teaspoon malt vinegar
few drops red food colouring
vegetable oil for the plate

1 Remove the stalk from each apple and push a 6 inch/15 cm wooden skewer into each from the base along the core. Make sure each apple is secure. Set aside. Lightly oil a large plate and set aside.
2 Place the remaining ingredients, except the food colouring, into a heavy-based saucepan. Add enough water to just cover the sugar and place the pan over high heat until the sugar melts. Add a few drops of food colouring, if desired.
3 Reduce the heat and cook until the sugar reaches 145C/295F, or the hard crack stage, on a sugar thermometer.
4 Immediately remove the pan from the heat and quickly dip each apple into the syrup, turning to coat evenly. Then place on the oiled plate to cool.
Note To add to the festive atmosphere, the toffee apples can be wrapped in brightly coloured paper and ribbons after the toffee hardens.

Pumpkin Tart
SERVES 8

1 lb/450 g fresh pumpkin, cut into small even-sized pieces or 1 lb/450g can of pumpkin purée
4 oz/100 g demerara sugar
5 egg yolks
4 fl oz/125 ml double cream
1 tablespoon molasses
½ teaspoon Cognac or brandy
1 teaspoon ground allspice
pinch of salt
2 oz/50 g pumpkin seeds, shelled
whipped cream, to serve (optional)
Sweet Pie Pastry
6 oz/175 g plain flour
3 oz/75 g icing sugar
½ teaspoon salt
4 oz/100 g chilled unsalted butter, diced
2 egg yolks

1 To make the pastry, sift the flour, sugar and salt on to a work surface or marble slab. Add the butter and rub in until the mixture resembles crumbs.
2 Make a well in the centre and put the egg yolks into the middle. Quickly mix together incorporating all the flour.

Toffee Apples   Pumpkin Tart

Form into a ball, wrap in cling film and rest in the refrigerator at least 30 minutes before rolling out.

3 Place the pumpkin into a steamer in a covered saucepan with just enough simmering water to steam. Simmer gently until the pumpkin is very soft. Drain well, then purée in a blender or food processor, or work through a fine sieve with the back of a wooden spoon.

4 Combine the pumpkin purée or canned purée and the sugar, egg yolks, cream, molasses, brandy, allspice and salt in a pan. Place over low heat and cook, stirring constantly, until the mixture is hot and slightly thickened. Do not allow to boil.

5 Heat the oven to 200C/400F/Gas 6.

6 Roll out the pastry on a light floured surface and use to line a 10 inch/25 cm

flan dish or quiche ring. Pour the purée into the dish and sprinkle over the pumpkin seeds.

7 Bake for 15 minutes. Lower the temperature to 170C/325F/Gas 3 and continue cooking for another 15 minutes or until the centre of the tart is firm to the touch.

8 Leave the tart on a wire rack to cool. Serve with whipped cream, if desired.

GUY FAWKES' NIGHT

Guy Fawkes was born in York, the son of a wealthy Protestant family. Soon after his father's death, Fawkes converted to the Catholic faith and, at an early age, left England to join the Spanish army. The King of Spain, who was the leader of a strong Catholic country, was on good terms with English Catholics and encouraged a bond in the hope that they would overthrow the British Protestant-ruled government, giving Spain an opportunity to rule.

King James I was forced by his Protestant ministers to pass harsh laws penalizing Catholics. Discontent grew and Robert Catesby, a Catholic, conceived a plot that would end the persecution of Catholics with one blow. Two other men were involved in the Gunpowder Plot, as it was known, and Fawkes, now a colonel in the Spanish army and an expert on using gunpowder, was invited to help. Thomas Percy, one of the king's courtiers, rented a house next the Houses of Parliament and the men began to dig a tunnel into the building. Digging equipment and barrels of gunpowder were carried across the river each night by boat.

The conspirators were waiting until the king and all his ministers assembled to open the Houses of Parliament, then they planned to light a slow burning fuse to the explosives, before making their escape by boat. Unfortunately the opening of Parliament was delayed from 31st October to 5th November and during this time one of the men sent a letter to his friend, Lord Mounteagle, warning him not to attend the opening. Suspicions were aroused and a search of the rooms carried out. On 5th November, just before the opening ceremony, Yeomen Guards searched the buildings and found 36 barrels of hidden gunpowder.

Fawkes was arrested along with some of the other conspirators and tortured for more information. The conspirators were tried and found guilty of treason, then hung, drawn and quartered on 31st January, 1606. King James I was so overjoyed at discovering the Gunpowder Plot that he declared the day a public holiday and the first record of the bonfire celebration was in 1607.

Today, Yeomen of the Guard still follow the traditional ceremony of inspecting the Houses of Parliament and its vaults before the opening. Once this has been done, the Queen is notified at Buckingham Palace that she can make her way to the House.

The burning of fires and effigies was a fairly common occurrence in the Middle Ages when villagers relished the extra holiday. Enormous potatoes called 'roasters' were saved to bake on the fire at 'Bunfireneet'. Treacle toffee and gingerbread, or parkin, were also made specially for the occasion.

Gingerbread

MAKES 10 PIECES

4 oz/100 g butter
6 fl oz/175 ml treacle
2 fl oz/50 ml golden syrup
¼ pint/150 ml milk
2 eggs, beaten
½ teaspoon salt
½ lb/225 g plain flour
½ tablespoon ground ginger
½ teaspoon bicarbonate of soda
vegetable oil for greasing the baking pan

1 Heat the oven to 150C/300F/Gas 2. Lightly grease a 6 × 11 inch/15 × 28 cm baking pan.
2 In a heavy-based saucepan, gently heat the butter, treacle, syrup and milk together until all the ingredients are combined and well blended.
3 In a bowl, beat the eggs with the salt. Sift the dry ingredients into a bowl and gradually add the eggs. Mix well, then add the melted buter and syrup mixture. Beat until well blended, then pour into the prepared baking pan.
4 Bake for 30-40 minutes or until a skewer or fork inserted into the centre comes out clean. Turn out on to a wire rack to cool. Cut into squares when cold, then wrap in aluminium foil and store in an air-tight container.

Treacle Toffee

MAKES 1¾ lb/800 g

1 lb/450 g demerara sugar
¼ teaspoon cream of tartar
3 oz/75 g butter
7 oz/200 g treacle
butter for the baking pan

1 Butter a 11 × 7 inch/28 × 18 cm baking pan.
2 Put the sugar and ¼ pint/150 ml water into a heavy-based saucepan and stir over low heat until dissolved. Add the remaining ingredients, increase the heat and bring to the boil.
3 Using a brush dipped in water, brush the sides of the saucepan to dissolve the sugar crystals. Cook, without stirring, until the syrup reaches 132C/270F, or the soft crack stage, on a sugar thermometer.
4 Pour the toffee into the buttered pan. Cool slightly, then mark into squares and leave to set. When cold, gently break into squares.
Note On a chilly November night, mugs of warming soup are always appreciated. A thick cream of chicken or mushroom soup is ideal.

CHRISTMAS

Throughout the centuries there have been many festivities to celebrate the end of the year. In northern Europe, barbarians held a yule festival where great logs were burned in honour of the gods Oden and Thor. Horns full of mead were passed to the people gathered round the fire, while poets and minstrels sang and told ancient legends.

After the birth of Christ, these pagan festivities were gradually absorbed into the celebrations of the Catholic church. The yule-log continued to be burnt, mistletoe was still used as a decoration and great feasting and merry making continued.

In the Middle Ages, the most splendid feast of the year took place at Christmas time. The banquet hall was filled with branches of evergreen and holly and mistletoe, or the 'kissing bush' as it was called, hung from the ceiling. Noticeably absent was the Christmas tree, not introduced to England from Germany until the 19th century.

Festivities began with guests parading underneath the kissing bush. They were careful, however, not to cross a green line marked on the floor near the high table. Nobody was allowed to cross it until the first-foot, or lucky bird, had leapt over. Before the feast began, the letting-in Christmas ceremony took place. The first-foot appeared at the back of the hall, dressed in green with dark hair, wearing ankle bells and carrying an evergreen bough. He skipped towards the high table, jumping the line with a flourish, then paused to collect money in his cap from all guests.

The next ceremony was the lighting of the yule candle. This enormous candle took 12 months to make and was created from multiple colours of wax. The candle was lit to cheers of 'wassail' and then used to light the yule-log. The largest log possible was put in the hearth and lit. The log was supposed to burn for all 12 days of Christmas and one small part of it was reserved for lighting the first fire of the New Year.

With the ceremonies over, the grand procession of food was carried into the hall. On one large tray was the centrepiece, a boar's head with an apple or lemon in its mouth and surrounded by greenery. Ducks, capons, geese, peacocks and swans were also served. The popular Christmas drink was the wassail, a hot ale spiced with nutmeg, cloves, ginger and sugar, with eggs and roast apples mixed in. Wassail, meaning 'to your health', came from the Saxon words *was hail*.

Poorer families ate more frugally with a bird such as capon, goose or chicken as the main dish. Turkey was first introduced to England from Mexico in the 16th century and was not a popular Christmas dish until the 1900s.

A special Christmas dish eaten by both lords and peasants was humble pie, 'umble being the innards of an animal, nowadays known as tripe. The innards were cooked for a long time and then baked in a pie with a sweet crust.

Mince pies are another popular Christmas treat dating to medieval times. They were brought back to England by soldiers returning from the crusades. Originally they were oblong shaped (known as 'coffins') and were supposed to represent the manger. The spices in the mincemeat, which actually included meat and suet, were symbolic of the gifts given by the three kings.

By the 17th century mince pies contained eggs, raisins, orange and lemon zest, sugar and spices, as well as chopped chicken or beef tongue. The meat gradually disappeared and the pie changed to its present circular shape. People followed the superstition of eating a mince pie for each of the 12 days of Christmas and saying 'happy month' before the first bite, to ensure a happy year.

Another popular dish was plum porridge, porridge mixed with raisins, spices, breadcrumbs and fruit juice, and served with the first course of Christmas dinner. The Christmas pudding we serve today is a Victorian version of the plum porridge.

When making the Christmas pudding, it was traditional for everyone in the family to take a turn at stirring. It had to be stirred clockwise, because this is the direction in which the sun moves round the earth. To stir 'widdershins' was thought to invite trouble. Tokens were also folded into the mixture; a silver coin signified wealth, a button meant bachelorhood, a thimble indicated spinsterhood and a ring meant marriage. The finder of a token would see these meanings as a prediction of their future.

CHRISTMAS DAY LUNCH

Cream of Celeriac Soup
or
Oysters in Orange and Garlic Cream

Roast Turkey with Sage and Onion Stuffing

Brussels Sprouts and Chestnuts

Old-Fashioned Mince Pies

Christmas Pudding with Brandy Butter

Christmas is a time for family gatherings, and everyone will be expecting traditional Christmas fare, with only the subtlest of alterations. Traditional Christmas dishes, as we know them today, have been included in this menu. Oysters, which were used in the early 1900s as a cheap filler in meat pies, are added here as a luxurious touch warranted by the occasion. Cream of Celeriac Soup is a more economical alternative and a delicious way of serving this root vegetable while in season.

The Sage and Onion Stuffing is a classic combination with turkey, and an undeniable favourite. Brussels sprouts are naturally on the menu, but glamourised for the occasion by being served with fresh chestnuts. Other side dishes, such as roasted sweet potatoes, glazed carrots and onions, kohlrabi cooked in cream with cheese grilled on top, or steamed broccoli could be served.

The Old Fashioned Mince Pies offer an unusual variation. In this mincemeat recipe, which dates back to medieval times, cold roast beef and beef suet are included with the dried fruits. It really wouldn't be Christmas without the Christmas Pudding, and the chilled Brandy Butter can also be served with the warmed mince pies.

Oysters in Orange and Garlic Cream
SERVES 8
6 large oysters, per person
finely grated zest and juice of 1 orange
2 cloves garlic, crushed
7 fl oz/200 ml double cream
pinch of cayenne pepper
4 oz/100 g butter, cut into small pieces
4 tablespoons ground almonds
fresh dill sprigs, to garnish

1 Wash the oysters under cold running water. Open the shells and scoop out the oyster, tipping it into a sieve placed over a bowl to catch the juices. Wash

Cream of Celeriac Soup   Oysters in Orange and Garlic Cream

the deep half of the shells and place them in a grill tray or roasting pan spread with rock salt or baking beans, so the oysters stand firm. Wash the oysters in salted water and transfer them to the shells on the tray.

2 To make the sauce, combine the oyster juices, orange juice and zest and garlic, then put into a large saucepan. Boil gently until reduced to 1 tablespoon liquid. Add the cream and cayenne pepper, and return the sauce to the boil. Whisk in the butter, adding a few pieces at a time, taking the pan on and off the heat. Do not allow the sauce to boil or it will curdle. Stir in the ground almonds and mix well.

3 Heat the grill to high.

4 Spoon the sauce into the shells around the oysters, then place them under the grill. Grill until lightly browned. Garnish with fresh dill sprigs and serve at once.

Cream of Celeriac Soup
SERVES 8

1 lb/450 g celery
2 tablespoons butter
1 lb/450 g celeriac, trimmed and
*   finely sliced*
1 small onion, thinly sliced
salt and pepper
2½ pints/1.4 litres chicken stock
1 bouquet garni
pinch of sugar (optional)
12 fl oz/350 ml double cream
fresh parsley sprigs, to garnish

1 Cut four 2 inch/5 cm lengths from the celery sticks and finely shred. Reserve these and any small yellow leaves in a bowl of water to use as garnish. Finely slice the remaining celery.

2 Melt the butter in a large saucepan, add the celery, celeriac and onion, then season. Cook over low heat, stirring occasionally, for 15 minutes or until soft but not browned.

3 Add the stock and bouquet garni. Bring to the boil, then simmer gently for 15 minutes, skimming occasionally.

4 Remove the bouquet garni and purée the soup in a blender or food processor. Taste for seasoning and adjust if necessary. Add the sugar, if desired.

5 To serve, bring the soup and the cream to the boil in separate pans. Stir the cream into the soup. Do not allow the soup to return to the boil or it will curdle. Ladle the soup into warmed soup bowls and garnish with the reserved celery leaves and parsley sprigs. Serve hot.

Brussels Sprouts and Chestnuts   Roast Turkey

Brussels Sprouts and Chestnuts

SERVES 8

2 lb/900 g fresh chestnuts
1 chicken stock cube
bouquet garni
½ onion, stuck with 2 cloves
½ stalk celery, chopped
1 small carrot, chopped
salt and pepper
2 lb/900 g Brussels sprouts, trimmed
2 tablespoons butter
pinch of sugar
vegetable oil for the baking tray

1 Heat the oven to 240C/475F/Gas 9. Lightly oil a baking tray.
2 Score around the chestnut shell with a small, sharp knife. Heat the baking tray in the oven and cook the chestnuts in small batches for 1-2 minutes, until they pop. Immediately peel off the outer shell and the brown skin covering the nut. Repeat until all are peeled.
3 Place the chestnuts in a saucepan with enough water to cover. Crumble over the stock cube and add the bouquet garni, onion, celery, carrot and seasoning. Bring to the boil, then reduce the heat and simmer for 20-30 minutes, until the chestnuts are cooked through but not crumbling. Drain.
4 Meanwhile, cook the Brussels sprouts in boiling, salted water until just tender. Drain.
5 Heat the butter in a saucepan until foaming, then add the sugar, Brussels sprouts and chestnuts. Season. Toss over medium heat until well glazed.

Roast Turkey with Sage and Onion Stuffing

SERVES 8

10 lb/4.5 kg oven-ready turkey
4 oz/100 g butter, cut into 6 equal-sized pieces
salt and pepper
6 rashers bacon
vegetable oil
fresh parsley for garnish
Sage and Onion Stuffing
2 tablespoons butter
½ onion, finely chopped
½ tablespoon dried sage
9 oz/250 g pork sausagemeat
the turkey liver, finely chopped
4 oz/100 g fresh breadcrumbs
salt and pepper

1 Loosen the flap of the skin around the turkey's neck and work your fingers under the breast skin to loosen it. Place 3 pieces of butter on each side of the breast. Season the cavity from the rear.
2 To make the stuffing, melt the butter in a saucepan, add the onion and sauté for about 5 minutes, until soft but not coloured. Stir in the sage, then remove the pan from the heat.
3 Add the sausagemeat to the pan with the liver. Mix well. Add the breadcrumbs, season well and mix until the ingredients are thoroughly blended. Spoon the stuffing into the neck cavity of the turkey. Do not pack it too tightly as the stuffing expands during cooking. Pull the flap of neck skin over the

stuffing and secure with a skewer or sew in place.

4 Heat the oven to 200C/400F/Gas 6. Place the bacon rashers over the breast, brush the bird with vegetable oil and seasoning. Cook for 3-3½ hours, basting frequently. If the breast browns too quickly, cover it with aluminium foil.

5 The turkey is cooked when a skewer or fork is inserted into the thickest part of the thigh and the juices run clear. Transfer to a warmed serving dish and rest for 10 minutes before carving.

Old-Fashioned Mince Pies

MAKES 20

2 oz/50 g shredded beef suet
2½ oz/60 g cold cooked roast beef, finely
    chopped
2 oz/50 g demerara sugar
2 oz/50 g seeded raisins
2 oz/50 g currants
2 oz/50 g sultanas
2 oz/50 g mixed candied peel
1 oz/25 g apple, peeled and grated
finely grated zest and juice of ½ orange
½ teaspoon ground allspice
2 teaspoons Cognac or brandy
2 teaspoons rum
2 teaspoons Madeira
1 tablespoon milk, to glaze
2 tablespoons caster sugar
extra butter for greasing the moulds

Pastry

12 oz/350 g plain flour
7 oz/200 g icing sugar
¾ teaspoon salt
6 oz/175 g chilled unsalted butter, diced
6 egg yolks

1 Combine the suet, roast beef, sugar, raisins, currants, sultanas, candied peel, apple, orange zest and juice, allspice, Cognac, rum and Madeira in a bowl. Cover with cling film and leave in the refrigerator for 1-2 days to marinate.

2 To make the pastry, sift the flour, sugar and salt into a bowl. Add the butter and rub in with your fingertips until the mixture resembles fine breadcrumbs. Make a well in the centre and add the egg yolks. Mix together until it forms a firm dough, then wrap in cling film and leave in the refrigerator for 30 minutes to rest.

3 Heat the oven to 200C/400F/Gas 6.

4 Roll two-thirds of the pastry out to a ⅛ inch/.25 cm thickness. Using a 3½ inch/9 cm cutter, stamp out 20 rounds and line 2½ inch/6.5 cm buttered tartlet moulds.

5 Roll out the remaining dough and cut out another 20 rounds. Brush the edges

with the milk. Spoon the mincemeat into the moulds and cover with the lids. Cut a cross in the top of each pie and brush the tops with milk.

6 Bake for about 20 minutes or until the pastry is cooked and golden brown. Dust with the caster sugar and leave to cook on a wire rack. Serve hot or cold.

Christmas Pudding with Brandy Butter

SERVES 8

4 oz/100 g apple, peeled and grated
4 oz/100 g seedless raisins
4 oz/100 g currants
4 oz/100 g sultanas
3½ oz/90 g mixed candied peel
2½ oz/60 g blanched almonds, chopped
4 oz/100 g demerara sugar
2 tablespoons molasses
finely grated zest and juice of ½ lemon
finely grated zest and juice of ½ orange
1½ teaspoons ground allspice
4 fl oz/100 ml brandy or rum
4 fl oz/100 ml stout
2 eggs
4 oz/100 g plain flour
9 oz/250 g fresh white breadcrumbs
4 oz/100 g unsalted butter, cut into small
    pieces
4 oz/100 g shredded beef suet
butter for greasing the bowl

Brandy Butter

6 oz/175 g unsalted butter, softened
6 oz/175 g caster sugar
6 tablespoons brandy

1 The day before making, place the apple, raisins, currants, sultanas, candied peel, almonds, sugar, molasses, lemon and orange zest and juices, allspice, brandy and stout into a large bowl. Cover with cling film and leave in the refrigerator overnight.

2 Add the eggs to the fruit and stir well. Mix the flour with the breadcrumbs in another bowl and add the butter and suet. Mix with your fingertips until the mixture resembles fine breadcrumbs.

3 Lightly butter the sides and bottom of a 3 pint/1.7 litre pudding mould.

4 Pour the flour over the fruit and stir until well combined. Pour the mixture into the prepared greased pudding mould. Cover with aluminium foil, pleating the top to allow for expansion during steaming. Secure tightly with string.

5 Place the mould into a large saucepan and pour in enough boiling water to come three-quarters of the way up the sides of the mould. Cover the pan tightly and steam for 6 hours. Top up with boiling water as necessary.

6 Keep the pudding in a dry, unheated cupboard for 1-3 weeks before eating. Reheat by steaming as above for 1½-2 hours, before serving. Serve with the Brandy Butter.

7 To make the Brandy Butter, beat the butter until it is very soft and smooth. Beat in the sugar, a little at a time, until it is all used. Add the brandy, a little at a time, beating well after each addition so the mixture doesn't curdle. Cover with cling film and chill until is is time to serve Christmas Pudding or Mince Pies.

Christmas Pudding with Brandy Butter   Mince Pies

BOXING DAY

There are many different customs and traditions associated with Boxing Day. Boxes were introduced in Britain by the Romans, who used them to collect the money that spectators paid to watch athletic games. In Britain, they were first used in churches as collection boxes.

The name Boxing Day stems from medieval times, when the priests emptied their alms boxes the day after Christmas and distributed the money to the poor people of the parish.

Servants and apprentices also kept boxes. Throughout the year they saved the money they received as gifts and tips in their boxes. As money became a more common Christmas gift, they delayed opening their boxes until the day after Christmas when no more contributions could be expected. And, until recently, the 26th of December was the day for giving small boxed gifts and tips to the postman, dustman and paper-boy.

Many sports are also associated with this day, and in earlier centuries there were squirrel hunts and bird shoots. Fox and hound hunts were also held, and this tradition is still continued today.

This Boxing Day menu forms the basis of a buffet that can be added to with salads and vegetables, depending on the number of people. All the main dishes have been designed to serve 8-10.

After the Christmas meal there is often leftover food, and this pie is a good way of using up any remaining turkey. The pie can also be made with duck or chicken, using the more economical cuts such as drumsticks or thighs.

The pâté, gammon and trifle dishes can all be prepared a few days in advance. They are ready to serve as is, with no reheating required. A buffet also reduces the amount of work for the cook since once the food is served, the guests can help themselves.

By using produce in season at this time, the buffet can be supplemented with dishes such as fennel à la grecque, braised endive, avocado salad, sweet potatoes or sautéed leeks.

BOXING DAY LUNCH

Kipper Pâté

Glazed Gammon
or
Turkey Pie

Potato and Parsnip Gratin

Trifle

Kipper Pâté
SERVES 8-10
1 lb/450 g unpeeled potatoes
1 tablespoon butter
½ lb/225 g back bacon, roughly chopped
1 lb/450 g onions, sliced
2 lb/900 g kipper fillets, skinned and boned
1 egg
2 tablespoons Drambuie
1 tablespoon Scotch whisky
grated nutmeg, to taste
salt and pepper
extra butter for greasing the mould

1 Put the unpeeled potatoes into a pan of cold, salted water. Bring to the boil and simmer for about 30 minutes or until the potatoes are just tender. Drain and peel under cold running water.

2 Meanwhile, melt the butter in a saucepan over low heat. Add the bacon and onions and cook on a low heat for about 15 minutes, stirring occasionally until the onions are soft but not browned.

3 Heat the oven to 200C/400F/Gas 6. Lightly butter a 3 pint/1.7 litre terrine.

4 Put the kipper fillets into a blender or food processor with the potatoes, bacon, onions, egg, Drambuie, whisky, nutmeg and pepper. Season with a little salt, if necessary. Blend until the mixture is blended but still chunky. Taste and add more seasoning or Drambuie and whisky, if wished. Alternatively, mash the potatoes with a fork, and finely chop the kippers, bacon and onions, then add the flavourings.

5 Spoon the mixture into the prepared mould, pushing it down lightly. Cover

with buttered aluminium foil and place a lid on top. Place the terrine in a larger roasting pan and pour enough boiling water to come three-quarters up the side of the mould. Cook for about 1 hour. Cool completely.

6 Transfer the terrine to the refrigerator for at least 1 day to let the flavours develop before serving. Serve with toast fingers, if desired.

Note The terrine will keep for up to one week in the refrigerator if you pour a thin layer of clarified butter on top.

Kipper Pâté

Glazed Gammon

SERVES 8-10

6 lb/2.7 kg gammon
1 onion, stuck with 4 cloves
1 carrot, chopped
4 cloves garlic
1 stalk celery, chopped
12 black peppercorns

Glaze

4 tablespoons demerara sugar
1 tablespoon fruit juice, cider or vinegar
1 teaspoon ground cloves
3 teaspoons Dijon mustard
salt and pepper

1 Soak the gammon overnight in cold water, changing the water at least twice.
2 Drain and place the gammon in a large saucepan with enough fresh water to cover. Add the remaining ingredients. Bring to the boil, lower the heat and simmer gently for 2-2½ hours, skimming occasionally.
3 To make the glaze, place all the ingredients into a small bowl and mix.
4 Remove the gammon from the pan and carefully peel off the rind, leaving the fat on the meat. Using a sharp knife, score the fat into a diamond pattern and brush generously with the glaze.
5 Heat the oven to 230C/450F/Gas 8. Place the gammon in a roasting pan and cook for 20-30 minutes, basting occasionally with the juices in the pan. When the gammon is well browned,

transfer to a warmed serving dish. Alternatively, serve cold.

Potato and Parsnip Gratin

SERVES 8-10

2 lb/900 g potatoes, peeled and thinly sliced
2 lb/900 g parsnips, peeled and thinly sliced
salt and pepper
7 fl oz/200 ml double cream
7 fl oz/200 ml milk
grated nutmeg, to taste
½ lb/225 g Emmenthal cheese, grated
2 tablespoons freshly grated Parmesan cheese
butter for greasing the dish

1 Heat the oven to 200C/400F/Gas 6. Lightly butter a shallow ovenproof dish.
2 Arrange the potato and parsnip slices in the prepared dish. Use the most even-sized slices for the top layer. Lightly season each layer.
3 Bring the cream and milk to the boil in a heavy-based saucepan over medium heat. Season lightly with salt and pepper and the grated nutmeg.
4 Pour the sauce over the potatoes and parsnips. Sprinkle over the Emmenthal cheese, then the Parmesan.
5 Place the dish in a roasting pan and pour in enough boiling water to come half way up the sides of the dish. Bake for 1-1½ hours. If the top browns too quickly, cover it with aluminium foil. The dish is cooked when a skewer or fork penetrates the layers with ease.

6 Keep warm until ready to serve, then reheat under a hot grill until the cheese is brown and bubbling.

Turkey Pie

SERVES 8-10

the leftover cooked turkey carcass, stripped and roughly chopped
1 bottle dry red wine
8 rashers lean back bacon
2 tablespoons butter
12 oz/350 g button mushrooms
salt and pepper
1 lb/450 g button onions
pinch of sugar
2 tablespoons vegetable oil
2¼ lb/1 kg cooked turkey meat
2 tablespoons plain flour
2 tablespoons brandy (optional)
9 oz/250 g frozen puff pastry, defrosted
1 egg, beaten, to glaze

Mirepoix

1 onion, roughly chopped
1 stalk celery, roughly chopped
1 carrot, roughly chopped
1 bay leaf
sprig thyme
3 parsley stalks
6 black peppercorns

1 Put the turkey carcass, any left over gravy and juices, wine, 1 pint/600 ml water and all the ingredients for the mirepoix into a large saucepan. Bring to the boil. Skim the surface. Lower the heat and simmer for 1 hour or until 1 pint/600 ml liquid remains. Strain and reserve.
2 Roll the bacon into 8 rolls and secure with wooden cocktail sticks. Place in a large pan of cold water and bring to the boil. Boil for 2 minutes, then remove the rolls with a slotted spoon and reserve.
3 Melt half the butter in a casserole, then add the mushrooms and sauté for 3-4 minutes or until just cooked. Season with salt and pepper and set aside.
4 Add the remaining butter to the pan with 4 fl oz/100 ml of the reduced stock, the onions, seasoning and the sugar. Cover and cook over gentle heat for 5-10 minutes or until the onions are tender. Remove the lid and boil rapidly until all the liquid has evaporated and the onions are coated in a shiny red glaze. Reserve.
5 Put the oil into the pan and when hot, add the turkey meat. Season and toss in the oil for 1 minute. Sprinkle over the flour and cook for 1 minute more. Add the brandy, if using, then the reserved stock. Stir until the sauce boils and

Potato and Parsnip Gratin   Turkey Pie

1 Split the sponges in half and spread with the jam. Place the two halves back together and cut each into ¾ inch/ 2 cm cubes.

2 Place the sponges in the bottom of a 3 pint/1.7 litre capacity bowl and sprinkle over half the sherry. Cover with fruit, then cover with cling film and set aside.

3 Heat the remaining sherry in a large bowl placed over a pan of simmering water. Sprinkle over the gelatine and stir until dissolved. Add half the sugar and the egg yolks, then whisk. Take the bowl on and off the heat, whisking constantly, until the mixture has thickened to the consistency of lightly beaten double cream. Don't overheat or stop whisking, or the yolks will curdle. Remove from the heat and set aside.

4 Beat the egg whites with the remaining sugar until stiff peaks form.

5 Gently fold the whipped cream into the yolk mixture, then spoon one quarter of the whites into this mixture and fold in gently. Pour the mixture over the fruit, cover and chill for 4 hours or until the trifle is set.

6 Before serving, decorate the top of the trifle with rosettes of whipped cream and the almonds.

thickens, then cover and lower the heat. Simmer for 15 minutes.

6 Remove from the heat and stir in the reserved mushrooms, bacon and onions. Taste for seasoning and adjust if necessary. Pour into a 4-4½ pint/2.3-2.5 litre pie dish. Leave to cool completely before covering with the pastry.

7 Heat the oven to 200C/400F/Gas 6.

8 Roll out the puff pastry to ¼ inch/0.6 cm thickness and use to cover the pie. Re-roll the trimmings and use to make decorations. Brush the surface with beaten egg, arrange the pastry decorations, then brush with beaten egg again. Bake for 30 minutes or until the pastry has risen and is golden.

Trifle
SERVES 8-10
½ lb/225 g trifle sponges
1-2 tablespoons raspberry or strawberry jam
8 tablespoons cream sherry
1 lb/450 g fresh fruit salad or tinned fruit
   cocktail, drained
1 teaspoon gelatine
4 oz/100 g caster sugar
4 eggs, separated
¼ pint/150 ml double cream, whipped
Decoration
¼ pint/150 ml double cream, whipped
2 oz/50 g flaked almonds, toasted

Trifle

HOGMANAY

In Scotland, Hogmanay, or New Year's Eve, is celebrated in traditional fashion. Haggis and whisky are served and Scottish Black Bun, which is prepared weeks beforehand, is brought out of its wrappings in readiness for the first-footers who will be calling throughout the night.

This popular custom actually started in the 16th century. Beggars used to go from church to church crying for hogmanay bread and cheese.

Guises, or children with blackened faces and wearing bizarre clothes, also went from door to door singing or reciting begging rhymes. Nowadays, groups of children visit houses on hogmanay morning and are given cake or small gifts, such as oranges or lemons stuck with cloves.

Years ago Scots would gather in the local marketplace and wait for the peal of bells announcing the arrival of the new year. At the sound of the bells, the bagpipes were played and much revelry took place. The crowd then dispersed to start first-footing. In small groups, people visited the homes of friends and relatives where they would drink whisky and a hot pint and eat traditional foods, such as bannock (a round unleavened bread), haggis and Scotch currant bun. First-footing continued all night until every house in the neighbourhood had been visited.

According to tradition, the first first-footer into any home had to be a tall dark man who carried in a piece of coal and black bun. This custom meant that a year of warmth and food would follow. Women were not allowed into the house first because it was considered bad luck. If any first-footers were barred from entering a house, they had to tramp round the building, stamping their feet to shake off any dust on their shoes. Carrying that dust into another house was believed to bring bad luck.

Scottish Black Bun

SERVES 4-6

½ lb/225 g self-raising flour
3 teaspoons ground allspice
pinch of black pepper
1 lb/450 g seedless raisins
1 lb/450 g currants
2 oz/50 g chopped mixed peel
4 oz/100 g chopped almonds
4 oz/100 g demerara sugar
juice and grated zest of 1 orange
¼ pint/150 ml Scotch whisky
4 tablespoons milk
1 egg
1 egg, beaten, to glaze

Pastry
9 oz/250 g plain flour
1 teaspoon salt
4 oz/100 g chilled unsalted butter, diced

1 To make the pastry, sift the flour and salt into a mixing bowl. Add the butter and rub it into the flour until the mixture resembles fine breadcrumbs. Stir in 2-3 tablespoons cold water to make a firm dough. Cover with cling film and refrigerate for 30 minutes.

2 Roll out two-thirds of the dough to a 14 inch/35.5 cm circle about ⅜ inch/.75 cm thick. Use to line an 8 inch/20 cm deep spring-release cake tin, with ½ inch/1.2 cm pastry overlapping at the top. Cover with cling film and chill while preparing the filling.

3 Meanwhile, sift the flour, allspice and pepper into a bowl. Stir in the dried fruit, mixed peel, almonds, sugar and orange zest. Add the whisky, milk, orange juice and egg and mix until well blended.

4 Spoon the mixture into the lined mould, folding over the overlapping pastry. Roll the remaining pastry into a circle, large enough to cover the top. Moisten the edges of the pastry circle with half the beaten egg, then cover the pie, sealing the edges well. Using a skewer, make 4 or 5 holes round the cake, right down to the base. Cut a cross in the centre and brush with the remaining beaten egg to glaze.

5 Heat the oven to 180C/350F/Gas 4. Bake for 2-2½ hours or until a skewer inserted into the centre comes out clean. Cover the top of the cake with aluminium foil if it browns to quickly.

6 Cool completely on a wire rack. Wrap in aluminium foil and leave in a cool dark place to mature for 2 weeks.

Scottish Black Bun

DIET AND NUTRITION

Your health is one of your most precious assets, and your diet plays an important part. By learning the basics of good nutrition, and paying attention to the food you eat, you can keep your health in peak condition.

Today, the types of illness and disease that we suffer from are dramatically different from those of the last century. Where once the killers were viral infections like tuberculosis, the big killers now are heart disease and cancer. Even those who avoid these two major diseases cannot, in the main, be termed healthy. Many suffer from smaller complaints such as haemorrhoids, varicose veins, migraines or depression.

Many experts believe that diet is one of the key factors in ill health. During World War 2, it was noted that people were healthy because they had a controlled, but totally balanced diet. Although the food was rationed, the amount of fat, sugar and meat was worked out by nutritionists as being the least the body could exist on and still remain healthy. Coupled with the home-grown fruits and vegetables from the allotments, it amounted to a nation virtually free from the heart and other related diseases that plague our society today. It has been estimated recently that about three-quarters of all people living in London suffer from diet-related illness.

Our diet has changed a lot over the past 150 years. Wholemeal bread, grains and fresh vegetables, with occasional meat and no sugar was once the norm. This was a healthy diet, since the foods provided all that was needed — vitamins, minerals, carbohydrates, protein and fibre.

Today, the typical British diet is highly processed. Food is canned, frozen or freeze-dried. More often than not, it has preservatives, additives and colouring in it. When food is processed it loses a lot of its basic vitality, flavour and colour. The food industry sometimes tries to compensate for this by adding colouring, flavouring enhancers, sugar and salt. But once food has been stripped of its basic nutrients, it can no longer benefit the body in the same way as it could in its fresh state.

The so-called convenience foods may, in the long term, turn out to be a great inconvenience to our health. Take, for example, the British sliced white bread loaf. Although handy for toasting and frying, it is very constipating. All the dietary fibre has been sifted out of the flour, leaving it white and lacking in nutrients. Some of the missing nutrients are added in the baking process, and some which where never there to begin with are also added — such as chalk, which is used as a bleaching agent to make the bread whiter than white, flour enhancers and preservatives.

Most of the foods we eat today have changed in quality over the last century, and many for the worse. Cattle are now reared intensively, leading to fattier meat — a crucial factor in heart disease. They are fed hormones and antibiotics that remain in the meat when it is eaten. Seas and rivers are polluted, resulting in poor quality fish. Fruits and vegetables are sprayed with chemicals which may be harmful. The soil in which they are grown is often of poor quality, and leads to substandard produce.

This picture is not as grim as it sounds. You can avoid the worst by learning how to find nutritionally good foods, and by following certain recommendations that have come about as a result of a serious concern about the British diet.

The National Advisory Committee on Nutritional Education (NACNE) was set up in 1979 to analyse the British diet and to correlate its effects on the health of the British people. It aimed to give guidelines on changing and improving our diet by evaluating how much fat, sugar, salt and fibre was eaten.

The report came out in its final form in 1983, with specific recommendations for improving the nation's health (see chart below). But what does all this mean, and how do you incorporate these changes in your diet?

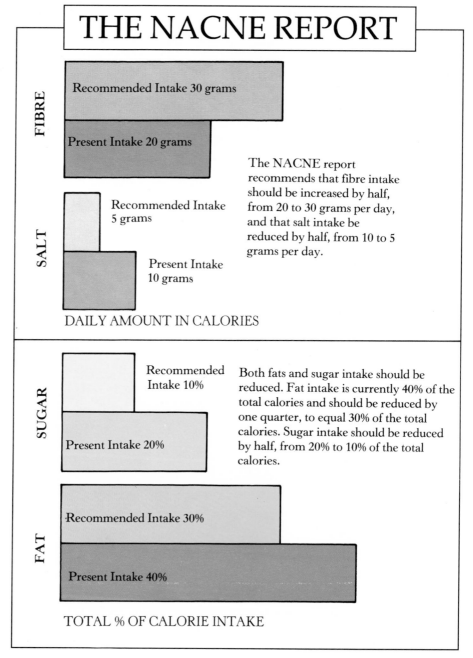

THE NACNE REPORT

FIBRE
Recommended Intake 30 grams
Present Intake 20 grams

SALT
Recommended Intake 5 grams
Present Intake 10 grams

DAILY AMOUNT IN CALORIES

The NACNE report recommends that fibre intake should be increased by half, from 20 to 30 grams per day, and that salt intake be reduced by half, from 10 to 5 grams per day.

SUGAR
Recommended Intake 10%
Present Intake 20%

FAT
Recommended Intake 30%
Present Intake 40%

TOTAL % OF CALORIE INTAKE

Both fats and sugar intake should be reduced. Fat intake is currently 40% of the total calories and should be reduced by one quarter, to equal 30% of the total calories. Sugar intake should be reduced by half, from 20% to 10% of the total calories.

KNOW YOUR NUTRIENTS

Fats

Fat is essential in your diet because it helps to carry the fat-soluble vitamins around your body. There are some fats that are good for you, and some that are harmful. Too much of the wrong sort of fat can lead to obesity and heart disease, and you should learn to distinguish between the different types.

Each type of fat or oil contains three different fatty acids in different proportions: saturated, monounsaturated and polyunsaturated fatty acids. It is the proportion of these that is the vital factor in determining how good or bad a certain fat is for you.

The ones with a high proportion of saturated fatty acids are unhealthy and should be avoided. They make your blood more viscous and can damage arterial walls. Over the years this can lead to arterial obstruction and heart attacks. Those fats with a high proportion of monounsaturated fats don't affect the arteries at all, and fats high in polyunsaturates play an important part in keeping the cell membranes healthy and the nerves in good order. The chart, below, gives you a rough guide as to which fats are high in polyunsaturates. New labelling regulations are coming into effect in 1986, and fats and oils that are high in polyunsaturates will say this on the label. Look for these brands when you are shopping.

Sugar

There are many forms of sugar — sucrose, glucose, fructose, and lactose, for example. Sucrose is the sugar that we usually eat, in granulated, cube or icing sugar form. Glucose is sugar that occurs naturally in fruits and vegetable juice, and we manufacture it in our bodies. Fructose is twice as sweet as sucrose, and is contained in honey as well as some fruits and vegetables. Lactose is sugar found in milk.

Manufacturers are adding more and more sugar to various food products each year. Since sugar occurs naturally in so many foods, there is no need to add extra to the diet. Sugar, while it does provide energy in the form of calories that can be utilized by the body, contains no nutrients — they are called empty calories. It is a contributory factor in tooth decay, obesity and

hyperglycaemia. Too much sugar can also lead to behavioural disturbances.

Salt

Salt, or sodium, is essential to life. But the average person eats almost 10 times more than is needed. For good health, a balance of sodium, chlorine and potassium is necessary since the three work in unison to balance your body fluid. Salt is found naturally in all food, so there is no need to add it when cooking. Eating too much salt can lead to high blood pressure — it disrupts the potassium level and chlorine balance, which in turn overworks the pancreas.

Fibre

Fibre is found in all whole grains, fresh fruits and vegetables, pulses and nuts. Eating a diet low in fibre has been found to be an important factor in the development of bowel cancer, as well as causing more minor problems such as constipation or piles. When there isn't enough fibre in the diet, the food passes along the intestines very slowly and unhealthy bacteria can then multiply in the intestine. Fibre speeds up the digestion process.

Proteins

Proteins repair cells in the body, and also produce hormones and enzymes. They are made of chains of amino acids. There are 20 known amino acids, of

which 12 can be synthesized in the body. The remaining eight have to be obtained from food. Animal protein is complete protein, and contains all the essential amino acids. Plant protein is incomplete, and needs to be eaten in combination with other proteins to become complete.

Carbohydrates

Carbohydrates supply energy, and are found in sugar, starch and fibre. But not all carbohydrates are the same in terms of your health. Fibrous carbohydrates, such as potatoes, wholemeal bread, whole grains and dried or fresh fruit, are better for you than carbohydrates from biscuits, sweets or white bread.

Vitamins

These are organic compounds found naturally in food. There are 40 known vitamins, of which 12 are vital to health. They are important because they work with enzymes to bring about the necessary chemical changes in the body.

Minerals

Minerals are inorganic substances found in food and water. There are 20 essential minerals in all, which work to regulate the body fluids and balance the chemicals in the body. A deficiency in any one mineral can lead to illness — an iron deficiency can lead to anaemia, and an iodine deficiency can lead to goitre.

FATTY ACIDS IN FOODS

	POLY. FATTY ACIDS %	MONO. FATTY ACIDS %	SATURATED FATTY ACIDS %
VEGETABLE OILS			
Safflower oil	78	13	9
Sunflower oil	72	16	11
Corn oil	59	27	13
Maize oil	59	28	14
Soya oil	52	25	15
Sesame oil	43	41	16
Peanut oil	32	43	17
Palm oil	9	44	47
Olive oil	8	74	16
Palm kernel oil	2	16	82
FATS			
Butter	3	32	60
Lard	9	44	40
Beef fat	4	49	45
Lamb fat	5	41	52
Pork fat	8	48	42
Chicken fat	15	48	35
Duck fat	13	57	29
Turkey fat	34	27	36
Mackerel oil	29	41	27
Herring oil	20	56	22

HEALTHY EATING

There are a number of ways to improve your diet. For optimum health, you should include all the different foods and nutrients each day. Eating a wide range of foods will help ensure this, and having fresh, unprocessed and unrefined food whenever possible will also aid your health.

Vitamin and mineral supplements

The debate as to whether or not you should take vitamin and mineral supplements has been raging for some time. Ideally, a balanced diet should provide you with all the essential vitamins and minerals your body needs.

However, it is important to know whether or not your body is assimilating the food it is getting. If you are tired or run down, your body will be less efficient at obtaining the nourishment from foods than if it is well rested and unstressed. If you are rested and eating whole, fresh foods, there should be no reason for supplements.

Some argue that because the soil in which fruits and vegetables are grown has become so demineralized, the resulting produce has little nutritional value. They recommend that you take supplements. If in doubt about the quality of the food you are eating, try and find a source of organically grown fruit and vegetables that have been grown on mineral-rich soil, and which have not been sprayed with pesticides.

If you decide to take supplements, it is best to buy them from a good chemist or health food shop. These stores usually stock a wide range of supplements made from natural products that are additive-free. Always check the label carefully, and if you have any doubts about supplements, ask your physician.

What to drink

One of the best drinks you can have is water. Try drinking mineral water, or if you prefer tap water, buy a water filter which will purify it. Fresh fruit and vegetable juices are also good for your health.

If you are a coffee drinker, try and cut down on how much you consume. Obviously, it would be ideal if you could eliminate it all together. Coffee is a stimulant that has far-reaching effects on your eating habits. When you get a 'high' from coffee, your body secretes insulin, which makes your blood sugar fall, and you often crave something sweet. In addition, drinking coffee can block your absorption of vitamin B. Try drinking coffee substitutes, or switch to a decaffeinated brand.

Herbal teas are another option, and there is a large choice available. As well as being delicious, they often have

HEALTHY COOKING

There are many simple ways to improve your diet without having to make drastic changes in the foods you eat or in the way you cook. The two meals shown here illustrate the point.

The meal on the right is fried steak with a rich cream sauce, fried potatoes, mushrooms and tomatoes, white bread and butter, and Black Forest cake. This meal is high in saturated fat. Most of the dishes have been fried in butter, and they contain little fibre.

The meal on the far right consists of a poached chicken breast stuffed with courgettes and carrots, a baked potato and yoghurt, steamed french beans and carrots and fresh fruit for dessert. The cooking methods preserve the essential vitamins and nutrients, as well as the texture and flavour of the foods. Yoghurt is a much better choice for baked potatoes than soured cream, and chicken is lower in saturated fat than beef. The fruit salad adds fibre, vitamins and minerals.

Although there may be times when you would prefer steak and fried potatoes, eating this type of food on a regular basis is detrimental to your health and should be avoided.

unusual characteristics of their own. Chamomile is a soporific, peppermint tea is good for upset stomachs, and some, like rosehip tea, are rich in vitamin C. You can also chill herbal teas to make cooling summer drinks.

Try and keep your alcohol consumption to a minimum. Not only is it fattening, adding extra calories and sugar, but it is bad for the liver. Drinking in excess can also change your eating habits so dramatically that you stop getting enough nourishment from your food.

Cut down on fat

For a healthier diet, most people need to cut down on the amount of fat they eat. A few modifications to your diet will make a world of difference.

First, look at the amount of dairy products you eat. Instead of using full-fat milk, buy skimmed or semi-skimmed milk. This contains all the same nutrients as ordinary milk —

protein, vitamins and calcium — but without the fat. Learn to substitute healthy alternatives like natural yoghurt for cream or soured cream. It can be used in soups and stews as well as with fruit. Go for more soft, low-fat cheeses such as cottage, curd and ricotta cheese rather than the creamy French cheeses. Change to a good polyunsaturated margarine. Remember to read the label carefully and make sure it isn't hydrogenated, and if possible, is salt-free. Don't use lard for cooking, but choose a good vegetable oil instead. Cut down on the amount of meat you eat — even the leanest cuts are often 70% fat. Choose white meat, such as chicken, instead of red meat, and eat more fish.

Cut down on sugar

Sugar is addictive, so it is not surprising that some people find it difficult to wean themselves off it. Unfortunately, it is added to a lot of pre-packaged foods, from bread to mayonnaise, from soup to

ketchup. Read the labels carefully, and if possible opt for a sugar-free band. If the label reads glucose, syrup, fructose, maltose or lactose, beware — these are still sugars. Many supermarkets now stock sugar-free brands of jam, ketchup and baked beans, as well as sugar-free canned fruit in natural juice. Cut down on the amount of sugar you use when cooking. Start making fruit breads instead of cakes, using bananas, apples or carrots for sweetening.

Cut down on salt

Eating salty foods is also a habit that is difficult to break. Adding salt to the water that vegetables are cooked in is unnecessary. Start by cutting this out. Try not to automatically add salt to food that is on your plate. Again, when you buy prepared foods, read the label carefully — many products have salt added. Avoid preserved, pickled or smoked foods. All of these may rely on salt for their distinctive flavours.

VEGETARIANISM

Vegetarians are people who don't eat meat or fish. There are two types of vegetarians — the lacto-ovo vegetarians, who eat plants, dairy produce and eggs, and the vegans, who eat only plant produce. Very strict vegans won't eat honey because it is made by bees, even though it comes from a plant.

Some people turn to vegetarianism on humanitarian grounds, some for religious reasons, some for economic reasons and some for health. Research shows that vegetarians suffer less from heart and bowel problems than meat eaters, since the vegetarian's diet is naturally high in fibre and low in fat.

Meat eaters often think that the vegetarian diet is deficient in protein. Recent research shows that you only need about 1¼ oz/30 g of protein a day. In fact, eating too much protein can damge your health — it puts a strain on the pancreas and causes vitamin and mineral deficiencies.

There are two types of proteins — complete and incomplete — and vegetarians derive their protein from both. Complete proteins are found in animal products like eggs and cheese, while the incomplete proteins are found in plant produce such as nuts and pulses.

The body needs 20 essential amino acids to be healthy. Eight of these are derived from food, and the remainder the body produces itself. The essential eight are all present in complete proteins, but not incomplete ones. Vegetarians, therefore, need to combine certain foods to obtain complete proteins. Combining two of the following foods each day will make a complete protein: pulses, nuts and grains. For example, a slice of wholemeal bread spread with peanut butter will give you a perfect protein balance.

Another thing that people sometimes worry about with vegetarianism is a vitamin B12 deficiency. B12 is found primarily in meat and eggs, and some vegans do take supplements. Sea vegetables are an excellent source of B12, as well as providing iodine, potassium, iron, calcium and magnesium.

Many people have misconceptions about vegetarian food. They think it is difficult to prepare, that it requires special ingredients or that it is just plain uninteresting. But the truth is that vegetarian food can be just as varied and appealing as dishes with meat.

Vegetarian meals can be prepared without needing special foods or supplies. They can, with some planning, be balanced and nutritious and add a whole new range of dishes to your cooking and eating pattern.

Vegetarian cooking is not all salads and nutburgers. It is a rich cuisine, full of marvellous dishes with definite characteristics, and lends itself to many structures. It can be as simple or as complex as you like. First of all, you must forget the meat and two veg system of eating, since there are a number of alternatives. For example, minestrone soup served with cheese, wholemeal bread and a salad makes a satisfying meal. Jacket potatoes, quiches, pancakes with a tomato and mushroom sauce or pizzas are all healthy, delicious and vegetarian.

Some of the most exotic dishes are vegetarian, and books on Middle Eastern and Indian cooking will provide lots of new ideas. There are a number of excellent books on vegetarian cooking, and you can find new ways to combine foods so that your diet is balanced and you health improves.

For example, spicy chick peas served with wholemeal tagliatelle makes a wonderful meal. For a Greek-style menu, as we have shown here, serve hummus with crudités, wholemeal pitta bread, a Greek mushroom salad, spanakopitta — triangles of pastry stuffed with spinach and cheese — and finish off with a fresh fruit salad.

MENU

Hummus
Greek Mushroom Salad
Spanakopitta

Mediterranean Fruit Salad

Hummus
SERVES 8
½ lb/225 g chick peas, soaked overnight and drained
juice of 3-4 lemons
2 cloves garlic, crushed
5 tablespoons olive oil
2 tablespoons tahini
salt and pepper
natural yoghurt for thinning (optional)
paprika, black olives and parsley sprigs, to garnish
wholemeal pitta bread, cucumbers, celery and extra black olives for serving

1 Place the chick peas in a saucepan with just enough fresh water to cover. Bring to the boil, then cover and

Diet and Nutrition

minutes, stirring occasionally, until the sauce is thick and coats the mushrooms.
4 Transfer to a serving dish and set aside until cold. Sprinkle with the parsley just before serving.

Spanakopitta
SERVES 8
9 oz/250 g butter
1 bunch spring onions, trimmed and chopped
1½ lb/675 g frozen chopped spinach, thawed
6 oz/175 g feta cheese, crumbled
2 oz/50 g Parmesan cheese, grated.
4 eggs, beaten
ground nutmeg, to taste
salt and pepper
14 oz/400 g package phylo pastry

1 Melt 2 oz/50 g butter in a large saucepan and sauté the onions until soft, but not coloured. Add the spinach and cook rapidly, stirring frequently, until no liquid remains.
2 Remove from the heat and cool. Stir in the cheeses, eggs and season with nutmeg, salt and pepper.
3 Heat the oven to 180C/350F/Gas 4.
4 Melt the remaining butter and arrange half the pastry in a layer in a baking pan about 10 x 8 inches/25 x 20 cm, brushing melted butter between each sheet. Spread the filling over the pastry, then repeat the layering process, again brushing melted butter between each sheet of pastry.
5 Brush the top with melted butter, then with 1 tablespoon water. Carefully cut the top of the pastry into 8 triangles, then bake for about 45 minutes until crisp and golden. Serve warm or cold.

Easy Mediterranean Fruit Salad
SERVES 8
15 oz/425 g can mandarin oranges
½ medium-sized melon, seeded, peeled and chopped
½ medium-sized pineapple, peeled, cored and chopped
½ lb/225 g strawberries, hulled and halved
½ lb/225 g seedless green grapes
4 oz/100 g fresh dates, halved and stoned
1 pomegranate

1 Combine the mandarin oranges with their juice with the remaining fruit, except the pomegranate, in a large bowl. Add any juices from the fruits.
2 Halve the pomegranate and use a teaspoon to scoop out the seeds and juice. Add to the other fruits and stir gently to combine.
3 Cover with cling film and chill until ready to serve.

simmer for about 1 hour, until tender.
2 Remove from the heat and set aside until cold. Then drain, reserving the cooking liquid.
3 Place the chick peas in a blender or food processor with the juice of 2 lemons, the garlic, olive oil and tahini. Blend until smooth, adding small amounts of the cooking liquid to make a good consistency.
4 Adjust the seasoning, adding more lemon juice, if desired, or natural yoghurt to make a creamier consistency.
5 Transfer to a serving dish and garnish with paprika, black olives and parsley sprigs. Serve with strips of wholemeal pitta bread, chunks of celery and cucumber and more black olives.

Greek Mushroom Salad
SERVES 8
4 tablespoons olive oil
2 onions, roughly chopped
2 cloves garlic, chopped
1 lb/450 g button mushrooms
4 tablespoons tomato purée
2-3 tablespoons lemon juice
salt and pepper
4 tablespoons chopped fresh parsley for serving

1 Heat oil in a large frying pan. Cook onion and garlic until transparent.
2 Add the mushrooms and cook, stirring, for several minutes, then add the tomato purée, 4 tablespoons water and the lemon juice to taste.
3 Cook over medium heat for 10-15

—— 99 ——

FOODS FOR SPECIAL DIETS

Foods have a chemical effect on the body. Because of this, including or excluding certain foods from the diet can be crucial to health, particularly when a debility has already set in. There are a number of books available on cooking for special diets. Here are a few hints on catering for people with special dietary needs, but check with your doctor before making any drastic changes in your diet.

Heart Disease

People suffering from heart problems need to keep their cholesterol level down and their blood pressure as low as possible. Cholesterol is found naturally in the body, and a certain level is necessary, but too much can lead to high blood pressure.

Avoid foods that are high in saturated fats, such as red meat, egg yolks and dairy products. These are thought to encourage the production of cholesterol. Salt also contributes to high blood pressure, so avoid using it whenever possible. Garlic is excellent for lowering the blood pressure, so use it as a flavouring.

Diabetes

In diabetics, the pancreas doesn't supply enough insulin to the body. Insulin helps the body digest the sugar that is eaten, and helps to maintain normal body functions. In some cases of diabetes, insulin injections are given and the diet is strictly controlled.

In the past, diabetics were taught to restrict their sugar and carbohydrate intake. The ideas behind the diabetic

diet have been radically revised over the past 20 years. It is now recognized that diabetics benefit from a diet high in starches with large amounts of dietary fibre, since this has been shown to improve blood sugar levels. The best foods to serve are things such as jacket potatoes with their skins, fresh vegetables like corn on the cob, pulses, brown rice and fruit. Diabetics should keep their intake of pure sugar to a minimum, since sugar is rapidly absorbed into the blood.

Arthritis

There are many different theories on what foods are best avoided by arthritics. However, one diet that is widely followed suggests cutting out processed foods, fruit, including tomatoes, egg yolks and dairy produce. Meat, with the exception of chicken breast, fish and shellfish, is also excluded.

Intestinal problems

Many people suffer from a host of different intestinal complaints. These range from ulcers and colitis to constipation and piles. For all of these, a high fibre diet is ideal. Foods to avoid are those that are highly spiced or deep-fried.

Coeliac Disease

Gluten, a protein found in wheat and certain other cereals, is harmless to most people. However, with coeliac disease, it damages the small intestine to such a degree that food is no longer absorbed properly. Therefore, a gluten-free diet is necessary for successful treatment.

Many foods are gluten free, including dairy products, meat, fish, eggs, pulses and fresh fruit and vegetables. Products containing gluten, such as wheat, barley, pasta, bread and flour must be avoided at all costs. Special gluten-free foods are available, and a number of supermarkets will provide a list of their products that are gluten free.

Food Allergies

The study of food allergies is a relatively new science. Although it is obvious that some people suffer adverse reactions to certain foods, in most cases there is little understanding of what is involved.

Doctors now believe that a variety of physical and mental symptoms can be caused by food allergies, including depression, anxiety and headaches. Some reactions are immediately obvious, such as a swelling of the lips or nausea. These symptoms appear within an hour of eating the food, and it is easy to pinpoint the cause. In other cases, when symptoms, such as skin rashes, don't appear until hours or even days after the food is eaten, the allergy or food intolerance is more difficult to diagnose. Allergy tests are time consuming and not always exact, and should never be undertaken without professional advice.

Certain foods are more likely to cause problems than others, such as cow's milk, fish and shellfish, chocolate, nuts, coffee and tea. With an immediate reaction, the food can be identified and eliminated from the diet. But for other symptoms allergy tests may be needed.

Migraine is a symptom that can be traced to food, although this is not necessarily an allergy. Coffee, chocolate and oranges are well-known triggers of migraine headaches.

GET THE MOST FROM YOUR FOOD

Food should be treated with respect to get the best nutritional value from it. How you buy, store and prepare food is very important. Here are a few guidelines.
● When buying fresh fruit and vegetables, buy little and often. This will help ensure that you get the freshest produce possible.
● Choose sound fruit and vegetables. Unsound produce — split celery stalks are a sign of mineral deficiency in the plant — will be no good to you.

● Wash fruit and vegetables well before eating them. Whenever possible, eat the skin as well.
● Avoid cooking with aluminium, it can irritate the bowel. Use stainless steel or cast-iron pans instead.
● Don't leave prepared vegetables soaking in water. The vitamins leak out into the water, and unless you drink the cooking liquid, they will be wasted.
● Steam rather than boil vegetables. This helps retain their vitamins, and

makes it easier to control how cooked they are. Ideally, vegetables should still be crunchy when served.
● If boiling vegetables, don't add salt, and save the cooking liquid for making stock.
● Use non-stick cookware, which reduces the amount of fat you need for frying.
● Remove the skin from chicken and turkey. When cooking red meat, choose leaner cuts.
● Don't fry or deep-fry. Poach, grill, steam or roast instead.

KITCHEN EQUIPMENT

Complete your kitchen with the latest in small appliances and novelty gadgets. New items have been introduced that fit every budget and help make cooking a greater pleasure for every cook from beginner to gourmet.

FOOD PROCESSORS

Food processors are well established as a standard kitchen appliance. The models introduced this year are more compact, taking up less valuable storage and counter space and featuring useful optional attachments.

Kenwood's Gourmet Variamatic (model A 535) food processor has been designed with an easy-to-use sliding speed control selector and a unique soft ice cream maker. It has the capacity to process 1.4 pints/800 ml liquid and chops, slices, minces, blends and shreds as well as making the ice cream and whisking egg whites.

The processor is sold with 12 attachments, including the special whisk and freezer tray for making soft ice cream. It also comes with a sample package of ice cream powder, which is the base for the mixture. Other packages, however, have to be ordered from the manufacturer.

Other attachments and accessories included in the purchase price are an acrylic bowl and cover, food pusher with graduated measure, spatula, steel blade, shredding plate, slicing plate, egg whisk, chipper plate, whisked sponge beater, fine shredding plate, cover and a useful blade storage rack.

The Oskar food processor from Sunbeam is also compact with a spherical bowl and can be purchased with an optional juice extractor attachment.

Only 12 inches/28 cm tall, the juice extractor comes complete with a special pusher, grater and filter basket. The

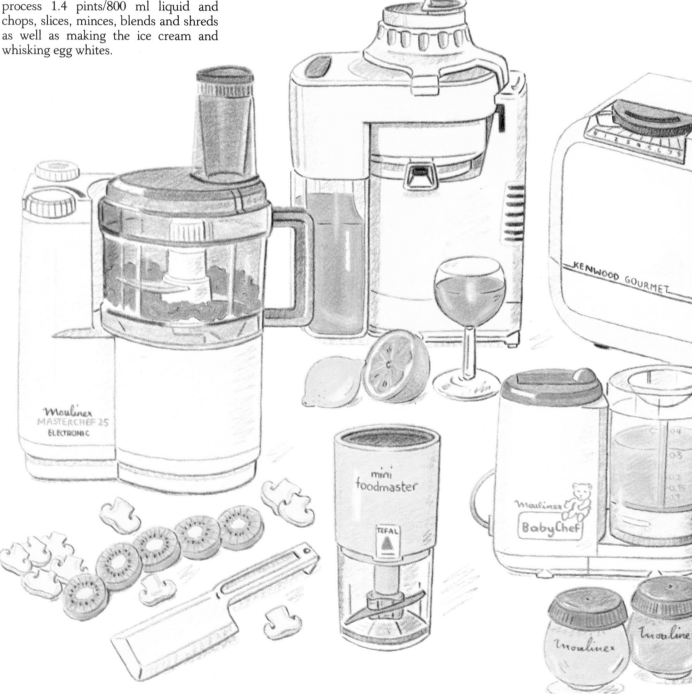

acrylic pulp collection container aids in easy disposal of the pulp after processing. As the fruit or vegetables are fed through the extractor the juice comes out of a small spout on the side of the processor, capturing the flavour and vitamins of freshly-squeezed juice without any of the pulp or seeds. Depending on personal taste, fruit can be processed without first being peeled, however, the juice will have a slightly bitter taste.

The food processor alone has the capacity to mince 1 lb/450 g lean meat

or mix a two packet cake mix.

Moulinex, the French electrical appliance manufacturer, has introduced another compact food processor, the electronic Masterchef 25. Despite the small size, it is capable of blending about 1½ pints/850 ml liquid, whisking 4 egg whites, kneading up to 1 lb/450 g bread dough and chopping, grating or slicing 11 oz/300 g dry ingredients.

Masterchef 25 is available in two models, 813 and 814. Model 814 (illustrated) features a variable speed control as well as a standard on/off switch and a useful accessory storage tray.

The full-colour cookery book included with Masterchef 25 contains over 90 recipes for every occasion – even how to use your food processor to make delicious jams, marmalades and chutneys. For a newcomer to using food processors, the book includes clear instructions on what blades to use.

Also from Moulinex is the ¾ pint/.4 litre capacity Baby Chef. This mini food processor is designed for making baby foods and is ideal for chopping and puréeing.

Baby Chef comes complete with three air-tight storage jars for the processed food, as well as a small plastic scraper. The plastic snap lids for the jars are an attractive baby blue.

For chopping and puréeing small amounts of foods, Tefal have introduced the Mini-Foodmaster. Much smaller than a food processor, only about 6½ inches/17 cm tall, it can easily be stored in a cupboard or drawer and is ideal for chopping herbs, nuts and small amounts of vegetables for puréeing.

KENWOOD GOURMET VARIAMATIC (MODEL A 535)
Available from leading department stores.
Approximately £60.00

SUNBEAM OSKAR FOOD PROCESSOR
Available from Fenwick Department Stores and Woolworths Stores
Approximately £33.00 : optional juice extractor approximately £16.00

MOULINEX MASTERCHEF 25 (MODEL 814)
Available from Boots Cookshops and specialty kitchen shops
Approximately £44.00

MOULINEX BABY CHEF
Available from Boots Cookshops and specialty kitchen shops
Approximately £19.00

TEFAL MINI-FOODMASTER
Available from Underwood branches.
Approximately £13.00

ICE CREAM MAKING

Use the Kenwood Gourmet Variamatic to make quick-and-easy soft ice cream – bound to be a family favourite.

Soft Ice Cream
SERVES 2-3
1 sachet Kenwood Ice Cream Powder
wafers and whole strawberries, to serve

1 Assemble the ice cream making attachment.
2 Add 8¾ fl oz/240 ml cold water and the contents of the sachet to the food processor bowl and mix on speed 1 for about 10 seconds.
3 Pour the mixture into the freezer trays and freeze for at least 5 hours.
4 Remove from the freezer and let stand for 5 - 10 minutes. Reassemble the ice cream making attachment and pass the ice cream down the feed tube. Process on speed 2 for 10-15 seconds, until light and creamy. Garnish and serve at once.

POTS AND PANS

No kitchen is complete without a set of heavy-based, sturdy pots and pans.

Le Creuset, known for its high-quality cast-iron pans and casseroles, have introduced Castoflon, a durable range of pots and pans with non-stick lining. For persons on special diets to cut down on fats and cholesterol, as well as weight watchers, the non-stick lining is a real bonus. It also prevents foods 'catching' during simmering.

The Castoflon manufacturing process includes three coats of Du Pont Silver-Stone on the cast-iron base and the exterior coating of coloured enamel.

The new range includes wooden-handled frying pans, saucepans with two pouring lips and skillets, as well as the marmitout pan. This can be used as a saucepan as well as a casserole.

The Crystale range from Tower also features a non-stick lining. Made from heavy-gauge aluminium, the saucepans have a micro-scrolled base which allows even heat distribution as well as preventing hot spots. New to this range from Tower are the see-through lids. The stylish red and white design fits into a contemporary kitchen and it is also available in beige and brown.

The British Home Stores have introduced nine natural beech-handled pans as part of their basic range, including a Teflon-coated non-stick omelette pan and non-stick frying pan with lid. Suitable for use on both gas and electric cookers, the pans are made from aluminium and feature a satin-finish exterior, which helps to hide small scratches.

CASTOFLON COOKWARE BY LE CREUSET

Available from leading department stores and specialty kitchen shops.

Approximately £16.50 for a 10½ inch/26 cm wooden handle frying pan, £22 for a 3 pint/litre marmitout pan and £13.50 for a 10½ inch/26 cm skillet.

CRYSTALE RANGE BY TOWER

Available from leading department stores and specialty kitchen shops.

Approximately £17.00 for an 8 inch/20 cm saucepan with lid, £9.00 for an 6¼ inch/16 cm milkpan and £19.00 for a 10½ inch/26 cm frying pan with lid.

BEECH-HANDLED PANS

Available from selected branches of British Home Stores.

Approximately £6.00 for medium-size saucepan with lid; £5.00 for non-stick omelette pan and £7.00 for non-stick frying pan with lid.

TABLE-TOP COOKERS

Table-top ovens are ideal for persons living on their own or those without space for a conventional oven in their kitchen.

The Ovenpan from Mellerware takes up no more counter space than an electric frying pan but is versatile enough to fry, roast, boil, braise, stew, casserole and even bake a cake. It is compact and still capable of roasting a 3 lb/1½ kg chicken with potatoes.

A detachable thermostat and heating element mean the Ovenpan is suitable for serving from at the table. Other features include a non-stick lining and chip-proof exterior.

ICTC's Big Mini Roasting Oven features a glass front panel and top interior heating element suitable for browning dishes, although it does not replace a conventional grill. The oven rack is adjustable to allow enough room for roasting joints and baking cakes and soufflés. The sleek cream casing includes the thermostat, neon power indicator light and on/off switch.

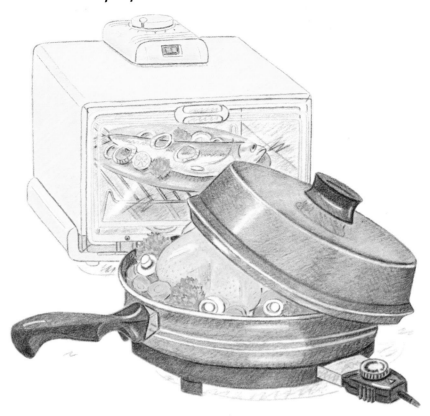

BIG MINI ROASTING OVEN
Available from Boots Cookshops, Selfridges, London W1, and other leading department stores. Approximately £45.00.

OVENPAN
Available from Fenwick Department Stores, Selfridges, London W1, and specialist kitchen shops. Approximately £26.00.

FOCUS RANGE

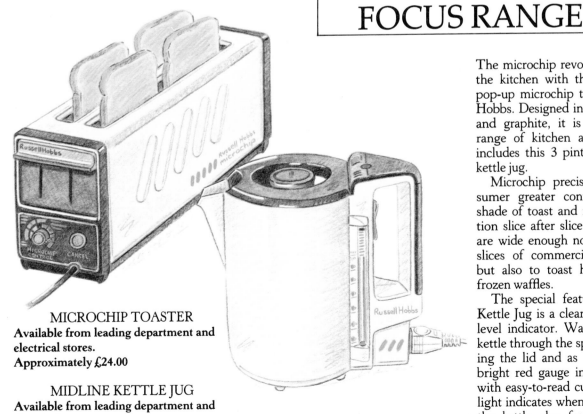

MICROCHIP TOASTER
**Available from leading department and electrical stores.
Approximately £24.00**

MIDLINE KETTLE JUG
**Available from leading department and electrical stores.
Approximately £20.50**

The microchip revolution is at home in the kitchen with this stylish four-slice pop-up microchip toaster from Russell Hobbs. Designed in stylish French grey and graphite, it is part of the Focus range of kitchen appliances that also includes this 3 pint/1.7 litre automatic kettle jug.

Microchip precision gives the consumer greater control over the final shade of toast and maintains the selection slice after slice. The toaster's slots are wide enough not only to hold four slices of commercial pre-sliced bread but also to toast hand-cut bread and frozen waffles.

The special feature of the Midline Kettle Jug is a clear, easy-to-read water level indicator. Water is added to the kettle through the spout without removing the lid and as the kettle fills up a bright red gauge indicates the amount with easy-to-read cup symbols. A neon light indicates when the kettle is on and the kettle also features an automatic cut-off switch when the water is boiled.

FOREIGN COOKING

Savouring the flavours of foreign foods at home has never been easier. A variety of appliances have been introduced to help produce authentic-tasting dishes.

Pasta-making machines to simplify the time-consuming pasta-making process have been available for several years. Ictc's PastaMatic 700, however, goes even one step further, eliminating the guesswork in achieving the correct proportion of eggs to flour. The sleek Italian-designed machine includes a clear plastic measuring jug with a guide for the exact amount of eggs to be added to varying flour weights. This assures smooth, perfect-textured pasta every time.

Easy to use, the flour is placed in the machine and the eggs are added directly from the measuring jug through an opening in the top while the machine is operating.

PastaMatic 700 also comes with a recipe book and six blades for shaping all types of pasta from spaghetti to lasagne. It even makes dough for making breadsticks, to complete an Italian-style meal at home.

Flavourful and crunchy Oriental stir-fry dishes are even quicker and easier to prepare with the new non-stick Chinese Wok. Distributed through department and kitchen stores throughout the UK by William Levene Ltd., the carbon steel wok has a non-stick interior coat-

ing – a real bonus for dieters and persons cutting down on their cholesterol intake. The traditional shape has been slightly modified with a flat base so the wok can be used on electric or gas burners.

The non-stick wok also features wooden handles and a lid, and comes with a wooden stirrer and a recipe book filled with tempting Chinese-style recipes.

Fans of spicy Mexican food will be pleased with the new four-piece Mexican Cooking Set from Habitat. Favourite Mexican specialities, such as tacos and enchiladas, have always been difficult to prepare at home, but this new set contains all the required equipment. It includes a stainless steel tortilla press, special tongs for deep-frying and a wire rack for serving assembled tacos. The recipe book includes ideas for hot and spicy dishes made with a variety of chillies and taco sauce and endless combinations of interesting taco fillings (see page 11 for other ideas).

Also from Habitat is a Tandoori Oven Set for making the delicious dry-roasted Indian dishes. The terracotta pot comes with a metal charcoal container, grid and six skewers, as well as an instruction and recipe booklet and a sample of tandoori mix spices, the essential ingredients of successful tandoori dishes.

ICTC PASTAMATIC 700
Available from leading department stores and specialist kitchen shops.
Approximately £90.00.

NON-STICK CHINESE WOK
Available from Alders, Asda Superstores, selected Boots Cookshops and leading department stores and kitchen speciality shops. Also available by mail order from the manufacturer.
For details of shipping cost and exact price, write to William Levene Ltd., 36/38 Willesden Lane, London NW6 7ST.
Approximately £16.25.

MEXICAN COOKING SET
Available from Habitat stores.
Approximately £13.00.

TANDOORI OVEN SET
Available from Habitat stores.
Approximately £29.00.

USING A TACO MAKER

Tacos
MAKES 12
For the tortillas
½ lb/225 g masa harina
1 teaspoon salt

Mix the tortilla ingredients in a bowl with 4 fl oz/125 ml water. Form into 12 balls and flatten between greaseproof paper in press.

Lightly fry each tortilla on the skillet, then keep warm in a moist towel.

Using the special tongs, deep fry the tortillas, then place in rack to fill.

For the filling
1 lb/450 g lean minced beef
2 tablespoons ground mild red chillies
½ teaspoon each oregano, cumin and salt
1 clove garlic, crushed
shredded lettuce, chopped onion and tomato and grated cheese, to finish

1 Fry the beef until brown, then add the spice, herbs and seasoning. Cook for 2 minutes, stirring.
2 Heat oven to 180C/350F/Gas 4.
3 Place the beef mixture in the tortilla shells and top with remaining ingredients. Bake until the cheese melts.

OVEN-TO-TABLEWARE

The increasing number of oven-to-tableware ranges reflects the growing popularity of this versatile style of cookware. Cooking and serving in the same dish saves on washing up and most new ranges also have the advantages of being freezerproof, microwaveproof and dishwasher safe.

Some of the styles introduced this year are only available in decorative serving pieces, while others extend to co-ordinated dinner services.

Royal Worcester, one of Britain's leading porcelain manufacturers, has launched several new patterns of oven-to-tableware that are as attractive as they are useful. Gourmet is a range of pure white porcelain with a distinctive raised pattern of wild barley. Some of the pieces available in this range are a large oval casserole with a 6 pint/3.4 litre capacity, as well as two sizes of flan dishes and a round casserole.

Two other new Royal Worcester patterns, Fleuri and Blue Bow, are part of a range of fluted oven-to-tableware designed to match existing tableware ranges. Fleuri is a delicate pattern of a garland of flowers on a white background with a thin green border, and Blue Bow features deep blue brushstroke flowers on a plain white background. These ranges extend from a 3½ pint/2 litre casserole to 3¼ inch/8 cm ramekins available in boxed sets of four or six. The other pieces are a round casserole, deep soufflé dish, oval baking dish, gratin dish, lasagne dish and a flan/quiche dish.

Also new from Royal Worcester this year are new pieces to the well established Evesham range, including an elegant asparagus dish.

Royal Doulton and Wedgwood are two other premier British manufacturers to have added to their ranges.

The Fresh Flowers range of Lambethware from Royal Doulton has been extended with the Chelsea and Hampstead patterns. Both are soft floral designs, with Hampstead featuring delicate waterlilies and Chelsea a bouquet of pale pink and lavender spring blossoms.

All the pieces in these two patterns are available individually and can also be bought in three-piece and five-piece place-settings, as well as a 15-piece

coffee set and a 21-piece tea set.

Individual pieces in these co-ordinated ranges include a 4 pint/2.7 litre oval or round casserole, a selection of soufflé dishes, vegetable dishes, a sauce boat and stand, as well as plates and cups and saucers. The sets can be completed with matching salt and pepper shakers, egg cups, and mugs.

For the more contemporary styled home, Wedgwood has introduced the Peach and Boulevard patterns as part of its Sterling oven-to-tableware range. Boulevard is a sleek pattern with thin

red and blue lines bordering plain plates, casseroles and cups and saucers. Peach is a more decorative design, featuring the ripe fruit on branches. Both patterns are available in dinner services as well as additional serving pieces. All pieces are dishwasher safe and can also be used in microwave ovens.

British Home Stores have added to the kitchen department ranges with an attractive range of earthenware oven-to-tableware. Each piece features a pale blue trim and label in on the base. The set includes an individual pie plate,

include a soufflé dish, quiche dish and loaf dish.

Another useful serving dish from Pyrex by Corning is the oval 12 inch/30 cm oven dish with an attractive wicker basket. It is ideal for baked dishes such as lasagne for a large crowd. This dish is also safe for using in conventional and microwave ovens.

ROYAL WORCESTER RANGES
Available from all leading department stores and china specialist shops. Approximately £40.00 for the large oval casserole in Gourmet, £10.40 for a 1¾ pint/1 litre soufflé dish in Blue Bow, £4.70 for round-eared dish in Fleuri and £15.00 for asparagus dish in Evesham Gold.

CHELSEA AND HAMPSTEAD LAMBETHWARE BY ROYAL DOULTON
Available from all leading department stores and china specialist shops. Approximately £4.25 for 10 inch/25 cm dinner plate, £2.45 for 6½ inch/16.25 cm plate and £4.45 for a cup and saucer.

PEACH AND BOULEVARD BY WEDGWOOD
Available from Wedgwood Rooms in leading department stores. Approximately £4.25 for 10 inch/25 cm dinner plate, £2.50 for 6¼ inch/16 cm plate and £5.00 for a cup and saucer.

BLUE AND WHITE EARTHENWARE FROM BRITISH HOME STORES
Available from selected branches. Approximately £2.50 for individual pie plate and £5.99 for quiche dish.

PYREX CLASSICS BY CORNING
Available from Boots Cookshops. Approximately £1.65 for two ramekins, £2.60 for a 2½ pint/1.4 litre soufflé dish.

soufflé dish, quiche dish, and oblong roaster. The range is microwave safe and can be washed in a dishwasher.

Pyrex is a well-established name in the kitchen. Pyrex Classics by Corning is a new range of clear glass bakeware that has replaced the previous standard range. Safe for use in microwave ovens and conventional ovens, the items are also dishwasher safe.

Ramekins are available in sets of two and other items in the Classic range

1 Corning baking dish; 2 Royal Worcester Blue Bow; 3 Wedgwood Boulevard; 4 Wedgwood Peach; 5 Royal Doulton Chelsea; 6 Royal Doulton Hampstead; 7 Royal Worcester Evesham; 8 Pyrex Classics; 9 Royal Worcester Fleuri; 10 British Home Stores earthenware; 11 Royal Worcester Gourmet

GADGETS

THE COMPLETE CURRY SET AND THE COMPLETE BREAD MAKER

The Complete Curry Set and Bread Maker are two of the new culinary sets introduced by Simple Cook. Attractively packaged, they are useful additions to any kitchen as well as making much-appreciated gifts for any keen cook.

Freshly ground spices are the essential ingredients of authentic-tasting curries, and The Complete Curry Set includes six whole spices and a ceramic mortar and wooden pestle for grinding the spices. It also includes a selection of delicious recipes to help you capture the true flavour of Eastern cooking.

The Complete Bread Baker is as healthy as it is useful. In addition to the terracotta bread mould, the set includes three prepared bread mixes, each with high fibre content, and recipes for other home-made breads.

Available from Reject Shops, Alders, The John Lewis Partnership stores and Liberty and Co, London, W1
Approximately £4.00

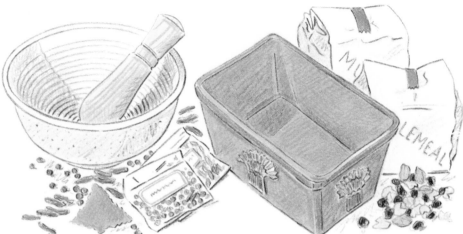

TALKING TOASTS

Start the day with a cheerful message. Talking Toasts, from WL, presses the messages 'I Love You', 'Smile' or 'Have A Good Day' on slices on bread before they are toasted.

Available in brightly-coloured dishwasherproof plastic, Talking Toasts are certain to bring smiles to sleepy faces.
Available as for Spaghetti Measuring Dispenser
Approximately £1.25

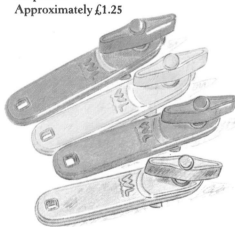

SELF-CLEANING GARLIC PRESS

Designed in Italy, the Self-Cleaning Garlic Press solves the problem of how to remove the garlic skin from the press after the garlic clove has been crushed. Available in bright red or white, this handy item features a perforated plastic side, which pushes the skin away from the grate. The easy-grip handle helps apply enough pressure to extract all the juice from the garlic, making sure there is full flavour in the prepared dish – not left behind in the base of the press.
Available as for Spaghetti Measuring Dispenser
Approximately £3.75.

BAG CLIP

Bag Clip is the answer to the question of what to do with opened packages of dried pasta, rice, biscuits and frozen vegetables.

This sturdy red clip seals the packages to

LIFT OFF CAN OPENER

The Lift Off Can Opener from WL comes in a range of seven colours – red, green, yellow, white, black, grey and beige – to co-ordinate with any kitchen design.

As the name implies, this handy kitchen accessory lifts off can lids, eliminating the danger of cutting fingers on sharp edges.
Available as for Spaghetti Measuring Dispenser
Approximately £3.89

retain freshness and flavours, as well as preventing annoying spills all over cupboard shelves or the freezing compartment of the refrigerator. The tight spring grips the bag without damaging the packaging and is wide enough to seal most bags.
Available as for Spagehetti Measuring Dispenser
Approximately £0.99

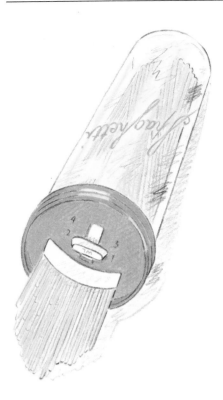

FREEZE, HEAT AND SERVE

Freeze, Heat and Serve is a range of low-cost, re-usable cookware that has been introduced by Anchor Hocking. Available in sets of two, the range includes a bowl, casserole, plate and platter, each of which is suitable for using in conventional ovens as well as microwave ovens. They are freezer-proof as well as dishwasherproof.

Available from House of Frazer stores and Boots Cookshops.
Approximately £2.00 for sets of two.

FISH SCALER CRINKLE CHIP CUTTER AND ALUMINIUM BAKING BEANS

As part of this year's expansion of Boots Cookshops, a range of own-brand professional cookware has been introduced. Made from stainless steel with sturdy, dishwasherproof handles, this fish scaler and crinkle chip cutter are among the kitchen gadgets in the range that make cooking more of a pleasure. Re-usable aluminium baking beans are from the selection of baking accessories that help the home baker achieve professional results. Aluminium beans are recommended over dried beans because they do not absorb flavours and also help keep the base of the flan flat.

Professional Cookware range available from selected Boots Cookshops.
Approximately £1.25 for the crinkle chip cutter and £3.50 for the baking beans.

SPAGHETTI MEASURING DISPENSER

The Spaghetti Measuring Dispenser eliminates all the guesswork of how much spaghetti to cook for one through four persons.

The clear plastic tube is a useful storage container for dried spaghetti and the adjustable guide in the lid controls the amount of spaghetti cooked. This saves on waste and means you can see at a glance how much spaghetti you have on hand.

Available from Alders, Asda Superstores, selected Boots Cookshops and leading department stores and kitchen specialty shops. Also available by mail order from the manufacturer. For details of shipping costs and exact price, write to William Levene Ltd., 36/38 Willesden Lane, London NW6 7ST.
Approximately £1.59

VICTORINOX

The Swiss firm of Victorinox is world famous as the manufacturers of top quality Swiss army knives and excellent domestic knives. This year they have introduced into Britain the seven-piece Kitchen Economy Range, which features red or black dishwasherproof nylon handles and finest quality stainless steel blades.

Available by mail order from Lesway, 3 Clarendon Terrace, London W9 1BZ.
Approximately £25 plus shipping costs.

DRAGON MOULD AND BISCUIT CUTTERS

This 1 pint/600 ml dragon jelly mould and these biscuit cutters are perfect for a child's birthday party or to liven up a teatime snack. Available in red or buttermilk, they are dishwasherproof. The biscuit cutter designs include a gingerbread man, a train, an aeroplane and a ship.

Available from selected Sainsbury Supermarkets. The dragon mould is £0.95, the ginerbread man biscuit cutter £.45 and the other biscuit cutters are £0.29.

HOT DRINK MACHINES

Designers of this year's hot drink machines haven't gone off the boil with their ideas.

Salton's Cappuccino/Espresso maker (model EX8) means coffee connoisseurs can enjoy two of their favourite continental drinks at home. It is a compact white appliance, complete with a glass jug with a lid for pouring as well as the special filter and filter attachments and a unique two-cup attachment. A steam jet froths milk for an authentic cup of cappuccino.

The EX8 has the capacity to make four demitasse cups of coffee.

The space-age look is brought into the kitchen with Melita's Aroma Art coffee machine. More advanced in design than any other model on the market, Aroma Art uses paper filters and has a 10-cup capacity. The round glass jug rests on a hotplate so the coffee doesn't cool off. The most unique feature of the Aroma Art is the striped red and white water level indicator. As the water is added to the tall water tank on the side, the striped pole floats up through an opening in the lid to indicate how many cups are being made.

Electronic precision has been introduced to the age-old tradition of tea-making. Krups have launched TeaTime with an electronic control to set the brewing time at 2-12 minutes.

After adding water to TeaTime, the process is automatic. Even the tea cosy could become a relic of the past with the hotplate. TeaTime boils up to 1¾ pints/1 litre water in seven minutes, then immediately passes the water into the filter container for brewing.

Yet, however you make your hot drinks, Thermos have introduced a stylish way to keep them hot. Coffee Butler comes in four designs. It keeps coffee hot as guests linger after dinner or while sipping throughout the day.

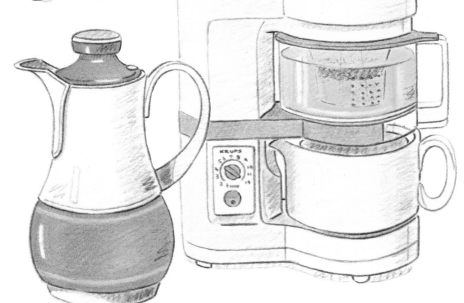

SALTON CAPPUCCINO/ESPRESSO
MAKER (MODEL EX 8)
**Available from John Lewis Partnership
stores and Selfridges, London W1.
Approximately £38.00**

MELITA AROMA ART
**Available from leading department stores
and selected Boots Cookshops.
Approximately £22.00.**

KRUPS TEATIME
**Available from Selfridges, London W1,
and House of Fraser stores.
Approximately £50.00.**

THERMOS COFFEE BUTLER
**Available from selected Tesco Stores
Limited and Boots Cookshops.
Approximately £14.00**

MICROWAVE COOKING

Microwave cookers have so much to offer. Once you become familiar with them, and learn to take advantage of their speed, versatility and efficiency, microwaves will change your attitude towards cooking dramatically.

Microwave cookers have been with us now for many more years than most people realize. They were developed as a result of research into radar during World War 2, and they have been used for over 30 years by many restaurants and hotels. But they have only become popular domestically in recent years. Microwave cookers are only just now being regarded as a natural addition to a kitchen, rather than a luxury gadget.

Unfortunately, so many people who buy a microwave cooker have great enthusiasm for it in the first few months, but then lose their enthusiasm and proclaim that it is only good for reheating, defrosting and cooking jacket potatoes! This is very sad, for when used to its fullest, a microwave cooker is a boon to any household, both large and small, for everyday cooking for the family to haute cuisine.

Much of the blame for this lost enthusiasm must lie with the manufacturers and their advertising. They have given the impression that a microwave cooker is some sort of magic box that does everything by itself, without any

MICROWAVE FEATURES

1 Metal grill
2 Temperature probe
3 Rating plate
4 Digital clock/timer
5 Power and timing control
6 Start button
7 Memory control
8 Turntable

ADVANTAGES OF A MICROWAVE

Speed – This is the major factor. Food is cooked so quickly that some cooking times are reduced by as much as 75 per cent. This makes it a very economical method of cooking, and can save as much as 25 per cent on the fuel bill for an average family.

Reheating – Plated meals can be reheated in minutes, without the food drying out or tasting stale and reheated. They are ideal for husbands or wives who come home late from work, and for teenagers who are never around at mealtimes.

Cooks in a hurry – Small portions of food for toddlers and children can be cooked or reheated in next-to-no time, which will keep hungry children happy since they won't have to wait long for their food. Microwave cookers are ideal for heating baby foods, too. They can be heated to exactly the right temperature with the help of a temperature probe which is fitted in some cookers.

Quick defrosting – They are wonderful for those who are always forgetting to remove frozen foods from the freezer for thawing.

People who live alone – Microwave cookers are particularly good for those who live alone. They make cooking for one less tedious, and certainly much cheaper.

Safe for children – Children can cook snacks for themselves, which they often enjoy doing. Their safe method of cooking makes them especially good for the elderly and the disabled. Their mobility makes them easy to be positioned in the kitchen.

More flavour – Foods such as vegetables, fruit and fish retain much more flavour – and more nutritional value – since little or no water is used during cooking.

Quick and easy to clean – Because microwave cookers are quick and easy to clean, they save on time and energy. They also save on the washing up, since many foods can be cooked or reheated in their serving dishes, and many dishes suitable for freezing can be used safely in a microwave cooker.

input from the user. It is when people realize that they have to learn new cooking techniques, and have to contribute quite a lot, that they lose interest.

Cooking food by microwave energy requires the same love and attention as it does when cooking by conventional methods. Probably more so, since it is an entirely different form of cooking, and one that needs to be understood thoroughly to be able to use it to its fullest advantage. A microwave cooker will never replace the conventional cooker, but it can be used entirely alone for cooking, or be used in conjunction with a gas or electric cooker.

HOW A MICROWAVE WORKS

A conventional oven cooks food by the conduction of dry heat, produced by electric heating elements or a gas flame, within the oven itself. The oven temperature is regulated by a thermostat, which is set to the required temperature by a control knob on the front of the cooker. The heat gradually penetrates from the outside of the food to the centre, giving a crisp exterior when the food is not covered. Food is browned to different degrees determined by the type of food and the oven temperature.

In a microwave cooker, food is cooked by an invisible source of energy in the form of microwaves, which create heat within the food itself. Microwaves are similar to radio waves, but shorter. As they penetrate the food, they cause the water molecules within the food to vibrate so rapidly, about 2,450 million times a second, that the friction creates heat which in turn cooks the food. When the food is placed inside the cooker, cooking begins immediately the cooker is switched on, unlike a conventional cooker that has to be preheated before cooking begins.

Microwave cookers do not need to have heavy duty wiring or a special power supply, as does an electric cooker. They can be plugged into any 13 amp socket. The electricity from the socket is converted inside the cooker by a magnetron (the most important part of the cooker) into microwaves. The microwaves are then directed into the cooker cavity by a waveguide, and are then evenly distributed by a stirrer or paddle.

Microwaves cannot pass through metal, so once they are inside the cavity, which is lined with metal, they are reflected off the sides in a zig-zag pattern. But they can pass through any other material that does not contain water molecules without having any effect on it – in the same way that light can pass through a window. The microwaves do effect substances that contain water molecules, so when a dish containing food is placed inside a microwave cooker, the microwaves reflect off the sides of the cooker and pass through the dish into the food. Foods containing fat and sugar attract and absorb microwaves very quickly, and heat up much more quickly. Some people have the false idea that microwaves are left behind in food, thinking that we eat them. As soon as cooking is finished or the power is switched off, the microwaves disappear – in the same way that light from an electric light bulb does when the electricity is turned off.

Microwaves will only penetrate to a depth of 1½-2 inches/4-5 cm all round food. Therefore, when foods are thicker than this, the heat will be transmitted to the centre by conduction. This is why a standing time is allowed, to give time for the cooking to complete.

DIFFERENT TYPES OF MICROWAVES

All microwave cookers work on the same basic principle, but differ from one to another in the way in which the microwaves are controlled, or distributed, within the cooker. This is quite a

WHAT MICROWAVES CAN OFFER

● Microwave cookers come in various sizes and colours. It should be easy to find one to fit in with most kitchens.

● The output will be either 500 watt, 600 watt, 650 watt or 700 watt. This simply means that those with the higher output will cook more quickly than those with the lower output.

● Most cookers have a glass door and a light which comes on when the cooker is operating. This allows you to see just what is happening inside.

● The interior linings are either stainless steel or acrylic – both are easy to clean. Since the oven linings do not become hot, food splashes do not burn on, and they can simply be wiped clean with a damp cloth.

● One of the most confusing things to a person buying a microwave is that the controls vary so much. All the cookers have on/off switches and a timer – either a normal clock timer or a digital timer. The simplest cookers just have Defrost and Cook settings. Others vary, offering from three to twelve settings. These settings are either numbered or given names, such as Warm, Defrost, Simmer, Roast, etc. The settings give you the choice and control over the amount of microwave energy that is used to cook the food, ranging from 100% power down to as little as 10% power. You select the level of power in exactly the same way you would select the cooking temperature on a gas or electric oven.

The more sophisticated cookers have electronic touch-sensitive control panels. Some have a micro-processor and an electronic brain, which enables you to put in food from frozen and programme the cooker to defrost, and then cook, and also to cook at one

power level and then change to another – all without having to manually reset the control.

Some of these cookers have a buzzer to remind you when to stir or when to add ingredients. Some even allow you to set the time you would like the cooking to start. That way, you can go out for the day and come home to a cooked meal. It is these refinements that increase the cost of the cooker.

● Cooking by microwave energy is a moist form of cooking, and foods do not generally brown. Some models are fitted with a browning element to help you overcome this problem. However, it is just as easy to brown before or after cooking under your conventional grill, or you can buy a special browning dish.

● Some cookers have a turntable, others do not. If you are buying a cooker without a turntable, it is better to buy one of the models where the microwaves are directed in such a way that you do not have to manually turn the dishes during cooking. Cookers without a turntable are more versatile – they are not so restricting on the size and shape of the dish you can use. With a turntable you must use dishes that allow enough room for turning. Some cookers have a shelf to enable cooking on two levels, making it easier to cook a complete meal at once.

● To make for more accurate cooking, some models are fitted with an auto-sensor, which senses the temperature of the air and automatically turns the oven off when the food is cooked. Some have a temperature probe that can determine when cooking is complete by temperature and time, or by temperature alone.

difficult process, and is still being improved. Some manufacturers use their own particular method as an important sales feature.

Because the pattern of microwaves reflecting off the cooker walls is not perfectly even, some cookers have a turntable to assist even cooking. With many that do not have a turntable, it is necessary to manually turn dishes during cooking. More up-to-date models

have improved methods of directing microwaves evenly, eliminating both a turntable and the need for turning.

ARE MICROWAVES SAFE?

A microwave cooker is probably one of the safest pieces of equipment in our kitchens. Many people are afraid that microwaves will leak out of the cooker and damage their health. Microwave cookers will only operate when the door

TYPES OF MICROWAVE

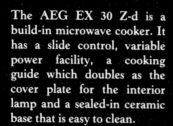

The AEG EX 30 Z-d is a build-in microwave cooker. It has a slide control, variable power facility, a cooking guide which doubles as the cover plate for the interior lamp and a sealed-in ceramic base that is easy to clean.

The Toshiba 7800 Deltawave has a special auto-defrost facility, which provides staged defrosting. It starts at a high level and, as the ice particles start to dissolve, automatically reduces the power – in three stages – to provide energy appropriate to the level of defrosting. For food that requires no further preparation after defrosting, a pre-set cooking programme can follow on immediately the defrost cycle is complete.

The Belling Triplette is a combination cooker, which is a combined microwave and fan oven. It can be used as a microwave, as a fan oven or a combination of both. The Belling Triplette has a turntable, electronic touch controls and a digital timer. The interior is stainless steel with a self-cleaning back panel.

The Philips Cooktronic is a 700 watt microwave oven, with a microprocessor control and a temperature probe. It has electronic variable power controls and features a rotating antenna for thorough and even cooking, eliminating the turntable.

is closed, and the door is sealed to prevent any leakage. Manufacturers have gone to great lengths to ensure their safety by fitting them with special interlocking safety switches, so that when there is even the slightest movement on the door the microwave energy will cease instantly.

Microwaves are present in ordinary light bulbs and fluorescent lights, and in the light and warmth from the sun. They are non-ionizing rays, which means that they do not produce any chemical change, and are therefore safe.

Every microwave cooker comes with a manufacturer's guide book. The instructions in the book regarding safety and maintenance should be followed implicitly. A microwave cooker should be tested regularly by a qualified engineer, just as you would have any other piece of electrical equipment tested.

CHOOSING A MICROWAVE

Each year seems to bring yet more electrical appliance manufacturers adding microwave cookers to their list of products. More and more refined models are coming on to the market, some with controls that look as though the user will have to be a computer wizard to understand them! With models from over twenty manufacturers, and with prices ranging from around £150 to £700, it really makes the task of choosing a cooker quite daunting.

Before buying, look at as many models as possible, and take the advertising leaflets home to read quietly. Don't buy on impulse, or be tempted by special offers. Make sure that you buy a cooker to suit your needs.

You must ask yourself why you want to have a microwave cooker, and give yourself an honest answer. Are you really only going to use it for defrosting and quick reheating? If this is the case, then it is foolish to buy one of the more expensive models. If you intend to become a microwave cook, using the cooker to its fullest advantage, then invest in one of the larger and more sophisticated models.

Study your kitchen carefully, and decide where you would like the cooker to be placed. They look quite small in the shops, but are really quite space-taking. If you are planning a new kitchen, it is possible to build in a microwave cooker just as you would a conventional oven. If you are short of worktop space, decide if you have room to build in a shelf to support the cooker,

but remember they are quite heavy.

Cooking by microwave is a moist method of cooking and will produce some condensation, so the cookers are made with vents. Look to see where the vents are placed. If they are at the back of the cooker it cannot be pushed right to a wall, and if they are on the top they cannot be covered too closely. One very important factor to note is which way the door opens, to the left or to the right. Make sure that you will not have to walk around the door to put in and take out dishes.

The latest additions to the range of microwave cookers are the combination cookers being produced by manufacturers. These combine both microwave cooking and conventional dry heat cooking. Combination cookers can be used as a microwave oven, as a conventional oven, or as a combination of the two with both methods working together at once.

Your microwave cooker will be supplied with an instruction manual, and in most cases with a recipe book. Read these very carefully before you use the cooker for the first time. Once you become familiar with your microwave cooker you will soon start to think 'microwave'. Remember, it always takes time to become familiar with a new gas or electric cooker, so be patient and give yourself time to master the new techniques necessary for perfect microwave cooking.

WHAT CAN BE COOKED IN A MICROWAVE

With very few exceptions, almost all foods can be cooked in a microwave oven.

Meat and Poultry
Large joints of meat can be cooked by microwave, but I have never found this to be really successful, probably because I am a traditionalist who prefers the smell and the flavour of roasted meat. However, there are many who will disagree with this. Boned and rolled joints of meat cook more evenly than those left on the bone. If you intend to cook a lot of larger joints in a microwave cooker, then it is a good investment to buy a special microwave cooker thermometer, unless your cooker is already fitted with a thermometer probe.

Meat that requires tenderizing by long slow cooking is still best cooked conventionally, but this does not mean that you cannot make casseroles. These will be very good providing that you use

FOODS TO AVOID

Foods that require dry heat, such as pastry, Yorkshire pudding and roast vegetables, are all best cooked conventionally to obtain crispness and flavour as well as browning. Choux or puff pastry especially, should be avoided.

Meringues cannot be cooked in a microwave oven. However, pre-baked pastry dishes such as pies, flans and sausage rolls can all be warmed through very well.

Never cook an egg, whether raw or cooked, in its shell in a microwave cooker. Pressure caused by the moving molecules will build up within the shell and the egg will explode.

Foods cannot be deep-fried in a microwave cooker. The temperature of the oil cannot be controlled, and it will overheat.

Don't dry fruit or flowers in a microwave cooker.

better quality, lean and tender, cuts of meat. Minced beef cooks very well, enabling you to make bolognese and curry sauces very quickly.

Poultry cooks extremely well. It stays moist and tender and retains all of its flavour. Unfortunately, the skin does not brown, but there is a special seasoning which you can sprinkle over the skin to help it brown and enhance the appearance. The skin can also be brushed with melted butter and sprinkled with herbs or paprika to give it an appetizing finish.

Small cuts of meat such as chops cook well, and can be browned in a browning dish. Or they may be seared, before cooking, in a frying pan. Bacon joints and rashers cook very well. Bacon rashers cook quickly and cleanly, and there are no messy grill pans to clean.
Fish
It is worthwhile buying a microwave cooker just to cook fish. It cooks in minutes, retains all of its flavour and keeps the kitchen free of strong odours.
Vegetables and Fruit
These are wonderful when cooked in a microwave cooker, and retain their colour, flavour and shape. They also retain more nutrients. They can also be cooked in their serving dishes.

EQUIPMENT

Having bought a microwave cooker, it is really not necessary to rush out and buy a lot of special cooking dishes. You will find that most of your existing dishes and plates will be quite usable. Almost anything other than metal can be used in a microwave cooker, such as heat-resistant glass, pottery (provided it is not too thick or deeply coloured), china, heat-tolerant plastics, wood, paper and wicker.

Never use any glass or china dishes with a metallic rim. Paper, wood and wicker should only be used for very short cooking periods, since they can catch fire if left for too long in the cooker. Clear, ovenproof glass dishes, with and without lids, are very useful.

A good supply of absorbent kitchen paper and cling film is essential for covering food, both to prevent splashing and to retain moisture. Kitchen paper is particularly useful for placing under foods such as potatoes, to absorb excess moisture.

Since the popularity of microwave cookers has increased, the amount of special microwave cooking equipment has been steadily growing. Unfortunately, some pieces can be very expensive, particularly browning dishes. Browning dishes are specially treated so that they will absorb microwave energy and become very hot, enabling foods to be browned. Some microwave cooking dishes are dual purpose. They can be used in a gas or electric oven as well, which makes them a good investment.

There are many cheap, lightweight containers available. They are made from high density polythene, offering good temperature tolerance and hardly

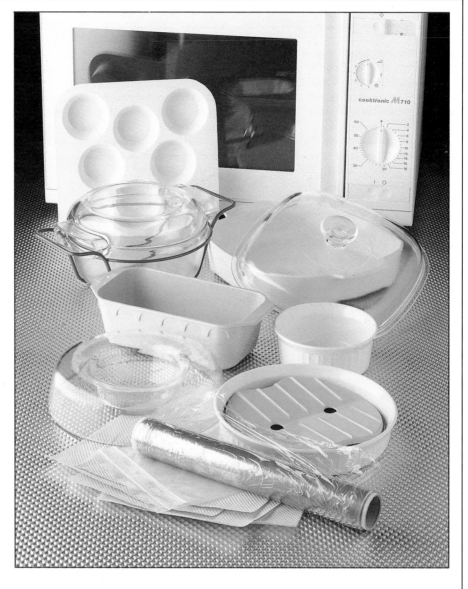

any resistance to microwave energy. They are very good for cakes, puddings, casseroles and freezer-to-microwave use.

Roasting dishes with a rack and cover are useful and roasting bags help to encourage browning. When using these bags, never use any metal ties –

always use plastic ties or string. Also, always puncture the bag to allow steam to escape.

Dishes that are specially designed for cooking cakes are a worthwhile purchase. Most normal baking equipment is made from metal and cannot be used in a microwave.

Cakes and Puddings
Sponge cakes and sponge puddings can be cooked with excellent results. Sponge cakes do not brown, but since most are usually iced when they are cold or filled with fruit and cream, this really doesn't matter. Fruit cakes are not quite so successful. They are more like steamed puddings, and are still best cooked in a conventional oven. Sponge puddings cook in minutes, and without filling the kitchen with steam. Christmas puddings can be cooked in a microwave oven in a

very short time, but they do not have the same appearance as those that are cooked in the traditional way by boiling.
Bread
Bread dough can be risen and cooked in a microwave oven, but it will not brown. It may be browned, after cooking, under a conventional grill.
Dairy Foods
Eggs and cheese can be cooked in a microwave oven, but care should be taken not to overcook them, since they quickly become tough and rubbery.

Cheese does not brown, but it can be browned under a conventional grill at the end of the cooking.

Milk to be served with coffee can be warmed through in its serving jug. Milk-based sauces, custards, and puddings all cook well, without any risk of burning. Sauces and custards must be stirred frequently during cooking to ensure their smoothness.
Preserves
Small quantities of jam, lemon curd, and chutney can all be made in a

microwave cooker. This enables small leftover quantities of fruit and vegetables to be used to good advantage.

Soups

These are easily made in a microwave cooker, and they retain the full flavour and colour of the ingredients.

Breakfast

Families who like to have cooked breakfasts need no longer be a problem. Bacon, tomatoes, mushrooms, and scrambled eggs can all be cooked on the serving plate in a few minutes (the eggs being placed in a separate container on the plate). Hot cereals can be made in their serving bowls. Try heating up muesli for a few seconds, it is delicious warm. Fresh bread and frozen bread rolls can be heated through in seconds.

Defrosting

Frozen raw foods, frozen cooked dishes, and pre-packaged convenience foods can all be defrosted quickly, for cooking later by conventional methods or for cooking by microwave. Many prepared frozen foods such as vegetables, fish fingers, pizzas, meat and fish in boil-in-the-bag containers can all be cooked quickly from frozen.

RULES FOR COOKING BY MICROWAVE

To achieve the best results from your microwave cooker, and to ensure even cooking, foods to be cooked should be of a uniform size. For example, vegetables should be trimmed into even-sized pieces, and when preparing meat for casseroles cut both the meat and the vegetables into comparable-sized pieces. When selecting chops, pick those that are of the same thickness, or ask your butcher to make sure that he cuts them to the same thickness. Choose fish that are of the same size.

Most foods will need to be covered to prevent splashing or to retain moisture. Dishes can be covered with lids or with cling film. When covering with cling film, always puncture the film to prevent ballooning, or vent the dish by pulling back one corner of the cling film to allow steam to escape.

Foods such as potatoes, cooking apples, tomatoes and fish that have a tight outer skin should always be pierced or slashed to allow the steam to escape and prevent exploding.

To ensure even cooking it will be necessary to reposition some pieces of food, or to stir two or three times during cooking. Keep a small plate by the side of the cooker on which to place a

stirring spoon. Sauces, custards and scrambled eggs must all be stirred very frequently during cooking. When cooking cakes, puddings and bread, it may be necessary to turn the dish during cooking to ensure even rising.

Most foods are best if seasoned after cooking since there is not normally enough time for the food to absorb the seasoning during cooking. Do not salt meat, since salt extracts moisture from the meat and makes it tough.

The larger the amount of food placed in a microwave cooker, the longer the cooking time will be. Smaller amounts of food receive more microwave energy and therefore cook more quickly. For example, one medium-sized jacket potato will cook in about 4 minutes on full power, and two would take about 6-7 minutes. Open-textured foods such as breads, cakes and puddings will cook more quickly than foods with a dense texture, such as meat.

When reheating foods that contain a high percentage of sugar and fat, such as mince pies, Christmas puddings and jam tarts, remember that the fat and sugar attract the microwaves and they will heat up very quickly. Also, the residual heat will go on heating for a while after they have been removed from the cooker. If they feel warm on the outside, you can be sure that they are very hot on the inside, so give them time to cool a little before serving.

Always keep a pair of oven gloves or an oven cloth by the side of your microwave cooker, just as you would by a gas or electric cooker. Although the cooking dishes themselves are not heated by the microwaves, the dishes can become very hot from the food cooking inside. Always take care when removing cling film from dishes, since very often there is a lot of steam trapped inside.

MENU PLANNING

Whole meals can be cooked in a microwave oven but, obviously, everything cannot be cooked together at the same time, so careful planning is necessary. If serving a hot main course, choose a starter that can be cooked ahead of time and then chilled. Or, if serving a cold main course that has been previously cooked in the microwave cooker, serve a hot first course. Desserts can be hot or cold since most can be cooked ahead of time to be chilled, or be ready for quick reheating.

The following recipes have been selected to show just how versatile a microwave cooker can be. There are also two complete menus for four people. The recipes were tested in a 650 watt cooker with a turntable. If your cooker has a lower output, allow a little longer cooking time, but do test at the end of the stated cooking time before adding any extra. If your cooker as a higher output, allow a little less time.

LITTLE GEMS

There is no end of small energy and time consuming tasks that can be done more quickly in a microwave cooker. They can help to speed up the preparation time as well as save on the washing up. Here are just a few.

● Butter can be softened for spreading within seconds. It can also be softened for creaming when making cakes by placing it in the mixing bowl and microwaving for a few seconds.

● Chocolate can be broken into small pieces and then melted in a small basin without the need for a saucepan.

● Flour can be warmed for breadmaking, to obtain a quicker rise. Bread dough can also be risen quickly in a microwave cooker.

● Dried fruits can be plumped up in minutes, without the overnight soaking.

● Fat for greasing cake tins can be quickly melted in a small cup.

● Packet jelly can be melted in a small basin without water. There is no need to boil a kettle.

● Hazelnuts can be heated through for skinning. They may also be browned in a microwave.

● Hard ice cream from the freezer can be softened without melting, to make scooping out easier.

● Fresh herbs can be quickly dried between sheets of kitchen paper.

● Jams can be quickly melted in a small basin, for glazing cakes and flans or for sauces.

● Tomatoes and peaches can be skinned easily after heating for a short time.

● Oranges that are warmed through for a few seconds are easier to peel.

MICROWAVE RECIPES

Here is a selection of recipes you can cook in a microwave oven. Included are two complete menus, plus a variety of other dishes – from simple starters and appetizing main courses to family favourite desserts.

MENU 1

Chilled Vichyssoise

Salmon Steaks with Caper Sauce

Oranges in Red Wine

This stylish menu uses a microwave oven to the fullest for carefree entertaining. The Chilled Vichyssoise and Oranges in Red Wine are prepared well in advance, and the impressive Salmon Steaks with Caper Sauce is finished off at the last minute. The salmon is scaled and the tarragon-flavoured butter and caper sauce are prepared before the guests arrive. All that remains to be done is five minutes of cooking in the microwave while enjoying the soup.

Chilled Vichyssoise
SERVES 4
Preparation time: 20 minutes
Cooking time: 26 minutes
Chilling time: 3-4 hours
2 oz/50 g butter
12 oz/350 g leeks, white parts only, thoroughly washed and thinly sliced
1 large onion, thinly sliced
1½ pints/850 ml hot chicken stock
salt and pepper
¼ pint/150 ml double cream
snipped fresh chives for garnish

1 Put the butter into a very large heat-resistant mixing bowl. Microwave on Full Power for 1 minute, until the butter has melted.
2 Add the leeks and onions to the butter and mix well. Microwave on Full Power for 5 minutes, until softened, stirring frequently.
3 Add the potatoes and stock to the

leek and onion. Cover three quarters of the bowl with cling film. Microwave on Full Power for 20 minutes or until potatoes are soft, stirring every 5 minutes.
4 Allow the soup to cool a little, then purée in a blender or food processor. Season well with salt and pepper, then refrigerate for 3-4 hours until chilled.
5 Stir the cream into the chilled soup. Garnish with the chives and serve.

Salmon Steaks with Caper Sauce
SERVES 4
Preparation time: 10 minutes
Cooking time: 4-5 minutes
Standing time: 3 minutes
4 salmon steaks, about ½ lb/225 g each
2 oz/50 g butter, softened
salt and pepper
lemon juice
2 teaspoons chopped fresh tarragon
lemon wedges and fresh tarragon sprigs for garnish
Caper Sauce
8 fl oz/225 ml soured cream
salt and pepper
2 teaspoons lemon juice
2 tablespoons pickled capers, drained
2 teaspoons Dijon mustard

1 Scrape the skin of the salmon with the back of a small knife to remove as many scales as possible.
2 Beat the butter until soft, then season with salt and pepper and lemon juice and mix in the tarragon.
3 Spread the tarragon butter evenly over the salmon steaks. Place in a shallow heat-resistant dish and cover with cling film, pulling back one corner.
4 Microwave the salmon on Full Power for 4-5 minutes, repositioning the steaks half-way through cooking. Remove from the cooker and allow to stand for 3 minutes.
5 Mix all of the ingredients for the sauce together, then spoon into a serving jug or bowl.
6 Arrange the salmon steaks on a serving dish and garnish with lemon wedges and sprigs of fresh tarragon. Spoon a little sauce over the salmon steaks and serve the sauce separately.

Note For delicious accompaniments to this menu, serve new potatoes and mange-tout. The potatoes may be cooked before the salmon, then covered and left to stand while cooking the salmon. Cook the mange-tout while you are allowing the salmon to stand. Reheat the potatoes for about 1-2 minutes on Full Power.

Oranges in Red Wine
SERVES 4
Preparation time: 10 minutes
Cooking time: 10 minutes
Chilling time: 2-3 hours
6 large oranges
¾ pint/425 ml red wine
6 oz/175 g caster sugar
2 inch/5 cm piece cinnamon stick

1 Very carefully remove the peel and all of the white pith from the oranges, then cut the oranges into thick slices.
2 Put the wine, sugar and cinnamon stick into a large heat-resistant mixing bowl or casserole dish. Microwave on Full Power for 5 minutes, until very hot. Stir well to dissolve the sugar.
3 Place the orange slices in the wine.

Cover with cling film, pulling back one corner to vent. Microwave on Full Power for 5 minutes.
4 Allow the oranges to cool, then refrigerate until well chilled. Spoon the oranges and wine into a serving dish.
Note To cook in advance, prepare and cool, then microwave on Full Power for 3-4 minutes to heat through.

Distinctive flavours highlight this quick and easy microwave menu. It is versatile enough to be an impressive dinner party as well as a family meal. Mushrooms à la Grecque and the Stuffed Chicken Breasts with Provençal Sauce capture the sharp flavours of the Mediterranean, and the Ginger and Apple Flan combines two wonderfully complementary flavours.

Mushrooms à la Grecque
SERVES 4
Preparation time: 5 minutes
Cooking time: 9 minutes
Chilling time: 4-5 hours or overnight
½ pint/275 ml chicken stock
1 tablespoon red wine vinegar
juice of 1 lemon, strained
3 tablespoons olive oil
2 cloves, garlic crushed
1 teaspoon dried mixed herbs
salt and pepper
1¼ lb/600 g button mushrooms, trimmed
finely shredded lettuce leaves and finely chopped fresh parsley for serving

1 Put all of the ingredients, except the mushrooms, into a large microwave casserole dish. Microwave on Full Power for 4-5 minutes, until very hot.
2 Add the mushrooms to the casserole dish and cover loosely with cling film. Microwave on Full Power for 5 minutes, stirring frequently.
3 Allow the mushrooms to cool, then refrigerate for 4-5 hours or overnight, until well chilled.
4 To serve, arrange shredded lettuce on four small serving plates. Lift the mushrooms from the cooking juices with a slotted spoon and arrange them on top of the lettuce. Moisten the mushrooms with some of the juices, then sprinkle with parsley.

Stuffed Chicken Breasts with Provençal Sauce
SERVES 4
Preparation time: 10 minutes
Cooking time: 22-24 minutes
Standing time: 5 minutes
2 oz/50 g butter, softened
juice of ½ lemon, strained
salt and pepper

½ lb/225 g peeled prawns
4 boneless and skinned chicken breasts, about 6 oz/175 g each
1 large onion, finely chopped
2 cloves, garlic crushed
1 tablespoon vegetable oil
14 oz/397 g can tomatoes
1 chicken stock cube
chopped fresh parsley for garnish.

back a corner to vent. Microwave on Full Power for 8 minutes, stirring twice. Remove and set aside.

5 Microwave the chicken breasts on Full Power for 7-8 minutes, turning and repositioning them every 2 minutes. Remove from the cooker, cover and leave to stand for 5 minutes.

6 Microwave the tomato sauce on Full Power for 2-3 minutes, until boiling hot.

7 Arrange the chicken breasts on a hot serving dish, then spoon the tomato sauce over. Garnish with the reserved prawns and chopped parsley. Serve with duchesse potatoes and steamed courgettes.

Ginger and Apple Flan
SERVES 4-6
Preparation time: 20 minutes
Cooking time: 9-9½ minutes
Chilling time: 2-3 hours
3 oz/75 g unsalted butter
1 tablespoon golden syrup
½ lb/225 g gingernut biscuits, crushed
2 lb/900 g cooking apples
6 oz/175 g caster sugar
2 oz/50 g preserved stem ginger, finely chopped
½ pint/275 ml double cream
preserved stem ginger for decoration

1 Put the butter and syrup into a mixing bowl. Microwave on Full Power for 1-1½ minutes, until the butter melts, stirring frequently.

2 Add the biscuits to the melted butter and syrup mixture, and mix thoroughly together.

3 Spread the mixture evenly over the base and up the sides of an 8 inch/20 cm pie plate or flan dish. Cover loosely with cling film and refrigerate while cooking the apples.

4 Peel, quarter, core and slice the apples. Put into a very large heat-resistant mixing bowl with the caster sugar and mix well. Cover three-quarters of the bowl with cling film. Microwave on Full Power for about 8 minutes, stirring every 2 minutes, until the apples are cooked, and are very fluffy.

5 Pour the cooked apples into a large nylon sieve placed over a bowl, to drain off the excess juice.

6 Mix the chopped ginger with the drained apples, then spoon into the chilled biscuit case. Refrigerate for 2-3 hours, until the filling is quite cold.

7 Whisk the cream until it is thick. Spoon or pipe the cream on top of the apple filling. Decorate with thinly sliced stem ginger. Refrigerate the flan until ready to serve.

1 Beat the butter with a little lemon juice and salt and pepper. Beat in three-quarters of the prawns, reserving the remainder for garnish.

2 Make a long horizontal slit through each chicken breast to make a pocket. Fill the pocket with the prawn mixture, then secure with wooden cocktail sticks to keep the filling enclosed. Place in a large shallow heat-resistant dish and loosely cover with cling film. Set aside.

3 Put the onion, garlic and oil into a large microwave casserole dish and mix well. Microwave on Full Power for 5 minutes, until the onion softens.

4 Add the tomatoes, including their juice, the stock cube and seasonings. Cover the dish with cling film, pulling

Curried Beef   Bolognese Sauce

Curried Beef
SERVES 2-3
Preparation time: 10 minutes
Cooking time: 13 minutes
Standing time: 2 minutes
1 lb/450 g lean rump or sirloin steak, trimmed
2 large onions, thinly sliced
2 cloves, garlic crushed
1 tablespoon vegetable oil
2 tablespoons curry powder
2 teaspoons paprika
1 teaspoon cumin seeds
1 tablespoon tomato purée
1 tablespoon sweet chutney, preferably mango
*   chutney*
½ pint/300 ml hot beef stock
1-2 teaspoons garam masala
salt and pepper
finely chopped fresh coriander or fresh parsley
*   for garnishing*
hot boiled rice for serving

1 Cut the steak into 2½ ¼ inch/6 cm 5 mm strips.
2 Put the onions and garlic into a large microwave casserole dish, add the oil and mix well. Microwave on Full Power for 5 minutes, until the onions are softened.
3 Add the curry powder, paprika and cumin seeds and mix well. Microwave on Full Power for 2 minutes
4 Place the steak on top of the onion mixture, then microwave on Full Power for 2 minutes, turning the meat after 1 minute.
5 Add the stock, tomato purée and chutney to the casserole dish and mix well. Cover the dish with cling film, pulling back one corner to vent. Microwave on Full Power for 4 minutes, until the meat is tender, stir half-way through cooking.
6 Remove the casserole dish from the cooker. Season the curry well with garam masala and salt and pepper. Cover and leave to stand for 2 minutes. Sprinkle the curry with coriander or parsley just before serving. Serve with hot rice.

Bolognese Sauce
SERVES 3-4
Preparation time: 5 minutes
Cooking time: 17 minutes
2 onions, finely chopped
2 cloves, garlic crushed
1 lb/450 g lean minced beef
1 tablespoon vegetable oil
1 beef stock cube
2 teaspoons dried mixed herbs
14 oz/397 g can tomatoes
1 tablespoon tomato purée
salt and pepper

1 Put in the onions, garlic and oil into a large microwave casserole dish and mix well. Microwave on Full Power for 5 minutes or until the onions are soft.
2 Mix the meat with the onions, then microwave on Full Power for 2 minutes, stirring after 1 minute.
3 Crumble the stock cube over the meat, then add the herbs, tomatoes, including their juice, and the tomato purée. Mix very well. Cover the dish

with cling film, pulling back one corner to vent. Microwave on Full Power for 10 minutes, stirring every 3 minutes.
4 Remove the casserole dish from the cooker and season with salt and pepper. Serve with hot pasta.

Lemon Sole with Dill Sauce
SERVES 4
Preparation time: 20 minutes
Cooking Time: 12¼ minutes
Standing time: 5 minutes
3 lemon soles, about 12 oz/350 g each
1 thick onion slice
1 bay leaf
salt and pepper
lemon juice
2 oz/50 g butter
1 tablespoon chopped fresh dill or 1 teaspoon
*   dried dill weed*
1 oz/25 g plain flour
4 tablespoons double cream
chopped fresh dill for garnishing

1 Carefully fillet each sole, to give 12 neat fillets. Discard the head and skin, but reserve the bones.
2 Break the bones in half and put them into a large heat-resistant bowl with ½ pint/300 ml cold water. Add the onion slice, bay leaf, ½ teaspoon dill and salt and pepper. Cover the bowl with cling film, then puncture to prevent ballooning. Microwave on Full Power for 5 minutes, then remove from the cooker and leave to stand for 5 minutes. Strain the stock from the bones and set aside. Discard the bones.
3 Season each sole fillet with salt and pepper and a little lemon juice. Roll up each fillet, with the skin-side inside, from the head to the tail, to make small neat paupiettes.
4 Put half the butter into a shallow heat-resistant dish and microwave on Full Power for about 45 seconds, until the butter melts. Turn each sole paupiette in the butter to coat it evenly. Arrange the paupiettes evenly in the dish. Cover with cling film, pulling one corner to vent. Set aside.
5 Put the remaining butter into a heat-resistant mixing bowl and microwave on Full Power for about 45 seconds, until the butter melts. Stir in the flour, then gradually whisk in the fish stock. Microwave on Full Power for 3½ minutes, stirring with a whisk every 30 seconds, until the sauce thickens and every trace of raw flour disappears.
6 Remove the sauce from the cooker, then stir in the cream and remaining dill. Season with salt, pepper and a little

lemon juice. Cover and set aside.

7 Microwave the sole for 3 minutes on Full Power. Strain the juices from the fish into the dill sauce, and stir well.

8 Pour the dill sauce evenly all over the paupiettes of sole. Sprinkle with dill, then microwave on Full Power for 1-2 minutes to heat through. Serve the lemon sole immediately, on a bed of hot rice, if desired.

Scampi Paprika
SERVES 4
Preparation time: 20 minutes
Cooking time: 13½-14½ minutes
1 lb/450 g large scampi
14 oz/397 g can tomatoes
1 large onion, halved and very thinly sliced
1 medium-size green pepper, deseeded, cored and very thinly sliced
2 tablespoons vegetable oil
1 tablespoon paprika
2 cloves, garlic crushed
1 vegetable stock cube
¼ pint/150 ml soured cream
salt and pepper
chopped fresh parsley for garnish

1 Make a cut through the back of each scampi and remove the black intestine.
2 Pour the tomatoes into a sieve placed over a small bowl to drain, then roughly chop. Allow the juice to stand for about 10 minutes, until a clear liquid rises to the top, then carefully spoon this liquid off, leaving behind the tomato juice.
3 Put the onion, pepper and oil into a large microwave casserole dish. Microwave on Full Power for 5 minutes, until the onion and pepper are soft.
4 Add the paprika, garlic and stock cube to the onion and mix well. Microwave on Full Power for 2 minutes.
5 Add the tomatoes and the strained juice to the dish and stir well. Loosely cover the dish with cling film and microwave on Full Power for 3 minutes. Add the scampi and microwave on Full Power for a further 2½ minutes, turning the scampi 2 or 3 times.
6 Stir the soured cream into the scampi mixture and season well with salt and pepper. Microwave on Full Power for another 1-2 minutes, until very hot. Sprinkle with parsley and serve.

Lemon and Raisin Pudding
SERVES 4-6
Preparation time: 10 minutes
Cooking time: 4½-6 minutes
Standing time: 2 minutes
4 oz/100 g butter or margarine
4 oz/100 g caster sugar
finely grated zest of 1 lemon
2 eggs, size 2
5 oz/150 g self-raising flour
3 oz/75 g seedless raisins
strained juice of 3 lemons
1½ oz/40 g granulated sugar
thin slices of lemon for decoration
extra butter for the mould

1 Lightly butter a 7 inch/18 cm microwave ring mould
2 Beat the butter, sugar and lemon zest together until very light and fluffy. Beat in the eggs, one at a time, beating well between each addition. Carefully fold in the flour, then fold in the raisins.
3 Spoon the sponge mixture into the prepared mould. Loosely cover the mould with cling film. Microwave on Full Power for 3½-4 minutes until well

Lemon Sole   Scampi Paprika

Chocolate Gâteau   Lemon Pudding   Coffee Cup-cakes

risen, yet still slightly moist on the top. Remove from the cooker and allow to stand for 2 minutes.

4 Meanwhile, put the lemon juice and the granulated sugar into a small mixing bowl. Microwave on Full Power for 1-2 minutes, until boiling. Stir well to dissolve the sugar.

5 Turn the pudding on to a hot serving plate, then spoon the boiling lemon syrup evenly over the pudding.

Chocolate and Orange Gâteau
SERVES 8
Preparation time: 15 minutes
Cooking time: 4½-5 minutes
Standing time: 2 minutes
3 eggs, size 2
3 oz/75 g caster sugar
2½ oz/65 g plain flour
½ oz/15 g cocoa
½ level teaspoon baking powder
2 oz/50 g unsalted butter, melted and cooled
4 oz/100 g plain chocolate
3 tablespoons orange juice
½ pint/275 ml double cream
finely grated zest of 1 orange
chocolate curls for decoration
vegetable oil for dish

1 Very lightly butter a 9 × 5 × 2½ inch/23 × 12.5 × 6.5 cm microwave casserole dish. Smoothly line the base with greaseproof paper, then lightly grease the paper.

2 Whisk the eggs and the caster sugar together until they are very thick and the mixture will hold a ribbon trail for at least 5 seconds.

3 Gently sift the flour, cocoa and baking powder on to the whisked mixture, then very gently fold together. Carefully fold in the cooled butter, a little at a time.

4 Pour the chocolate mixture into the prepared dish. Cover the dish loosely with cling film. Microwave on Full Power for 2½-3 minutes until well risen and set, yet still slightly moist on the surface. Remove from the cooker and allow to stand for 2 minutes. Very carefully turn the sponge on to a rack to cool completely.

5 Break the chocolate into small pieces, then put them into a small heat-resistant mixing bowl with the orange juice. Microwave on Low for 2 minutes, stirring every 30 seconds until the chocolate melts. Remove from cooker

and stir until the mixture is smooth. Set aside and allow to cool.

6 Whisk the cream and the orange zest together until thick, but not buttery. Add the melted chocolate and mix lightly, but thoroughly together.

7 Cut the cooled sponge cake in half horizontally. Place the bottom layer on a serving dish, and spread evenly with one third of the cream.

8 Place the second layer of sponge on top of the first layer, pressing the two gently together. Spread the remaining cream all over the cake, to cover it completely. Mark the cream into swirls. Decorate with chocolate curls.

9 Chill the chocolate gâteau very slightly before serving.

Note For an extra special occasion, the chocolate may be melted with an orange liqueur such as Cointreau, instead of the orange juice.

Coffee Cup-cakes
MAKES 24
Preparation time: 15 minutes
Cooking time: 1½ minutes per batch of 6 cakes plus 45 seconds for the icing
4 oz/100 g butter or margarine
4 oz/100 g caster sugar
2 eggs, size 2
1 tablespoon strong black coffee
5 oz/150 g self-raising flour
Icing
4-5 tablespoons strong black coffee
10 oz/275 g icing sugar, sifted
24 chocolate buttons for decoration

1 Beat the butter and sugar together until very light and fluffy. Beat in the eggs, one at a time, beating well between each addition. Beat in the coffee, then gently fold in the flour.

2 Spoon the mixture into 24 double thickness, paper cup-cake cases. Microwave on Full Power, in batches of 6 for 1½ minutes. Place on a cooling rack to cool. (If you have a bun tray suitable for use in a microwave, stand the paper cases inside the bun tray and this will help keep the cakes in a better shape.)

3 To make the icing, put the coffee into a cup and microwave on Full Power for 45 seconds until very hot. Mix the icing sugar with sufficient hot coffee to make an icing thick enough to coat the back of the spoon.

4 Spoon a little of the icing into the centre of each cake. Alternatively, pipe a rosette of coffee butter cream in the centre of each cup-cake and add the chocolate buttons. Leave to stand for about 1 hour until the icing is set.

KIDS IN THE KITCHEN

Making sure your children eat a balanced diet can often be difficult. By teaching them to cook, you can help them to appreciate good food and set the foundations for a lifetime of healthy eating.

'Kids in the kitchen' is a phrase which might fill many mothers' hearts with foreboding — images of mess, mountains of bowls and a nasty mixture of sugar and flour scrunching under your feet. Another phrase should perhaps override the first — we are what we eat. Just as our mothers instilled us with good eating habits, we should perpetuate this and let our kids in the kitchen to learn.

When your children get older, they will probably be taught cookery in school. Sadly, most of these classes tend to concentrate on fatty foods like Scotch eggs and puddings. Encourage them in your own kitchen to appreciate the difference between good and bad cooking. Children, as well as adults, should be made to understand the importance of healthy eating.

CHOOSING A BALANCED DIET

Very basically, the rules are simple. Just as adults need a balanced diet, so do children. Although the amount of sugar, saturated fats and salt should be reduced in *everyone's* diet, a child should not (unless for medical reasons) have low fat spread or skimmed milk. Both of these lack vitamin D, which is essential for the absorption of calcium.

Although bran can add much-needed fibre to an adult's diet, it passes through the body too quickly for a child to absorb much goodness from other foods eaten with it. Oats, on the other hand, are absorbed more slowly, and therefore a bowl of porridge is much better for children than a bran-based cereal.

Sugar is found naturally in a variety of foods, including root vegetables, fruits and even milk. This sugar provides energy, which should be enough

for the body. These foods also contain other nutrients essential for a balanced diet, such as vitamins and minerals. The problems with sugar begin when a child is allowed too many sweets, biscuits, cakes and canned fizzy drinks. Although the sugar in these foods also provides energy, they have no added nutritional value, and are called 'empty calories'.

Saturated fats, which contain cholesterol, should be limited. Not just when cooking, but also when choosing foods. Egg yolks, offal, canned meats, sausages, butter and cream are all examples of foods that are very high in cholesterol.

At every meal, you should try and serve something from each of the following food groups — protein (meat, chicken, fish, eggs, cheese), dairy products (milk, cheese, yoghurt, eggs), fibre (bread, pasta, potatoes, rice, pulses) and fresh fruit and vegetables. Although this is a rough guide, it is good to follow.

Always start the day with breakfast. Try and limit cooked breakfasts of bacon, eggs and sausages since these are high in fat. Grill, rather than fry these foods whenever possible. Cereals are an excellent choice, but avoid those that are sugar-coated or high in bran fibre. At lunch and dinner, provide plenty of green vegetables. Fruit, fresh or dried, and raw vegetables such as celery or carrot sticks, are excellent between-meal snacks.

If your child has a packed lunch at school, keep to the same rules when planning the meal. Use wholemeal bread for making sandwiches, and cut down on the butter. Unfortunately, the law requiring that a set school lunch had to provide one-third of the child's nutritional requirements has been abo-

lished. Keep this in mind when preparing dinner, since school lunches tend to overdo the fat and sugar. Try to aim for dinner between five and six o'clock. This will give your child adequate time to digest the food before bed.

Fluid is also important, since it clears the body of waste products. Children need about 2 pints/1.1 litres of liquid a day. This can be some milk, fresh fruit juice or water. Encourage them to drink the latter, because it does the best job — as well as being the cheapest.

When children get invited to parties, don't let the nutritional aspect slip. If possible, make sure your children have a balanced lunch before they go. Then, hopefully, they will not fill up on all those cakes and biscuits. In the same way, when you are giving a party, provide carrot and celery sticks, fresh fruit, and fresh fruit juice.

Lastly, older children who get pocket money will be tempted to rush out and spend it all on sweets. Although the purpose of pocket money is to teach independence, parents can steer children in the right direction.

GETTING KIDS TO EAT

- Sit down with the family. A lonely place setting appeals to no one.
- Serve smaller portions, and do not force older children to eat. They will feel a lot less conspicuous if left alone.
- Arrange the food attractively on the plate. Often special plates with a favourite cartoon character helps encourage younger children to eat.
- Make sure the chair is comfortable and the right height for the table.
- If younger children want to eat

with their fingers, let them. They will eventually learn to eat with knives and forks, usually when they go to school.
- Within reason, don't fuss about messy tables and floors. These can always be cleaned up afterwards.
- If your child is a particularly slow eater, then let him have the time he needs. Constant nagging is not productive.
- Do *not* have the television on.

One fact to remember is that eating and meals form a major part of a child's social upbringing. Meals eaten at the table with the entire family invite conversation — about the activities of the day and about the food itself. If the food is delicious, meals become a pleasurable experience and will promote thought about what is being eaten.

LET'S HAVE A PARTY

By the time a child reaches six or seven, he will have gained a certain amount of knowledge about the food he eats, and will naturally want to experiment in the kitchen. Watching a parent cook can instil deep-rooted foundations for an appreciation of food in later life.

Even if your child looks forlorn at the meal you have cooked, if he has cooked it himself it will seem much more appetizing. Why not let them have a try at the following recipes? Older children will probably be able to make all of the dishes, while younger ones may be able to attempt two or three.

SAFETY CODE

Before they start, it is important that the following rules are adhered to at all times. This basic training will remain with the child, providing a code of safety and neatness.

- Forbid children to cook anything unless supervised by an adult.
- Watch the pan handles. They should be turned inwards, otherwise, the pan can accidentally be knocked off the cooker.
- Don't let them touch any plugs or electrical appliances with wet hands.
- Have them grill or bake whenever possible, instead of frying.
- Help by putting dishes or baking trays in and out of the oven.
- Ensure that children put on an apron and wash their hands before they start.
- Washing up should be done as they go, but as long as it is done afterwards, that is what counts.
- If sharp knives are being used, you will need to supervise.
- Wipe up spills on the floor so no one will slip on them.

BUYING FOOD

In an ideal world, the majority of food you buy would be of the freshest quality. However, this is not always possible, and there are acceptable alternatives in packaged food lines.

Canned food In the case of fruit and vegetables, canning will have diminished the vitamin content but not fibre. Choose canned fruit in natural juice, with no sugar added. Buy canned fish in brine, not oil. Forget about canned soups, they are high in added sugar. Canned beans are excellent — they contain protein, fibre and minerals — but some brands contain added salt and sugar.

Frozen food Basic frozen foods such as vegetables, fruit, pastry, meat and fish lose very little nutrients during the freezing process, and they are excellent stand-bys in the kitchen. However, foods such as pies, burgers, fish fingers, cooked meals and pizzas should be regarded with suspicion. By law, the contents must be listed with the main ingredient first and you may be surprised in some cases just what it is.

Dried food Dried fruit makes an excellent snack for children. Not just the usual raisins, sultanas and currants, but also dried apples, bananas and apricots. Although the drying process invalidates the vitamin C content, dried fruit contains potassium, which provides energy for the body. Dried vegetables like beans are also excellent choices. Avoid dried food products where boiling water is poured over noodles or rice to make a simple meal — these are dangerously high in preservatives.

EAT UP!

These immortal words will often get you nowhere when trying to get children to eat. Remember, a child's stomach is considerably smaller than an adult's — what may not look like a lot of food to you can seem a positive challenge to a child.

A finicky child can be a problem, but it is often parents who fuel any aversion to one food by making a fuss. Although he or she may eat very little, as long as the foods being eaten are nutritionally sound, they will come to no harm.

COOKERY TERMS

To Baste
To spoon hot fat over food (usually meat) to keep moist during cooking.

To Beat
To make a vigorous circular movement with a wooden spoon, fork or balloon whisk to remove lumps, beat in air or make a mixture smooth.

To Bind
To add a liquid ingredient, such as water, egg or syrup, to make dry ingredients stick together.

To Blend
To add wet ingredients slowly to dry ingredients and then mix until smooth.

To Chop
To cut into small pieces.

To Cream
To beat butter or margarine with a wooden spoon to incorporate air until it is light in colour and fluffy.

To Dice
To cut food into small squares.

To Fold In
To mix one ingredient with another that has air in it. The mixture is cut and turned over very gently with a large metal spoon as few air bubbles as possible are broken.

To Garnish
To decorate a dish, such as a flan, with edible trimmings. Thin slices of cucumber and tomato or a little parsley are popular garnishes.

To Glaze
To brush food with liquid, such as beaten egg or milk, to give a shiny finish.

To Grate
To push food downwards against a grater to make small flakes. Most graters have fine and coarse sides.

To Hull
To remove the outer coating of podded vegetables, like peas, or the stalks of soft fruit, such as strawberries or raspberries.

To Knead
To use the hands to fold and push mixtures, such as dough, to make them smooth.

To Rub In
To rub into flour using the fingertips until the mixture looks like fine breadcrumbs.

Cheese Straws

The oven is used and younger children may need assistance with cutting up the pastry.

MAKES ABOUT 90

You will need...

4 oz/100 g plain flour, plus extra for the work surface
salt and pepper
1 teaspoon mustard powder
2 oz/50 g butter or margarine
3 oz/75 g mature Cheddar cheese
1½ tablespoons cold water

...and this equipment

sieve
mixing bowl
round-bladed knife
grater
measuring spoons
rolling pin
sharp knife
baking sheet
palette knife
wire racks

1 Ask a grown-up to make sure the shelf is at the top of the oven and to turn the setting on to 200C/400F/Gas 6.

2 Wash and dry your hands and put on an apron.

3 Sift the flour, salt and pepper and mustard powder into a mixing bowl.

4 Cut the butter into small pieces and rub in until the mixture looks like fine breadcrumbs.

5 Grate the cheese and stir into the mixture.

6 Gradually add enough water to make the mixture stick together.

7 Sift some flour on to a work surface, place the dough on it and knead until smooth.

8 Roll the pastry out to about ⅛ inch/3 mm thick.

9 Using a sharp knife, cut the pastry into strips, about 3 inches/7.5 cm long and ½ inch/1.2 cm wide. Gently twist each straw twice and put on the baking sheet.

10 Ask a grown-up to put the baking sheet in the oven. The cheese straws will take about 10 minutes to cook and will be golden brown. Do the washing up while they are cooking.

11 Ask a grown-up to take the baking sheet out of the oven. Ease the cheese straws off the sheet with a palette knife and leave to cool on a wire rack.

Gingerbread Men

The oven is used and young children will need help cutting out the gingerbread men.

MAKES 10

You will need...

a little vegetable oil for greasing the baking sheets and measuring spoon

½ lb/225 g plain flour, plus extra for the work surface

½ teaspoon bicarbonate of soda

1 teaspoon ground ginger

2 oz/50 g margarine

3 oz/ 75 g soft brown sugar

2 tablespoons golden syrup

1 egg

currants for decoration

...and this equipment

pastry brush

2 baking sheets

sieve

measuring spoons

mixing bowl

round-bladed knife

wooden spoon

small saucepan

rolling pin

gingerbread man or lady cutter

palette knife

wire racks

1 Ask a grown-up to check that the shelf is in the centre of the oven and to turn the setting on to 190C/375F/Gas 5.

2 Wash and dry your hands and put on an apron.

3 Brush the baking sheets with oil.

4 Sift the flour, bicarbonate of soda and ginger into a mixing bowl. Cut the margarine into pieces, then rub it into the flour until the mixture looks like fine breadcrumbs.

5 Add the sugar and stir well with a wooden spoon.

6 Oil a 1 tablespoon measuring spoon and use it to measure the syrup into a small saucepan. Heat gently on top of the cooker until it is runny. Turn off the heat.

7 Pour syrup and egg into the flour mixture. Mix thoroughly until you have a stiff dough.

8 Sift some flour on to a work surface. Place the dough on it and knead well. If the dough is too soft to handle, leave for a few minutes and it will firm up.

9 Roll out the dough to ¼ inch/5 mm thick. Use the gingerbread man cutter to

cut out as many figures as you can.

10 Lift the figures on to the baking sheets with a palette knife. Press the currants on to the gingerbread men to make eyes and buttons.

11 Ask a grown-up to place the baking sheets into the oven. They will take 10-15 minutes to cook and will be golden brown. Do the washing up while they are cooking.

12 Ask a grown-up to take the baking sheets out of the oven. Carefully lift the gingerbread men from the baking sheets with a palette knife and place them on wire racks to cool. Turn off the oven.

Peppermint Hearts and Rose Creams

Younger children will need help separating the eggs.

MAKES 35-40

You will need...

11 oz/300 g icing sugar, plus extra for the work surface

1 egg

peppermint essence

edible green food colouring

rose water

edible pink food colouring

...and this equipment

kitchen scale

large metal spoon

sieve

3 small bowls

mixing bowl

fork and wooden spoon

rolling pin

heart-shaped cutter

flower-shaped cutter

plate

1 Wash and dry your hands and put on an apron.

2 Measure 2 oz/50 g of the icing sugar and spoon it into a small bowl and set aside.

3 Place a sieve over a mixing bowl and spoon the rest of the icing sugar into the sieve. Sift into the bowl.

4 Separate the egg white and yolk. Do this over a small mixing bowl. Save the yolk for another recipe.

5 Beat the egg white with a fork until slightly frothy. Slowly stir it into the icing sugar in the large mixing bowl with a wooden spoon.

6 Divide the mixture in half and place in two small bowls.

7 Add a few drops of green colouring and peppermint essence to one bowl and a few drops of rose water and pink colouring to the other. Mix well.

8 Sift half the reserved 2 oz/50 g icing sugar into the green mixture. Work this in to make the mixture firm again. Sift the other half into the pink mixture and work in the same way.

9 Sift a little extra icing sugar over the work surface. Roll out each piece to about ¼ inch/5 mm thick.

10 Dip a heart-shaped cutter in the icing sugar and stamp out as many heart shapes as you can from the green mixture. If the cutter starts to stick, dip it in icing sugar again.

11 Repeat with the pink mixture using a flower-shaped cutter.

12 Put the sweets on a plate and leave to dry for 2 hours. Turn over and dry for another 2 hours. Wash up.

Strawberry Milk Shake
SERVES 6
You will need...
½ lb/225 g strawberries
2 pints/1.1 litres cold milk
2 tablespoons caster sugar
6 scoops strawberry ice cream
...and this equipment
nylon sieve
mixing bowl which fits neatly under the sieve
wooden spoon
spatula
measuring jug
large mixing bowl
measuring spoon
rotary beater
6 glasses
ice cream scoop

1 Wash and dry your hands and put on an apron.
2 Hull the strawberries (remove the little green stalks).
3 Press the strawberries through the sieve with a wooden spoon, using a stirring action. You will be left with a thick juice called a *purée.*
4 Scrape the purée into a large mixing bowl with a spatula.
5 Measure the milk and pour into the bowl. Add the sugar and whisk the mixture with a rotary beater until it is frothy.
6 Spoon into the glasses and add a scoop of ice cream to each glass before serving.
7 Wash up afterwards.

Mice in the Grass
Boiling water is needed for making the jelly and care should be taken when opening cans.
SERVES 6
You will need...
5 oz/150 g packet lime jelly
14 oz/400 g can pear halves
12 blue silvered dragees (balls)
12 flaked almonds
1 glacé cherry
6 long strands desiccated coconut
...and this equipment
measuring jug
saucepan
wooden spoon
large shallow dish
fork
6 small plates or 1 large plate
can opener
knife

1 Wash and dry your hands and put on an apron.
2 Make up the jelly according to the instructions on the packet. Pour it into a large shallow dish and set it aside until it is completely set.
3 When the jelly has set, break it up by mashing it with a fork. Spoon it on to the 6 individual plates.
4 Open the can of pears, drain and pour away the juice. Place one pear half, rounded side up, on top of the jelly.
5 Press two dragees on to the pointed end of the pears to make the eyes. Use 2 flaked almonds to make the ears.
6 Cut the glacé cherry into small slices and use for the mouths.
7 Finally, push piece of desiccated coconut into the back of each pear to make the tail.
8 Place in the refrigerator while you do the washing up.

Animal Sandwiches
Heat is used for hard-boiling the eggs and care should be taken when opening cans and cutting crusts off the bread.
MAKES 30-40 SANDWICHES
You will need...
4-5 oz/100-150 g butter or soft margarine
1 large thinly sliced white sandwich loaf of bread
1 large thinly sliced wholemeal sandwich loaf of bread
Fillings
12 eggs
14 tablespoons mayonnaise
OR 4 × 7 oz/200 g cans tuna fish
12 tablespoons mayonnaise
OR 6 oz/175 g jar crunchy peanut butter
...and this equipment
large saucepan
large spoon
bowl
2 mixing bowls
2 forks
measuring spoons
can opener
chopping board
round-bladed knife
metal animal shape biscuit cutters
serving plates
cling film

1 If using butter, take it out of the refrigerator at least 30 minutes before you need to use it, so that it will be soft and easy to spread.
2 Wash and dry your hands and put on an apron.
3 Prepare the fillings. Place the eggs in a large saucepan and pour in enough cold water to cover. Put the pan on the cooker, turn the heat to high and bring to the boil. Turn the heat down slightly and boil gently for 10 minutes. You may

need to use 2 saucepans or hard-boil the eggs in batches.
4 Turn off the heat and, with a large spoon, put the eggs in a bowl of cold water. Leave them until they are cold.
5 Gently tap the eggs and peel off the shells. Place in a mixing bowl and using a fork, mash with 14 tablespoons mayonnaise.
6 Open the cans of tuna fish and drain. Place the tuna in another bowl, if using, and using a fork, mash with 12 tablespoons mayonnaise.
7 You can spread the peanut butter straight from the jar, if using.
8 Spread a little butter or margarine on each slice of bread with the round-bladed knife. Spread a filling on half the slices of bread.
9 Place the other slices, butter side down, on top of the filling. Place on a chopping board and cut the crusts off.
10 Cut out as many shapes as possible from each sandwich. Arrange on plates. Cover with cling film and wash up.

8 Put the mayonnaise, yoghurt and lemon juice into a small serving bowl and mix well with a spoon to make a dressing.
9 Pour the dressing over the salad, then use a fork and spoon to toss the salad so that it is coated in dressing.
10 Cover with plastic wrap and chill in the refrigerator for 30 minutes. Do the washing up while you wait.

Tuna-Stuffed Eggs
Heat and boiling water are used to hard boil the eggs. Care should be taken opening the cans.
SERVES 4
You will need...
4 eggs
3 tablespoons mayonnaise
salt and pepper
4 oz/100 g can tuna fish
few green stuffed olives
watercress
...and this equipment
saucepan
metal spoon
2 small bowls
kitchen knife
chopping board
small spoon
measuring spoons
can opener
wooden spoon
absorbent kitchen paper
serving plate

1 Wash and dry your hands and put on an apron.
2 Hard-boil the eggs. See instructions on page 132 for Animal Sandwiches. Peel off the shells.
3 Cut the eggs in half on a chopping board and scoop out the yolks with a small spoon.
4 Put the yolks in a small bowl and mash them with a fork. Add the mayonnaise and salt and pepper. Stir well with a wooden spoon.
5 Wash the wooden spoon, the knife and the fork, then open the can of tuna fish. Drain off the oil.
6 Add the tuna fish to the egg mixture and beat well with a wooden spoon.
7 Carefully spoon the tuna mixture into each hollow egg white.
8 Put the olives on a chopping board and slice them thinly. Arrange them on top of the tuna mixture.
9 Break off the sprigs of watercress leaves. Rinse the leaves under cold running water, then drain and pat dry with kitchen paper. Arrange on a plate and garnish with watercress.

Coleslaw Salad
A sharp knife is needed to shred the cabbage finely.
SERVES 6
You will need...
½ small white cabbage
1 onion
1 large carrot
2 eating apples
salt and pepper
2 tablespoons mayonnaise
2 tablespoons yoghurt
1 tablespoon lemon juice
...and this equipment
long sharp knife
chopping board
colander
absorbent kitchen paper
grater
serving bowl
measuring spoons
small serving bowl
metal spoon
salad spoon and fork
plastic wrap

1 Wash and dry your hands and put on an apron.
2 Cut the cabbage in half, then into quarters on a chopping board. Cut the cabbage one quarter at a time. Place cut-side down on the board and slice into thin pieces. This is called *shredding* and you may want a grown-up to do it for you, as it is rather difficult you must be careful not to cut your fingers.
3 Put the cabbage in a colander and wash thoroughly under cold running water. Let it drain, then turn out on to absorbent kitchen paper. Pat dry with more kitchen paper.
4 Peel the onion and chop it into small pieces on the chopping board.
5 Peel the carrot and cut off the two ends. Grate it on to the chopping board.
6 Cut the apples into quarters. Cut away the core, then chop the rest of the apple into small squares. This is called *dicing*
7 Put the cabbage, onion, carrot and apple into the serving bowl. Sprinkle with salt and pepper.

Hamburgers

The grill is used as well as a sharp knife. The breadcrumbs are made in a food processor or blender.

SERVES 4

You will need...

½ lb/225 g lean minced beef
1 oz/25 g stale breadcrumbs
1 egg
pinch of mustard powder or Tabasco sauce
salt and pepper
a little plain flour for the work surface
4 hamburger rolls
4 lettuce leaves
1 small onion
2 firm tomatoes
tomato ketchup, relish and mayonnaise for
*   serving (optional)*

...and this equipment

mixing bowl
fork
wooden spoon
grill pan
fish slice
sharp knife
chopping board
absorbent kitchen paper
teaspoons
serving plates

1 Wash and dry your hands and put on an apron.
2 Put the meat in a mixing bowl and break it up with a fork.
3 Add the breadcrumbs, egg, mustard powder or Tabasco sauce and salt and pepper and stir well with a wooden spoon until thoroughly mixed.
4 Very lightly flour the work surface. Place the meat mixture on the surface and divide into four equal-sized balls.
5 Using your hands, shape the heaps into ½ inch/1 cm thick rounds.
6 Turn the grill on to high. Arrange the burgers on the grill rack in the grill pan. Grill for 6 minutes
7 Remove the pan from under the grill and place it on top of the cooker.
8 Turn the burgers over, using the fish slice. Grill the other side for 6 minutes.
9 While the burgers are cooking, cut the hamburger rolls in half with the sharp knife. Peel and slice the onion into rings on a chopping board. Slice the tomatoes. Wash and pat the lettuce leaves dry with absorbent kitchen paper.
10 When the burgers are cooked, put each one on the bottom half of a roll. Add a lettuce leaf, a few onion rings and a few tomato slices. Add teaspoonsful of tomato ketchup, relish and mayonnaise. Top with the other half of the roll. Wash up after you have eaten.

Rock Buns

A grown-up should help with the oven.

MAKES 6

You will need...

½ lb/225 g self raising flour
¼ teaspoon ground cinnamon
¼ teaspoon grated nutmeg
½ teaspoon ground mixed spice
pinch of salt
3 oz/75 g butter
3 oz/75 g caster sugar
6 oz/175 g mixed dried fruit
2 oz/50 g mixed candied peel
2 oz/50 g glacé cherries
2 tablespoons milk
1 egg
2 tablespoons lemon juice
vegetable oil for greasing the baking sheets

...and this equipment

pastry brush
2 baking sheets
sieve
mixing bowl
measuring spoons and jug
round-bladed knife
metal spoon
chopping board
sharp knife
fork
fish slice
wire rack

1 Ask a grown-up to put the shelf in the top of the oven and to turn it on to 200C/400F/Gas 6.
2 Wash and dry your hands and put on an apron.
3 Brush the baking sheets with oil.
4 Sift flour, cinnamon, nutmeg, mixed spice, and salt into a mixing bowl.
5 Cut the butter into small pieces and rub into the flour until the mixture looks like fine breadcrumbs.
6 Stir in the sugar, then the dried fruit and candied peel, using a metal spoon. Place the cherries on a chopping board and cut in half with a sharp knife. Stir into the mixture.
7 Measure the milk in a measuring jug and beat in the egg with a fork. Pour into the mixture with the lemon juice and mix to a firm dough.
8 Place 6 heaps on to baking sheets.
9 Ask a grown-up to place the sheets in the oven. The buns will take 10-15 minutes to cook and will be firm and golden brown. Do the washing up.
10 Ask a grown-up to take the baking sheets out of the oven. Leave to cool for a few minutes, then carefully lift the rock buns from the baking kheets with a fish slice and place them on a wire rack to cool. Turn off the oven.

THE PERFECT KITCHEN

Some people spend most of their time in the kitchen — not just cooking, but eating, entertaining and working. Home economist Jane Suthering combines imagination, experience, fantasy and fact to share her ideas for the perfect kitchen.

BLACK FOREST GATEAU

MAKES 8-10 SLICES

150 g/5 oz plain flour
2 teaspoons bicarbonate of soda
1 tablespoon coffee powder
1 tablespoon cocoa powder
6 eggs, seperated
150 g/5 oz castor sugar
1 teaspoon lemon juice
75 g/3 oz plain dessert,
  finely grated
pinch of salt
melted butter,for greasing

Home economist Jane Suthering cooks for a living. She spends most of her working day in kitchens — her own as well as kitchens in photographers' studios, where it is her job to make sure that the food being photographed looks its best. Here, Jane talks about her perfect kitchen. She also shares her ideas for the future kitchen — ideas that would make life easier for her and everyone who spends time in the kitchen.

MY PERFECT KITCHEN

I've often thought about 'My Perfect Kitchen', and wondered exactly what it would be like if I had all the money, but more importantly, the time necessary to produce it.

I look in amazement, and often with irritation, at many of the glossy advertisements for superb kitchens. They are immaculate show-pieces, but life in the kitchen isn't like that! I hate the rather clinical, pristine look of so many of these designs. Although I'm all in favour of modern technology and the advances in labour-saving equipment, I want my kitchen to be warm and welcoming. For me, it's the centre of my home and doubles as my 'office'. I spend more time in the kitchen than any other room in the house, and have often thought that my only requirements for a home are a large kitchen with a recessed sleeping area and a bathroom.

I have had four homes in the last 12 years, each move allowing me a larger kitchen. The first one was a tiny square in which I could pivot on the spot and almost reach everything I needed — labour-saving, but never anywhere to put anything once I'd finished with it. My conclusion was that I would love to have a huge kitchen.

I have always dreamed of a large family kitchen with plenty of natural light and double doors opening out on to a lovely garden. The working section would be at one end of the kitchen with the living area at the other. This would consist of a large sofa and plenty of cupboards and bookshelves to take all my china, glass and the innumerable cookery and reference books I continue to collect. I think I would also have to include a desk/table for my writing and

notes, as well as the telephone and answering machine, and some neat little cubbyholes for the telephone directories — very essential, but a nuisance.

The two ends of the kitchen would be brought together by a vast kitchen table, possibly refectory style, that would seat 12 comfortably. Close to the table there would be a serving table or perhaps a trolley. This would be very useful at meal times, and ensure that everything I need is close at hand.

JANE'S PERFECT KITCHEN

MY KITCHEN

I have recently moved into a new three-storey house. The ground floor consists of a fairly large kitchen, about 14 feet/4.5 metres square, an integral garage and a cupboard under the stairs which has become my cookery book library. There's no room in this particular kitchen for them, but at least they are within easy reach.

I keep a large fridge and upright freezer in the garage solely for work purposes. I chose an upright freezer because I find it far more convenient to store and locate food. A washing machine and a sink are plumbed in the garage — ideal for handwashing and soaking. Most of the wallspace is covered in shelves and cupboards — it is here that all my cake tins, large pieces of equipment, canned and bottled foods, wines and rarely used items are stored. Everything can be seen and reached easily. I love order, and ideally want a place for everything plus some extra room to allow for additions.

As people spend more and more time in the kitchen the attitude towards it changes continually. In houses like mine, which do not have a separate dining room, all the entertaining has to be done in the kitchen. I gave my kitchen a more sophisticated look by installing medium oak units and a wooden floor, and intend to make it more of a kitchen/dining room by adding a polished dining table, which can be protectively covered during the day when work is in full swing.

I have always chosen a gas hob for its efficiency and controllability, particularly when making delicate items such as sugar syrups, caramels, flambées, or when I need quick heat adjustments for fats and oils. The hob I've chosen this time is a Zanussi — not particularly expensive within the large range of hobs available, but I like its streamlined appearance, and there are no difficult nooks and crannies to clean. The pan stands are in two separate sections, each covering two burners, which means they will actually fit in the sink for cleaning. They are also dipped in enamel — never again will I buy a hob with chrome or aluminium pan stands, because they stain horribly and look most unsightly very quickly. There is also a splashguard between the hob and the controls which reduces the chance of them getting so dirty. Finally, the hob is shallow which means it will fit into the work surface without losing essential drawer space underneath.

I have realized that four burners just isn't sufficient for my needs so a two-ring Westinghouse electric hob is fitted next to the gas hob. Again it has a streamlined appearance and is shallow so no drawer space is lost. It is also useful for long slow cooking instead of using gas, which can sometimes blow out on a very low setting.

When you do as much cooking as I do, you will realize that ventilation is particularly important. I hate the smell of cooking pervading the rest of the house, but am constantly irritated by the noise of the cooker hood extractor. Surely it's possible for manufacturers to produce quiet, if not noiseless, extractors and cooker hoods.

Together with my assistant Anne, I spend at least two or three days each week preparing food for photography, testing, or creating recipes, so my choice of ovens is very important. I decided to install two this time, a Neff circotherm and a Bosch oven which can be set as a conventional oven or as a fan-assisted oven. I need to have both conventional and fan-assisted ovens to check temperatures and timings for recipe develop-

JANE'S NEW KITCHEN

ment. I had a Neff oven previously and was always very happy with its performance, apart from the grill which only has one setting and has to be regulated by moving the grill pan. The Bosch oven has a much stronger grill which can be regulated. What I'd really like to see developed is a grill pan which could be moved up and down to a suitable level by a simple lever or switch, and not this outdated method of moving the pan in and out on to a different set of grooves.

I don't use my Toshiba microwave a great deal, but have found it invaluable on many occasions, especially in my first few days of moving in to the house. It's particularly useful for defrosting and reheating, but also excellent for cooking fish and egg-based dishes. I'm often involved with photographic sessions for microwave recipe books and advertising, and that food must always be prepared in the microwave.

The other major appliances in my kitchen are the fridge/freezer and the dishwasher. I keep the fridge/freezer in the kitchen for my personal use. I'd really like to see a bit more imagination going into the development of these appliances. It seems that you have to buy an expensive one to get additions such as automatic ice cube makers and defrosters. I would also like to see the development of individual refrigerated drawers. It's so much easier to see items quickly in a drawer than on a shelf. Small, removable containers would also be a great boost for easy storage of prepared ingredients.

My dishwasher is made by Philips and I'd hate to be without it. I don't enjoy washing up and, although a certain amount has to be done throughout the day as we are working, I take delight in loading the dishwasher at the end of a busy day, wiping the kitchen floor and then just closing the door on the washing up! My only annoyance is that it doesn't take many of my stemmed glasses — a great shame since glass washes so beautifully in the dishwasher. Perhaps in time we'll see more adjustable shelves and baskets inside of dishwashers.

While I'm talking about washing up, I think it's important to talk about choice of sinks. Ideally, I'd like a double sink, of a decent proportion so that I can wash up awkward tins and pans easily, with a small central sink for cutlery which would hold the waste disposal. I'd also like to see elbow taps for those innumerable times when my hands are

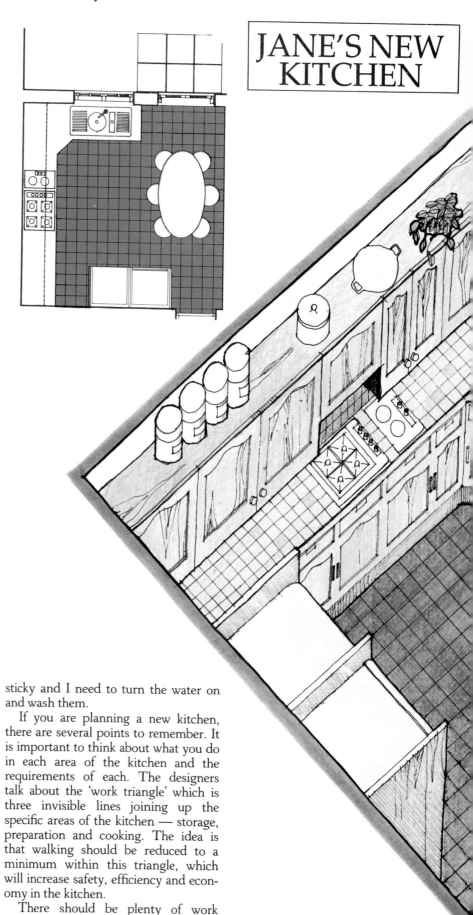

sticky and I need to turn the water on and wash them.

If you are planning a new kitchen, there are several points to remember. It is important to think about what you do in each area of the kitchen and the requirements of each. The designers talk about the 'work triangle' which is three invisible lines joining up the specific areas of the kitchen — storage, preparation and cooking. The idea is that walking should be reduced to a minimum within this triangle, which will increase safety, efficiency and economy in the kitchen.

There should be plenty of work surface on each side of a sink and hob, set at a suitable height. The suggested

'correct' height is about 1 inch lower than the bent elbow. The choice of tiles or laminate work surfaces is vast and this time I've chosen a large-scale tile. I would certainly not choose white laminate as I did in my previous kitchen, since it stained so badly and forever needed bleaching.

The work surface should be well supplied with electrical sockets and well lit by a series of concealed lights all the way along the work surface below the wall units. Strong central lights are also important, and these should be fitted with a dimmer control. I would also like a small shelf at intervals above the work surface to place ingredients or equipment so that they were at hand. I hate clutter and although I keep my food processor, kettle and toaster on the worktop, I prefer most things to be put neatly away.

If I have to follow a recipe there never seems to be anywhere convenient to put it to keep it away from the food. I like to use plastic covers for individual recipes and then attach these to bulldog clips which can be hung on cup hooks screwed into the base of the wall units. How nice it would be to have a concealed hinged shelf, large enough to hold an open book, which could be pulled out from the base of the wall unit rather like a lectern. It would also be good to see the development of cookery books with easy-wipe plastic pages.

Sensible use of storage space is important. Carousels in corner cupboards are very useful. Adjustable shelves are extremely important since all bottles and jars, china, glass and equipment varies so much in size. Fitted baskets, or those on runners, increase storage space dramatically. I personally prefer drawers to cupboards for many items. I tend to store small jars, filled with herbs and cake decorating equipment, in them. I label the lid of each jar or tub — that way it's much easier to find a particular jar at a glance. Deep drawers with dividers are ideal for storing baking trays, patty tins and roasting tins.

LOVES AND HATES

MY FAVOURITE EQUIPMENT
- plastic scrapers to clean out bowls and saucepans, and rigid scrapers to clean work surfaces
- a good selection of sharp knives, a palette knife and a swivel peeler
- my Le Creuset castoflon non-stick milk pan and saucepan
- pressure cooker
- hand held electric mixer, balloon whisk and hand-held blender
- my food processor and my Moulinex jeanette
- petal steamers and salad spinner
- sugar thermometer
- my Olafsröm saucepans

MY PET HATES
- chopping boards made from more than one piece of wood since they always split
- open shelves — they harbour dust and grease
- small sinks, even if you own a dishwasher
- single ovens with integral grills
- appliances which are difficult or awkward to clean, such as grinders, mincers and garlic presses
- non-stick cookware that doesn't stay non-stick for very long
- spice racks
- anything chipped or cracked

THE FUTURE KITCHEN

The future may hold a lot of surprises for us, but here are few ideas that come to mind for my kitchen.

● Cupboard doors that can be opened by pressure points on the floor, similar to the lavatory flush control on trains and planes.

● An oven timer/control to judge when food is cooked so that the oven can switch itself off, and perhaps open the door, to prevent further cooking.

● A complete waste disposal system which would dispose of all glass and packaging as well as perishables.

● Push-button instant convected heating. I dislike radiators since they take up valuable wall space and are usually unnecessary in a kitchen. There are times, however, when the kitchen is cold and needs instant heat.

● Complete computerization. This would control cupboards and pinpoint ingredients which could be brought to the front of the cupboard without having to hunt for them. It would hold information on stocks, recipes, techniques and preparation, local community information, shopping bargains and seasonal buys. It would also be able to order the actual shopping.

Automatic dishwasher and dryer. The dirty dishes are placed on the conveyor, they enter the machine and re-emerge clean and dry.

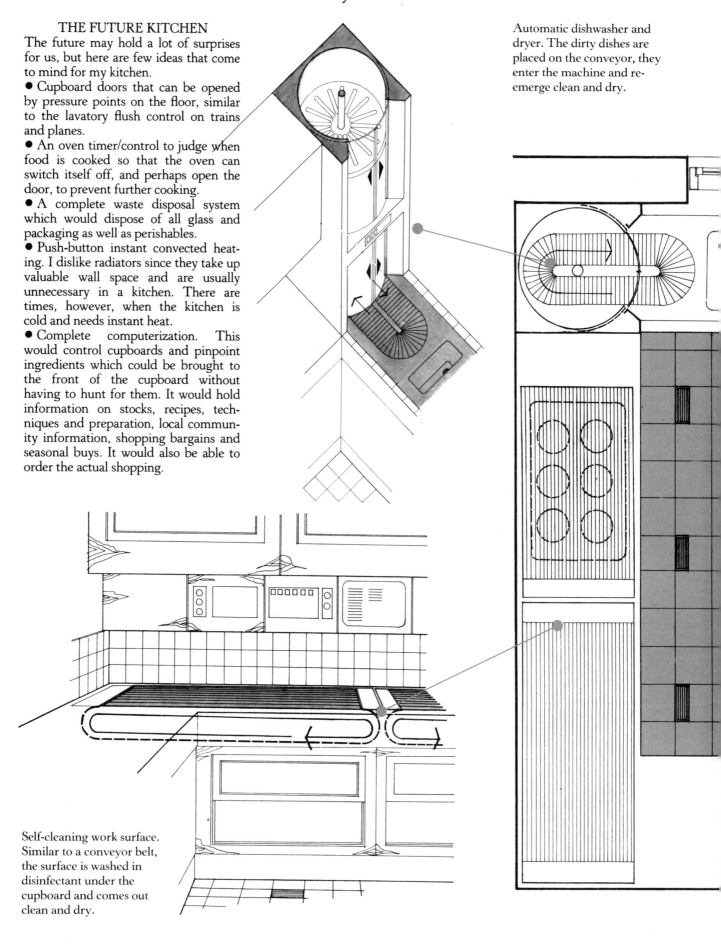

Self-cleaning work surface. Similar to a conveyor belt, the surface is washed in disinfectant under the cupboard and comes out clean and dry.

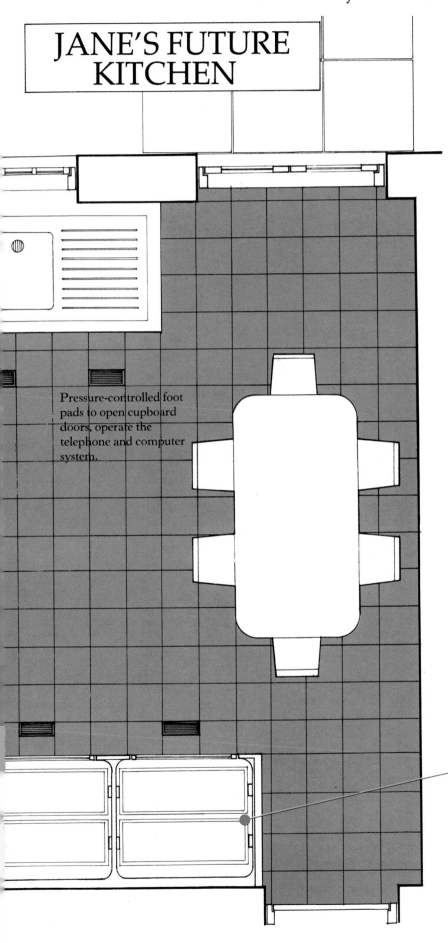

JANE'S FUTURE KITCHEN

Pressure-controlled foot pads to open cupboard doors, operate the telephone and computer system.

- An electrically controlled continuous conveyor work surface that would clean itself.
- An intercom-style memory system that you could speak into, either if a flash of inspiration came or if you remembered something you had to do. The memory bank would hold the information until such times as you required it.
- A foot operated telephone for incoming calls. That way I wouldn't need to pick up and hold the receiver.
- Ingredient dispensers that gave out specific weighed amounts when a button was pressed — much more convenient than using measuring scales.
- A wall kettle that could be filled automatically from the water pipe. This idea came from a friend of mine who is permanently irritated by filling and plugging in her kettle.
- A self-cleaning floor!

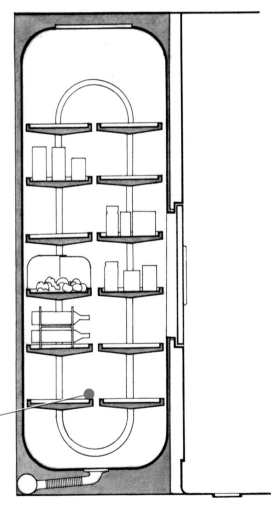

Computerized cupboard that brings items to the front on command.

IN THE SUPERMARKET
Page 7 Illustration by Jane Human
Page 9 Photography by Theo Bergstrom
Page 10 Photo supplied by The Fresh Fruit and Vegetable Information Bureau
Page 11 Photo supplied by C. Shippam
Page 12 Photo supplied by Sharwood's speciality foods company
Page 13 Photo supplied by Sharwood's speciality foods company
Page 14 Photo supplied by Findus /Lean Cuisine food products
Page 15 Photo supplied by St. Ivel Shape
Page 15 Photo supplied by Canderel Sweetener

CHEF'S CHOICE
Photography by Alan Duns

WINES AND SPIRITS
Page 23 Photo supplied by Anthony Blake
Page 24 Photo supplied by Food + Wine From France
Page 25 Photo supplied by Food + Wine From France
Page 26 Illustration supplied by The Wine Development Board
Page 27 Photography by Theo Bergstrom
Page 28 Photography by Theo Bergstrom, glasses supplied by Courtier at Liberty, London W1
Page 30 Photography by Theo Bergstrom, wine supplied by Berkmann Wine Cellars
Page 30 Illustration by Ray Leaning
Page 31 Illustration by Jane Human, wine supplied by the Victoria Wine Company
Page 32 Photo supplied by Scottish Tourist Bureau
Page 33 Photo supplied by BBC Hutton Picture Library
Page 34 Photography by Alan Duns

MENU PLANNING
Page 35 Photography by Alan Duns

Page 36-37 Illustrations by David Sim
Page 38-39 Photography by Alan Duns
Page 40-41 Illustration by Charlotte Wess, glasses supplied by Courtier at Liberty, London W1, china supplied by Josiah Wedgwood and Sons, Ltd, cutlery supplied by Butler of Sheffield at Liberty, London W1, fish knife and fork supplied by Helen Whitehead, goblet and vase supplied by Dartington Glass Ltd.
Page 42 Photographs by G. Rogers, The Image Bank (top); Anthony Blake (bottom)
Page 43 Photographs by A. Ginsburg, The Image Bank (top); Elizabeth Whiting and Associates (bottom)
Page 44 Photographs by Elizabeth Whiting and Associates

GREAT BRITISH COOKERY YEAR
Photography by Theo Bergstrom
Black and white illustrations supplied by Mary Evans Picture Library except page 73
Page 53 Candlesticks, candles and tablecloth supplied by Fortnum and Mason, cutlery supplied by Mappin and Webb.
Page 60-67 China supplied by Worcester Royal Porcelain Co.
Page 68-69 Car supplied by Jaguar Cars Ltd.
Page 72 China supplied by Worcester Royal Porcelain Co., hamper and cutlery supplied by Mappin and Webb.
Page 73 Photograph supplied by The Mansell Collection, glass bowls, milk jug and sugar bowl supplied by Mappin and Webb
Page 87 Toys supplied by Duplo

DIET AND NUTRITION
Page 93 Photography by Theo Bergstrom
Page 96-97 Photography by Theo Bergstrom, china supplied by Worcester Royal Porcelain Co.
Page 98-99 Photography by Alan Duns

KITCHEN EQUIPMENT REVIEW
Illustrations by Christina Wood
Page 108 Photography by Chris Knaggs

MICROWAVE COOKING
Photography by Chris Knaggs, except page 118 by Alan Duns
Page 116 Microwaves supplied by Toshiba (UK) Limited, Home Appliances Division, Belling & Co. Ltd., Philips, AEG
Page 118 Microwave equipment supplied by Corning

KIDS IN THE KITCHEN
Photography by Alan Duns
Page 127 Painting by Kelly McDonald, Ropsley C.E. School, Grantham, Lincs.
With thanks to the children Barney Dorman, Charlie Dorman, Harry Duns, Daniel Gordon, Joshua Gordon, Florence Robertson, Emma Wiley

THE PERFECT KITCHEN
Drawings by Ron Chapman
Page 135 Photography by Theo Bergstrom

Editorial Director	Maggi McCormick
Editor	Ricki Ostrov
Deputy Editor	Beverly Le Blanc
Art Editor	Steve Leaning
Designer	Ray Leaning
Picture Researcher	Vicki Walters
Production Coordinator	Robert Paulley
Production Controller	Steve Roberts
Home Economists	Lisa Collard
	Coralie Dorman
	Joyce Harrison
	Norma Miller
	Louise Pickford
	Jane Suthering
Stylists	Annabel Claridge
	Dawn Lane
	Penny Markham
	Marie O'Hara
	Sue Russell

L

Labelling, 9
   food additives, 8, 9
   nutritional, 8, 9
   wine, 26, 27
Lamb: roast lamb with garlic and
   parsley crumb topping, 66-7
   traditional Irish stew, 58-9
Lean Cuisine, 14
Leek: chilled vichyssoise, 120
Lemon: chilled lemon and pistachio
   soufflé, 55
   dressing, 54
   lemon and raisin pudding, 125-6
   lemon asparagus rolls, 72
Lentils: masoor dall, 12
Lighting, kitchen, 139
Lime, 10
Liqueurs, 33
Liver: hot chicken liver salad, 49

M

Madeira, 31
Mango, 10
Mangosteen, 10
Marrow kofta curry, 12
Marsala, 31
Masoor dall, 12
May Day cookery, 68-71
Meat, 97, 98
   microwave cookery, 117
   see also individual types of meat
Melting Snow, 16
Menu planning, 36-44
   microwave cookery, 119
Merlot grape, 25
Mexican cookery, 11, 107
Mice in the grass, 132
Microwave cookery, 113-26, 138
Migraine, 100
Milk: strawberry milk shake, 132
Mincemeat: old-fashioned
   mince pies, 87
Minerals, 95, 96
Mirepoix, 90
Monounsaturated fatty acids, 95
Mothering Sunday cookery, 60-1
Moules marinière, 54
Mulled red wine, 34
Mushroom: Greek mushroom salad, 99
   mushroom tart, 71
   mushrooms à la Grecque, 122
   turkey pie, 90-1
Mussels: moules marinière, 54

N

National Advisory Committee on
   Nutrition Education (NACNE), 15, 94
New Year cookery, 46-9, 92

O

Oats, 128
Old-fashioned mince pies, 87
Onion: blue cheese and onion tart, 48-9
   kipper pâté, 88-9
   roast turkey with sage and onion
   stuffing, 86-7
   Stilton and onion soup, 19
   turkey pie, 90-1
Orange: chicory and orange salad, 70
   chocolate and orange gâteau, 126
   orange sunset, 34
   oranges in red wine, 121
   oysters in orange and garlic
   cream, 83-4
Oven-to-tableware, 108-9, 111
Ovens,, 137-8
   microwave, 114-19
   table-top, 105
Oysters in orange and garlic cream, 83-4

P

Pancakes, 56-7
   Bolognese filling, 57
Papaya, 10
Paprika: scampi paprika, 125

Parsley: roast lamb with garlic and
   parsley crumb topping, 66-7
Parsnip and potato gratin, 90
Passion fruit, 10
Pasta-making machines, 106
Pastries: Eccles cakes, 61
   ham and Gruyère fingers, 72
   sardines in puff pastry, 66
Pastry: sweet pie pastry, 78-9
Pâté, kipper, 88-9
Paw paw, 10
Peanut butter: animal sandwiches, 132
Pears: mice in the grass, 132
Peppermint hearts, 131
Peppers: chicken breasts with sweet
   pepper, 54
Persimmon, 10
Pies: old-fashioned mince pies, 87
   Spanakopitta, 99
   turkey pie, 90-91
Pigeon breasts with blackberry
   sauce, 21
Pineapple, 10
Pistachio nuts: chilled lemon and
   pistacho soufflé, 55
Polyunsaturated fatty acids, 95
Pomegranate, 10
Pork: spare-ribs, 74-5
   sweet and sour pork, 13
Port, 31
Potato: chilled vichyssoise, 120
   crinkle chip cutters, 111
   kipper pâté, 88-9
   potato and parsnip gratin, 90
   potato balls, 54
   potatoes in cream, 66
   traditional Irish stew, 58-9
Pots and pans, 104
Poultry: microwave cookery, 117
   see also individual types of poultry
Prawns: seafood skewers, 75-6
   stuffed chicken breasts with
   Provençal sauce, 122-3
Prickly pear, 10
Processors, 102-3
Proteins, 95, 97
Provençale sauce, 122-3
Puddings, *see Desserts*
Pumpkin tart, 78-9

Q

Quiches, *see tarts, savoury*

R

Raisins: fruit scones, 61
   lemon and raisin
   pudding, 125-6
Rambutan, 10
Red wine, 24, 25
Refrigerators, 138
Rice: rice with chick peas, 12
   tangy rice and almond
   mould, 15
Rich chocolate cake, 61
Riesling grape, 25
Roast lamb with garlic and parsley
   crumb topping, 66-7
Roast turkey with sage and onion
   stuffing, 86-7
Rock buns, 134
Rolls, granary, 77
Rose creams, 131
Rose delight, 16
Royal Ascot, 72
Rum, 32
   apple rum cake, 21
   Caribbean kir, 34

S

Safety, children in the kitchen, 129
Sage: roast turkey with sage and onion
   stuffing, 86-7
St. Patrick's Day cookery, 58-9
St. Valentine's Day cookery, 52-5
Salad dressings: French, 49
   lemon, 54

Salads: avocado and crab salad, 54
   chicory and orange, 70
   coleslaw, 133
   Greek mushroom salad, 99
   hot chicken liver salad, 49
   tomato, 71
Salmon: salmon steaks with caper
   sauce, 120
   seafood skewers, 75-6
   smoked salmon soufflé, 47-8
Salt, 95, 97, 100
Sandwiches: animal, 132
   crab and cucumber sandwiches, 72
   lemon asparagus rolls, 72
Sardines in puff pastry, 66
Saturated fatty acids, 95, 128
Sauces: blackberry (savoury), 21
   Bolognese, 124
   caper, 120
   dill, 124-5
   Hollandaise, 63-6
   Provençale, 122-3
   yoghurt (sweet), 76
Scallops: seafood skewers, 75-6
Scampi: scampi paprika, 125
   seafood skewers, 75-6
Scones, fruit, 61
Scottish black bun, 92
Sea vegetables, 98
Seafood skewers, 75-6
Shape, 15
Sherry, 31
Shopping, 8-16, 100, 129
Shrove Tuesday cookery, 56-7
Sild: stuffed tomatoes in a parsley
   field, 19
Sinks, 138
Smoked salmon soufflé, 47-8
Soft ice cream, 103
Sole: lemon sole with dill
   sauce, 124-5
Soufflés: chilled lemon and pistachio
   soufflé, 55
   smoked salmon soufflé, 47-8
Soups: chilled vichyssoise, 120
   cream of celeriac, 84
   microwave cookery, 119
   Stilton and onion, 19
Spaghetti measuring
   dispenser, 111
Spanakopitta, 99
Spare-ribs, 74-5
Sparkling wines, 30
Special diets, 100
Spinach: Spanakopitta, 99
Spirits, 32-3
Starters: menu planning, 36
Steamed puddings: Christmas pudding
   with brandy butter, 87
Stilton and onion soup, 19
Stir-frying, 106-7
Storage, 139
   wine, 26
   see also Freezers
Strawberry milk shake, 132
Stuffed chicken breasts with Provençal
   sauce, 122-3
Stuffed tomatoes in a parsley field, 19
Stuffing, sage and onion, 86-7
Suet puddings: Christmas pudding with
   brandy butter, 87
Sugar, 16, 95, 97, 128
Sultanas: fruit scones, 61
Supermarkets, 8-16
Suthering, Jane, 135-41
Sweet and sour pork, 13
Sweet pie pastry, 78-9
Sweeteners, artificial, 16
Sweets, 128
   coffee and nut bonbons, 16
   Melting Snow, 16
   peppermint hearts, 131
   rose creams, 131
   rose delight, 16
   toffee apples, 78
   treacle toffee, 80

T

Table settings, 40-4
Table-top cookers, 105
Tacos, 107
   basic Mexican taco, 11
   Florida chicken taco, 11
   vegetarian taco, 11
Tangy rice and almond mould, 15
Tarts, savoury: blue cheese and
   onion tart, 48-9
   mushroom tart, 71
Tarts, sweet: almond and apricot tart, 22
   ginger and apple flan, 123
   pumpkin tart, 78-9
Tea: electric tea makers, 112
   herbal, 96-7
Toasters, 105
Toffee: toffee apples, 78
   treacle toffee, 80
Tomato: baked tomatoes and
   courgettes, 66
   Bolognese filling for pancakes, 57
   Bolognese sauce, 124
   scampi paprika, 125
   stuffed chicken breasts with
   Provençal sauce, 122-3
   stuffed tomatoes in a parsley field, 19
   tomato salad, 71
Tortillas, 107
Traditional Irish stew, 58-9
Treacle toffee, 80
Trifle, 91
Tropical fruits, 10
Tuna: animal sandwiches, 132
   tuna-stuffed eggs, 133
Turkey: roast turkey with sage and
   onion stuffing, 86-7
   turkey pie, 90-1

V

Vegetables, 100, 128
   aïoli and crudités, 75
   menu planning, 36, 37
   microwave cookery, 117
   mirepoix, 90
   see also individual types of vegetable
Vegetarian taco, 11
Vegetarianism, 98-9
Vermouth, 31
   orange sunset, 34
Vichyssoise, 120
Vintages, wine, 24-5
Vitamins, 95, 96, 97
Vodka, 33

W

Walnut and banana cake, 71
Water, drinking, 96, 128
Whisky, 32
   Scottish black bun, 92
White wine, 24, 25
Wimbledon, 73
Wine, 23-31
   Bolognese filling for pancakes, 57
   buying, 26
   decanting, 29
   fortified, 31
   glasses, 28, 41-2
   grapes, 25
   keeping, 25
   labels, 26, 27
   making, 24-5
   matching to food, 29
   mulled red wine, 34
   oranges in red wine, 121
   serving, 28-9
   sparkling, 30
   storage, 26
   turkey pie, 90-1
   vintages, 24-5
Woks, 106-7

Y

Yellow bean sauce, chicken in, 13
Yoghurt: fruit kebabs with yoghurt
   sauce, 76